CRIMINAL JUSTICE
POLICY MAKING

CRIMINAL JUSTICE POLICY MAKING

Federal Roles and Processes

BARBARA ANN STOLZ

PRAEGER

Westport, Connecticut
London

Library of Congress Cataloging-in-Publication Data

Stolz, Barbara Ann.
    Criminal justice policy making : federal roles and processes / Barbara Ann Stolz.
        p. cm.
    Includes bibliographical references and index.
    ISBN 0–275–97323–9 (alk. paper)—ISBN 0–275–97324–7 (pbk. : alk. paper)
    1. Criminal justice, Administration of—United States.   I. Title.
    HV9950.S745   2002
    364.973—dc21   2001034632

British Library Cataloguing in Publication Data is available.

Library of Congress Catalog Card Number: 2001034632
ISBN: 0–275–97323–9
        0–275–97324–7 (pbk.)

First published in 2002

Praeger Publishers, 88 Post Road West, Westport, CT 06881
An imprint of Greenwood Publishing Group, Inc.
www.praeger.com

Printed in the United States of America

The paper used in this book complies with the
Permanent Paper Standard issued by the National
Information Standards Organization (Z39.48–1984).

10 9 8 7 6 5 4 3 2 1

Contents

Acknowledgments

Preparing this book has given me the opportunity to collect the works of several special friends and colleagues—Barry C. Feld, Walter B. Miller, Nancy Marion, and Richard Ward. Several years ago, while researching the problem of drug-related police corruption, I met the Honorable Milton Mollen. Even at that time, I knew the work of the Mollen Commission would find its way into this text. To these individuals, I owe special thanks. I would also like to thank those authors whose work is included, whom I have never met. The work of the authors, included in this text, provided the tools with which to analyze the politics of criminal justice policy making.

This book was begun as a response to the complaints of my graduate students, who had to read article after article in the university's reserve section, because there was no text of readings on the politics of criminal justice policy making. This text is definitely a response to student demand. In particular, I would like to thank Jenna Battcher, former student and now colleague, who took the time to read the draft of the text and provide suggestions, based on a student's perspective.

In addition, I would like to express my appreciation to those who helped in the mechanics of producing this book. First and foremost, I would like to thank Suzanne Staszak-Silva, my editor, who guided and supported me throughout the project. I would like to thank my production editor Arlene Belzer, who saw the project through with great patience. And, I must give special recognition to the librarians who helped find copyright information, public documents, and websites, especially Mary K. Cummings.

Finally, I would like to thank my friends and family. This work is no Dostoevsky novel, but my Russian instructor's repeated inquiries about my progress and moral support kept me going. My family and friends have listened to my laments and stories of the challenges—learning to scan, dealing with the idiosyncrasies of Word, and consistent formatting—confronted during this project. For their patience and support, I thank them.

Chapter 1

Introduction

Criminal justice policies, structures, and systems are not preordained, but are human creations of the public policy-making process. Accordingly, to understand criminal justice policy, it is necessary to study not only the policy, but also how the policy is made and implemented. To do so involves examining the political structures and processes through which (1) behavior is defined as criminal, (2) policies, processes, and procedures regulating criminal behavior are determined, and (3) criminal justice policies are implemented. Such an analysis requires the application of the academic discipline of political science, as well as that of criminal justice.

Political science is the study of who gets what, when, where, and how. Political scientists describe government structures and the formal policy-making process within the institutions of government, as well as the informal processes that affect policy making. To analyze the policy making process, political scientists apply various conceptual frameworks, including symbolic politics, interest groups, political culture, and implementation. Using academic articles from political science and public policy literature, as well as government publications, this text attempts to provide an introduction to the politics of criminal justice policy making.

This chapter introduces the reader to key political science concepts and analytical frameworks that will be used throughout this text. The last section of this chapter provides a brief summary of the content of the chapters that follow.

POLITICAL SCIENCE, POLITICAL STRUCTURES AND PROCESSES, AND THE STUDY OF CRIMINAL JUSTICE POLICY

In the United States, governmental authority is distributed constitutionally among three levels of government—the federal, fifty state, and thousands of local governments. That is, the U.S. system of government is a federal system. At each level of government, policy-making authority is shared among three branches—the executive, legislative, and judicial. In the simplest of terms, the legislative branch enacts, the executive branch implements, and the judicial branch interprets laws and policies. Although each branch has distinct policy-making responsibilities, the branches are often also dependent upon each other to effect policy.

Federalism

Federalism defines the responsibilities of and relationships among federal, state, and local governments. The distribution of responsibilities and the relationships among the levels of government vary among policy areas, with the federal government bearing more responsibility in some policy arenas and state and/or local governments having primary responsibilities in others. For example, responsibility for international relations and military policy has fallen to the federal government, while state and local governments traditionally have borne the primary responsibility for education and criminal justice. The relationships among levels of government may, however, also vary over time within a particular policy arena. In recent decades the federal role in education has been expanded through a variety of mechanisms, for example, grants-in-aid. When studying a particular policy area, it is important to determine the following:

- What is the responsibility borne by each level of government?
- How have the respective responsibilities changed over time?
- How do the levels of government interrelate, for example, through joint jurisdiction or grants-in-aid?

Although traditionally criminal justice policy making has been primarily a function of local and state governments, in recent decades the federal government has become an active partner in addressing the problem of crime in American society. Not only has the federal government provided additional criminal justice resources to state and local governments, but it has also expanded the direct federal role in criminal justice. That role has expanded from the constitutionally established federal responsibilities for combating certain specified crimes—counterfeiting securities and currency, piracy and felonies committed on the high seas and offenses against the law of nations, and treason. Today, for example, federal anti-drug laws; grant programs providing state and local criminal justice agencies with funding for police; anti-drug, domestic violence, corrections, and juvenile justice initiatives; and funds for academic research have increased the federal government's involvement in criminal justice policy and practice. The expansion of the federal government's role in criminal justice policy making makes the federal sector an ideal laboratory for the study of criminal justice policy making. Studying the role of federal governmental structures and the processes within those institutions provides insight into how governmental institutions affect what the public knows as criminal justice policy.

Three Branches of Government

At all levels of government, the American system is characterized by the separation of powers among the three branches of government—executive, legislative, and judicial. Each branch of government plays a role and affects policy within a policy arena, by implementing, enacting, and interpreting policies, respectively. Since each branch has a different basic function, the processes and procedures of each branch vary from the others. The variations in processes and procedures, as well as the structure, of each branch affect the policies that emerge from each branch.

At the federal level, the executive branch includes the president and the executive branch agencies, commonly referred to as the federal bureaucracy. Modern presidents participate in policy making through their various roles, including chief administrator, chief legislator, and chief communicator. Presidents appoint top bureaucratic officials, with the "advice and consent" of the Senate. In so doing, presidents can exercise influence over agency priorities. A president may initiate policies; recommend policies to Congress that it, in turn, enacts into law; and educate the public regarding a policy issue.

Federal executive branch agencies carry out the policies over which the respective agency has responsibility, although often more than one agency may have responsibilities in a particular policy area. For example, although the Justice Department has primary responsibility for criminal justice policy, the Secret Service, the U.S. Customs Service, and the U.S. Coast Guard, among others, carry out criminal justice–related responsibilities. Agencies may also provide information about or carry out evaluations of the policies and programs under their jurisdictions.

Congress has responsibility for enacting federal legislation and confirming certain presidential appointments. Federal criminal justice legislation, generally, relates to the federal government's activities, for example, funding the efforts of the federal Drug Enforcement Administration. The Senate also must confirm many presidential executive branch nominees. While it usually defers to the president's choice, Congress does on occasion reject or create an environment, which leads the president to withdraw the name or causes the nominee to withdraw. In addition, through a variety of mechanisms, for example, grants-in-aid, however, Congress can also affect the policies and activities of state and local governments.

District, appellate, and the Supreme courts comprise the federal judiciary. The Supreme Court, through the power of judicial review, has the authority to determine whether a federal or state law is constitutional. In so doing, the Court acts as a policymaker. At the same time, through the power of appointment, the president and Congress exercise influence over who sits on the Court.

The structures and policy-making processes of each branch affect its role as policymaker and the policies promulgated, respectively. The Supreme Court can only address issues brought to it and is, generally, limited to the parameters of the case presented to it. If the Court wishes to address additional dimensions of an issue it is considering, it cannot "shop" in the lower courts for cases that address its concerns. Accordingly, judicial policy making tends to be fragmented and extended over time. For example, the criminal defendant's right to an attorney is a case in point. As we know it today, this right was developed through a number of Supreme Court decisions made over several decades.

Three Branches Share Functions

The three branches of government are separate institutions that share functions. For example, generally, legislation does not become law unless both houses of Congress pass the same bill and the president signs it. The bureaucracy implements the law and, thereby, affects policy, in practice. The courts interpret whether the law is constitutional; the court's decision may compel Congress to rewrite the law. On the one hand, this sharing of functions by the branches establishes a general need for cooperation among the branches if policy is to be enacted and implemented. On the other hand, sharing functions provides a check by each branch on the policy making of the other, at least in theory—the so-called checks and balances.

Policy making is also affected by the relationships among the branches at a particular point in time. One branch may seek to exert more influence than another in a particular policy arena. For example, in 1986, Congress took the lead in the drug policy area by drafting and enacting omnibus anti-drug legislation that the president then signed. Conflicts between branches also affect policy. For example, congressional disagreement with a Supreme Court decision may lead to the introduction of legislation, even the proposing of a constitutional amendment, to counter the Court's decision. For example, after a series of death penalty decisions, during the

1970s, overturning state statutes, Congress sought to revise federal death penalty laws to provide for constitutionally acceptable procedures.

Federal Government and Criminal Justice Policy Making

The federal government's role in the criminal justice arena has expanded, particularly since the 1960s. All branches of the federal government—the executive (the president and the bureaucracy), legislative (Congress), and judicial (federal courts including the Supreme Court) have participated in that expansion. The role of each branch in promoting this expansion has reflected the policy-making powers and processes of the respective branch.

The separation of powers and checks and balances affected the expansion of the federal criminal justice role. As a consequence of the separation of powers and checks and balances, cooperation among the branches has been necessary to effect changes in criminal justice. For example, within the executive branch, presidents in their role as policy initiator have introduced new federal criminal justice policies, directly through the bureaucracy or by sending proposed legislation to Congress. Congress has, through its lawmaking authority, on its own initiative or at the behest of the president, enacted legislation expanding federal criminal laws and federal criminal justice responsibilities. The federal criminal justice bureaucracy, charged with implementing the law, as part of the executive branch, has had to implement new federal criminal justice policies, enacted by Congress and/or promulgated by the president. The federal courts, through the interpretation of the law, have supported additional federal involvement in such criminal justice areas as drug policy, the rights of criminal defendants, and the response to juvenile delinquency.

In sum, federal criminal justice policy making is affected by the general characteristics of American government. The expanded federal role in criminal justice has been the result of policy making by all three branches of the federal government and reflects the respective policy-making processes of each branch. Accordingly, understanding federal criminal justice policy requires an awareness of American governmental institutions and how they make policy.

APPLYING POLITICAL SCIENCE FRAMEWORKS TO THE STUDY OF CRIMINAL JUSTICE POLICY

To analyze the policy-making process among the levels of government, among the three branches, and within each branch of government, political scientists employ numerous conceptual frameworks. Among the frameworks that have proved to be useful to the study of criminal justice or juvenile justice policy making, and that are discussed in this text, are symbolic politics, interest groups, political culture, and implementation. Each framework reflects different assumptions about how policy is made and, accordingly, emphasizes different aspects of the policy-making process. For example, the symbolic politics framework examines the influence of the public, as audience, and the interest group framework studies the influence of organized groups on policy. In general, these frameworks focus on those policy-making processes that can be observed readily. Commonsense, however, tells us that not all possible policies are subject to public debate. Such an observation suggests that some of the influences on policy and policy making may not be subject to direct observation. In an attempt to explain why certain issues may not appear on the public agenda, some scholars have applied an alternative framework—non–decision making—to the study of public policy.[1] Applying decision making and non–decision-making frameworks to the study of criminal justice policy enhances our understanding of the politics of criminal justice policy making.

Symbolic Politics

Among the frameworks political scientists, as well as sociologists, use to analyze policy making is symbolic politics.[2] From this perspective, political acts are viewed as symbols. It is assumed that these acts are directed toward an audience—usually the general public. Moreover, the substance of the act is less important than the audience's perception of and/or reaction to the act.

In general, political acts, as symbols, are said to serve to reassure or to threaten the onlooker.[3] Each political act reinforces the impression that the political system is to translate individual wants into public policy and, thus, symbolization instills a feeling of well-being. According to the literature,[4] political acts also perform a more general educative function. That is, symbolic politics may serve to educate the public about an emerging policy issue.

All three branches of government have been found to engage in symbolic politics. For example, legislators introduce bills to reassure the public that the legislature is addressing problems of public concern. Similarly, a chief executive—the president, a governor, a mayor, or county executive—may make public statements or recommend policy proposals. At times, however, whether or not legislation is enacted or policies are actually promulgated, is not as important as the fact that the legislation has been introduced or the policy has been proposed. At other times, policies may be enacted, but ultimately not address the problem. In either case the functions of symbolic politics may be fulfilled.

Criminal justice legislation has been found to perform four symbolic functions: reassurance/threat, general educative, moral educative, and model for the states.[5] Criminal laws and criminal justice policy making may reassure the public by communicating to the law abiding that something is being done about a crime problem.[6] Such legislation also communicates a threat to the potential lawbreaker. Political leaders may use policy proposals or the policy-making process, itself, to educate the public about a crime problem. During the 1990s, for example, Senate hearings on domestic violence sought to inform the public that such behavior was criminal and not simply a family matter.[7] Two other symbolic functions of federal criminal law are identified in the literature—moral educative and model for the states. Criminal justice legislation fulfills a moral educative function for the lawbreaker and the law abiding by communicating the line between right and wrong behavior. Criminal law also praises the law abiding and by praising teaches law abidingness.[8] Federal criminal justice legislation may also provide a model for the states.[9] For example, one purpose of federal death penalty legislation may be to provide for the states a model of "rational criteria" for imposing the death penalty. Or, the practices of the Federal Bureau of Prisons may be presented to the states as a model of enlightened correctional policies.[10] The symbolic politics framework and its relationship to criminal justice policy making is examined further in chapters 3 through 5.

Interest Groups

For decades political scientists have studied the role played by interest groups in policy making at all levels of government.[11] An interest group is generally defined as an organized body of individuals with shared goals who try to influence government policy. The activities of interest groups are protected by the Constitution. In the policy-making literature, the primary distinction made between the role of interest groups and the branches of government is that interest groups influence, but they do not govern.

Viewing policy making from the perspective of interest groups rests on certain assumptions regarding the distribution of power and how decisions are made. These assumptions are as follows:

- First, political power is distributed among a variety of actors/interests that express their opinions and attempt to influence policy through the legislative process— pluralism.
- Second, different groups participate in different policy arenas. Robert A. Dahl's famous study of New Haven, *Who Governs*, looks at different policy areas, for example, education and elections, and identifies different groups in each, respectively.[12]
- Third, public policy is a result of the conflict among these interests and its resolution.
- Fourth, the behaviors of actors are observable. Conflicts and preferences are revealed through participation.

• Fifth, interest groups fill in the gaps in the formal policy-making system, providing rewards and opinions. They are part of the informal policy-making system through which policy decisions, according to this perspective, are actually made.

Typically, researchers who study interest groups develop cases studies, using legislative documents, newspaper accounts, and interviews, to depict who participated in a particular policy decision. They describe and categorize interest groups according to their goals, resources, and how they participate in the political system. Interest groups have been found to vary with respect to the goals they seek. For example, some groups pursue material goals such as money; other groups pursue such intangible goals as prestige or psychological rewards; and still other groups act to achieve altruistic goals, such as the advancement of a cause. Interest groups vary in the resources at their disposal that may be used to influence policy. Among the resources identified in the literature are: (1) money or financial resources, (2) expertise or information, (3) membership (grassroots or elite), (4) leadership, (5) staff, and (6) political skills, for example, employing former politicians to advocate their position. Interest groups also differ in how they participate in the policy-making process. For example, groups may (1) testify at legislative hearings, (2) provide information or draft legislation to political officials, (3) communicate with public officials through letter-writing campaigns by their membership, (4) meet and advise public officials and/or their staff, (5) work in temporary or permanent coalitions, (6) participate in public demonstrations, or (7) (hopefully, less frequently) offer bribes. The differences in how groups participate usually reflect the resources of the particular group. Interest groups representing the professionals in a policy area, for example, may employ techniques that utilize their expertise, but those representing large groups of citizens may attempt to influence the policy-making process through letter-writing campaigns targeting policymakers or public demonstrations.

Although some attention has been paid to the role of interest groups in criminal justice policy making, the literature is somewhat sparse, nonsystematic, and diverse in its findings.[13] While discovering inconclusive and even contradictory evidence in the earlier criminal justice interest group literature, Erika S. Fairchild asserts several conclusions about interest groups in criminal justice.[14] She finds that criminal justice legislation generally is conceived by small numbers of influential legislators, administrators, and interest group representatives and enacted on a consensual basis by state legislatures. Furthermore, she observes that among the interest groups that attempt to influence criminal justice policy, those that are professionally concerned with the outcomes often exert more influence than those that have social service or public interest concerns. Barbara A. Stolz, however, suggests that nonprofessional groups may affect whether or not a policy becomes a matter for public debate.[15] Such groups may effectively block consideration of legislation or educate the public and members of Congress to the criminal character of social problems, for example, domestic violence. Interest groups have been found to affect criminal justice policy at all levels of government. The role of interest groups in criminal justice decision making is examined further in chapter 4.

Political Culture

A third framework applied by political scientists is political culture. Political culture refers specifically to political orientations—attitudes toward the political system and its various parts and attitudes toward the role of self in that system.[16] Underlying this approach is the assumption that the structures of government and the public's perceptions of what is expected of government are affected by the political culture. Researchers use techniques to determine a people's attitudes and behaviors toward government.

Although primarily applied to the study of comparative politics to compare and contrast the political cultures of nations, the political culture approach may be applied to the study of urban politics to explain differences in political attitudes and behaviors found between or among communities in the same society.[17] Since the criminal justice system and its constituent components are part of the political system, we may assume that political culture affects the structures of the criminal justice system and the public's perceptions of what is expected of that system and its components. James Q. Wilson[18] adapted the political culture approach to the study of police in four different communities. In addition to describing diverse political styles and their corresponding police styles, he points to the influence of a community's political style on the selection of its police administrator and posits the existence of a "zone of indifference" in which police are free to operate within a community. Employing this approach to study criminal justice policy contributes to our understanding of bureaucratic policy making and public perceptions of criminal justice policy. Political culture and its application to the study of criminal justice policy making is examined in chapter 6, which focuses on the role of the bureaucracy in implementing policy.

Implementation of Policy and the Street-Level Bureaucrat

The policy-making process does not end with the enactment of legislation. After the policy decision, the efforts to carry out that policy may be referred to as implementation. It is at this stage in the process where "so much can go wrong."[19] The reader may find it surprising that the study of policy implementation is relatively recent. Traditionally, it was assumed that once policies were enacted, they were implemented in the same way across communities. During the 1970s, a literature on social service delivery programs began to emerge. These studies generally involved a detailed investigation of what happened in the field when people tried to put into operation new programs or program modifications. Such studies also usually looked at the interplay of the various political, technical, bureaucratic, organizational, and socioeconomic factors that impinge on these efforts.[20] They found variations in the implementation of the same program in different communities.

One aspect of the study of policy implementation is to determine how those who provide the service to the client affect what the recipient views as the policy. It is assumed that those who have discretionary power in the direct delivery of services are more significant in the shaping of policy than the senator or agency executive.[21] According to Michael Lipsky,[22] for example, "street-level bureaucrats" affect policy because of the discretion they can exercise, a lack of organizational controls over their carrying out of policy, and ambiguity in service goals. Therefore, understanding public policy includes the study of the process by which policy is implemented, as well as the discretion exercised by the bureaucrat who delivers the service to the client.

In the criminal justice policy area, police, court officials, and correctional officers all deliver services. They implement policy and, in so doing, function as policymakers. The role of police, as policymakers, is perhaps most evident as they make decisions regarding when and when not to make an arrest and for what violations. Traditional texts and courses in criminal justice usually discuss police discretion as decision making, but do not necessarily set this discussion in the general context of criminal justice policy making. Viewing such grass-roots decisions in the broader context of criminal justice policy making, however, enhances our understanding of policy as formally established and policy in practice and as viewed by the public. The application of the implementation approach to the study of criminal justice policy making is discussed in chapter 6.

Non–decision Making and Criminal Justice Policy

Traditionally, political scientists have studied how policy is made. That is, they examine the policy-making process as it takes place in order to determine who participates in that process and how. Underlying this approach is the assumption that it is possible to observe power as it is exercised or that power and influence in the policy-making process is that which is exercised in the observable processes. Commonsense, however, suggests that not all potential policy issues are debated publicly, nor are all possible policy options discussed within a particular policy area.

An alternative framework, referred to as non–decision making, assumes that political organizations have a bias in favor of the exploitation of some kinds of conflicts and the suppression of others. That is, some issues are

organized into politics while others are organized out of politics.[23] Peter
Bachrach and Morton S. Baratz[24] refer to such decision making as the
"second face of power." The criticism of this approach that immediately
comes to mind is how does the researcher determine what issues or policy
conflicts have been suppressed—if they are suppressed they are not visible.
This author does not have a simple response to this dilemma. In the criminal justice area, however, there are a number of policies, one of the most
obvious being the legalization of drugs, that traditionally have not been
matters of public policy debate. Positing the suggestion that there may be
criminal justice policies that might be, but are not, being considered by
policymakers increases the awareness of criminal justice policy researchers
and the public that existing justice policies are not necessarily the only
policy options. This observation, in turn, may increase the likelihood that
at least some researchers or others may seek to identify such policies. The
question of non–decision making and criminal justice policy is further addressed in chapter 8.

TEXT PRESENTATION

The overall objective of this text is to provide an introduction to the
study of criminal justice policy making by drawing on the discipline of
political science and not to assess the merits of the criminal justice policies
that result from the policy-making process, as described. The text is organized according to the formal policy-making institutions of the federal
government—the executive branch (including the president and the bureaucracy), Congress, and the Supreme Court—that are involved in developing
federal criminal justice policy. Chapter 8 addresses the issue of non–
decision making and criminal justice policy making.

To accomplish the text's objective, each chapter includes selections from
the political science/public policy literature and government publications.
Through these sources, the reader will be introduced to (1) federal structures and processes that establish criminal justice policy; (2) key aspects
and issues of federal criminal justice policy making, related to the respective
branch of government; and (3) various political science frameworks, which
have been used to explain how government structures and processes affect
criminal justice policy. Although the articles and discussions in this text
focus primarily on the federal criminal justice policy-making process, the
concepts and many of the observations may be applied to criminal justice
policy making at the local and state levels. Each chapter includes an introduction; discussion questions; recommended readings and other sources,
including web sites, and excerpts from the academic literature and public
documents.[25] It should be noted that some of the readings include language
that reflects the fact that they were published in the 1960s and 1970s. These
articles are included because they are classic examples of the application of

a political science framework to criminal justice policy making. Spelling, punctuation, and capitalization of the original articles have been retained; however, the footnotes in the original articles are included as endnotes in the respective chapter and are renumbered accordingly.

Chapter 2 sets out the context of federal criminal justice policy making. The first selection by Suzanne Cavanagh describes the evolution of the federal role in criminal justice. The excerpt from an article by Walter B. Miller presents the ideologies (both conservative and liberal perspectives) reflected in federal criminal justice policy initiatives.

Chapter 3 considers the role modern presidents have played in criminal justice policy making. It includes selections related to President Johnson's 1965 crime commission, which many scholars would argue significantly influenced American criminal justice policy in the twentieth century. An excerpt from Nancy E. Marion's article, "Symbolic Politics in Clinton's Crime Control Agenda," analyzes President Clinton's criminal justice policy initiatives between 1992 and 1996, from the perspective of symbolic politics.

Chapter 4 examines the participation of Congress in criminal justice policy making. Specifically, the selections focus on interest group participation and the role of symbolic politics in the enactment of omnibus crime control legislation during the 1980s. The legislative history of the "Anti-drug Abuse Act of 1986" and statements from the hearings on the death penalty illustrate the issues raised in the academic article by Stolz.

Chapters 5 and 6 address the role of the federal bureaucracy in criminal justice policy making. Chapter 5 considers the evolution of the federal criminal justice bureaucracy's role in providing information to policymakers. Chapter 6 examines the implementation of criminal justice policy, as it is affected by political culture and the discretion of the street-level bureaucrat, particularly the police. The articles by James Q. Wilson and Michael Lipsky, respectively, provide the context for considering the possible relationship of these factors to police culture and the problem of police corruption, described in the excerpts from the reports of commission investigations in New York and Chicago.

The selections in chapter 7 consider the role of federal courts, particularly the Supreme Court, in criminal justice policy making. They include a summary of the Supreme Court decision, *In re Gault*, which transformed the procedural rights of juveniles before the juvenile court. The selection by Barry C. Feld focuses on how the Court has affected the rights of the juvenile defendant and the operation of the juvenile court, as we know it.

As suggested above, however, not all possible policies and policies options are considered in the policy-making processes observed by political scientists. In the criminal justice area, the legalization of drugs, for example, has generally not been a subject of congressional debate. The readings in-

cluded in chapter 8 examine the politics of non–decision making in the
criminal justice policy arena.

To fully understand federal criminal justice policy making, it is essential
first to examine the political structures and processes through which that
policy is created. Chapters 3 through 7 in this text examine the contribution
of each branch of the federal government to criminal justice policy making.
One must also, however, examine how the interaction between or among
the branches affects criminal justice policy. Chapter 9, the conclusion to
this text, briefly considers such issues. A fuller discussion of the effects of
the interaction among the branches on criminal justice policy must await
another text.

RECOMMENDED READING

Marion, Nancy E. *A Primer in the Politics of Criminal Justice*. Albany, NY: Harrow
    and Heston, 1995.

NOTES

1. Peter Bachrach and Morton S. Baratz, "Two Faces of Power," *American
Political Science Review*, vol. 56, no. 4 (December 1962): 947–52.

2. For example: Murray Edelman, *The Symbolic Uses of Politics* (Chicago: University of Illinois Press, 1964); Murray Edelman, *Politics as Symbolic Actor: Mass
Arousal and Quiescence* (New York: Academic Press, 1971); Joseph Gusfield, *Symbolic Crusade: Status Politics and the American Temperance Movement* (Urbana:
University of Illinois Press, 1963).

3. Edelman, *The Symbolic Uses of Politics*; Edelman, *Politics as Symbolic
Actor*.

4. Nancy E. Marion, *A History of Federal Crime Control Initiatives, 1960–
1993* (Westport, CT: Praeger, 1994), p. 14.

5. Nancy E. Marion, *A Primer in the Politics of Criminal Justice* (Albany, NY:
Harrow and Heston, 1995), pp. 23–24.

6. See, for example: Ralph Baker and Fred Meyers Jr., *The Criminal Justice
Games: Politics and Players* (Belmont, CA: Duxbury Press, 1980); Barbara A. Stolz,
"Congress and Capital Punishment: An Exercise in Symbolic Politics," *Law and
Policy Quarterly* (April 1983): 157–79.

7. Barbara A. Stolz, "Congress, Symbolic Politics, and the 1994 Evolution of
'Violence Against Women Act,' " *Criminal Justice Policy Review*, vol. 10, no. 3
1999): 401–28.

8. Walter Berns, *For Capital Punishment* (New York: Basic Books, 1979),
pp. 507–8.

9. Stolz, "Congress and Capital Punishment"; Barbara Stolz, "Congress and
Criminal Justice Policy Making: The Impact of Interest Groups and Symbolic Politics," *Journal of Criminal Justice*, vol. 13, no. 4 (1985): 307–19.

10. Stolz, "Congress and Capital Punishment," pp. 170–71.

11. Carol S. Greenwald, *Group Power: Lobbying and Public Policy* (New York: Praeger, 1977); Stolz, "Congress and Capital Punishment."

12. Robert A. Dahl, *Who Governs* (New Haven: Yale University Press, 1961).

13. See for example: Erika S. Fairchild, "Interest Groups in the Criminal Justice Process," *Journal of Criminal Justice*, vol. 9 (1981): 181–94; Michael A. Hallet and Dennis J. Palumbo, *U.S. Criminal Justice Interest Groups: Institutional Profiles* (Westport, CT: Greenwood Press, 1993); Marion, *A Primer in the Politics of Criminal Justice*; Albert P. Melone and Robert Slatger, "Interest Group Politics and the Reform of the Federal Criminal Code," in Stuart Nagel, Erika Fairchild, and Anthony Champagne, eds., *The Political Science of Criminal Justice* (Springfield, IL: Charles C. Thomas Publishers, 1983), pp. 41–55; Lloyd E. Ohlin, "Conflicting Interests in Correctional Objectives," in *Theoretical Studies in Social Organization of Prisons* (New York: Social Science Research Council, 1960); Stolz, "Congress and Capital Punishment"; Barbara Ann Stolz, "Interest Groups and Criminal Law: The Case of the Federal Criminal Code Revision," *Crime and Delinquency*, vol. 30, no. 1 (1984): 91 to 106; and Stolz, "Congress and Criminal Justice Policy Making."

14. Fairchild, "Interest Groups," p. 188.

15. Stolz, "Interest Groups and Criminal Law," p. 105.

16. Gabriel A. Almond and Sidney Verba, *The Civic Culture* (Boston: Little, Brown, and Company, 1965), p. 12.

17. James Q. Wilson, *Varieties of Police Behavior* (Cambridge, MA: Harvard University Press, 1968).

18. Ibid.

19. Walter Williams, *The Implementation Perspective: A Guide for Managing Social Service Delivery Programs* (Los Angeles: University of California Press, 1980).

20. Ibid., p. 11.

21. Ibid., pp. 11–12.

22. Michael Lipsky, "Street-Level Bureaucracy and the Structure of Work," in Willis Hawley and Michael Lipsky, eds., *Theoretical Perspectives on Urban Politics* (Englewood Cliffs, NJ: Prentice-Hall, 1997); Michael Lipsky, *Street-Level Bureaucracy: Dilemmas of the Individual in Public Services* (New York: Russell Sage Foundation, 1980).

23. Bachrach and Baratz, "Two Faces of Power," p. 949, citing E. E. Schattsneider, *The Semi-Sovereign People* (New York: Holt, Rinehart and Winston, 1960), p. 71.

24. Ibid., p. 949.

25. Note: web addresses and the information provided are subject to change.

Chapter 2

The Context of Federal Criminal Justice Policy Making: Responsibility and Ideology

INTRODUCTION

The distribution of crime control responsibility among the levels of governments in the United States—federal, state, and local—has changed over time. Today, crime control and, therefore, criminal justice policy making is not just a state and local function. The federal government plays an active role in the criminal justice policy arena, both directly, through the enactment and enforcement of federal criminal laws, and indirectly, through programs of assistance to the states and localities. The changing role of each level of government and the relationships among the levels of government in the criminal justice policy arena have evolved since the Civil War, but, particularly, since the 1960s; these changes continue. Underlying federal, as well as state and local, criminal justice policies are different ideological perspectives on crime. In simple terms, these perspectives may be characterized as conservative or liberal, each reflecting different views on the source of criminal behavior and associated methods for dealing with crime.

This chapter provides the context for the study of criminal justice policy making, as discussed in chapters 3 through 8 of this text. The articles included in this chapter describe the evolution of the federal role in criminal justice and the ideological perspectives reflected in these policies. They also provide analytical tools that can be applied to the study of future changes in the roles of the federal, state, and local governments in criminal justice policy making.

THE FEDERAL GOVERNMENT AS A LOCUS OF
CRIMINAL JUSTICE POLICY MAKING

While governmental responsibility for crime control in the United States traditionally has been vested primarily in state and local governments, the federal government's crime control efforts have expanded since the Civil War, but, especially, since the 1960s. The Constitution mentions only three areas of federal criminal justice responsibility: (1) counterfeiting securities and currency, (2) piracy and felonies committed on the high seas and offenses against the law of nations, and (3) treason. The initial expansion of federal criminal justice responsibilities focused on crimes with international or interstate dimensions; crimes on Indian reservations; and crimes against the nation, such as espionage. Moreover, despite this expansion, there remained a clear distinction between federal and state and local jurisdictions. More recent expansions in federal anti-crime responsibilities have sometimes blurred the boundaries of federalism between federal and state and local responsibilities.

Traditionally, the expansion of federal criminal justice responsibilities has been based on two powers of the federal government—the interstate commerce clause and the power to tax. In 1910, Congress enacted the White Slave Traffic Act, more commonly know as the Mann Act, which prohibited the interstate transportation of a woman or girl for the purpose of causing her to "give herself up to debauchery, or to engage in any other immoral practice." Although a congressional report found perhaps a thousand such cases a year, Congressman James R. Mann (Republican-Illinois) declared that "all of the horrors which have ever been urged, either truthfully or fancifully, against the black-slave traffic pale into insignificance in comparison with the horrors of the so-called 'white slave traffic.' "[1] Federal powers of taxation were used to regulate narcotics.[2] In part in response to the need to develop domestic legislation consistent with U.S. international anti-narcotics efforts, the Harrison Narcotics Act of 1914 was the first major federal drug control legislation with fines and imprisonment as penalties for noncompliance. Because it was a tax measure, enforcement responsibility fell to the Internal Review Service.[3] The prohibition of alcohol generated additional federal anti-crime laws. Since the 1960s, the federal government has further extended its criminal justice responsibilities in response to public concern over organized crime, street violence, drugs, and other social problems with new federal criminal laws and penalties.

The federal criminal justice role has also been expanded since the 1960s through the use of the "power of the purse," specifically grants-in-aid to the states and/or localities. This approach has included both the carrot and the stick. To promote certain policies or programs, the federal government may provide assistance to the states and localities to carry out those policies or programs—the carrot (e.g., by providing funds for education of local law enforcement or drug treatment or education programs). Or, the federal government may support or encourage state and local action by making federal funds contingent on the states or localities doing or not doing something—the stick (e.g., threatening to withdraw state highway funds if drugged driving laws are not enacted). The Law Enforcement Assistance Administration (LEAA) and its successors have provided assistance to state and local criminal justice agencies since the late 1960s, thereby expanding the federal role in the state and local administration of criminal justice.

Typically, although federal criminal justice efforts—justified on the basis of the interstate commerce clause or the power of taxation or through grants-in-aid—have become intertwined with those of state and local criminal justice agencies, distinctions among the criminal justice role of each level of government were maintained. Recent expansions of federal criminal justice responsibilities have, however, sometimes blurred jurisdictional lines among federal, state, and local governments. Although criminal offenses are framed in terms of jurisdiction, there may be some overlap. For example, a drug offender may be subject to prosecution under both federal and state statutes for the same activities. In the Controlled Substance Act of 1970, Congress reached beyond the limits of the interstate commerce clause. It asserted that drug trafficking, possession, and use have a substantial and detrimental effect on the health and general welfare of the American people. Further, since it was not feasible to distinguish between a controlled substance manufactured and those distributed intrastate, it was not feasible to distinguish in terms of control.[4]

Although the federal interpretation of the interstate commerce clause has expanded, the Supreme Court has defined the relationships among the levels of government and set limits on expansion. In *Perez v. the United States*,[5] the Court upheld the commerce clause jurisdiction over purely local loan-sharking based on a blanket congressional finding that loan-sharking is "in large part" controlled by organized crime and thus affects interstate commerce.[6] Later in *U.S. v. Lopez*,[7] however, the Court held that possession of a gun in a local school zone was not an economic activity that might have a substantial effect on interstate commerce.

It should be underscored that federalizing a crime does not mean that the particular crime has been nationalized. That is, implementation of federal anti-crime laws is carried out by federal law enforcement agencies and through the federal courts. A crime such as terrorism falls under the jurisdiction of federal law enforcement agencies. Sending a weapon through the mail is a federal crime, but all gun-related crimes are not federal and remain subject to state and local variations in law and law enforcement. Enacting federal death penalty legislation does not nationalize the death penalty, but provides for a federal punishment for certain federal crimes, for example or a killing during an aircraft hijacking by drug kingpins.

The expansion of the federal criminal justice role has not been the result of efforts by one, but by all three branches of the federal government, as will be described in the chapters that follow. For example, the executive branch through presidential proposals, based on the recommendations of commissions and other mechanisms, has increased federal criminal justice programs. The bureaucracy, as directed by Congress and the president, has expanded the federal criminal justice research agenda. Legislatively, Congress has enacted new federal criminal laws, based on presidential proposals or initiated by the Congress, itself. Judicially, the Supreme Court, through its interpretation of these laws, has played a part in defining the new federal role in criminal justice.

The expanding role of the federal government in criminal justice has not been heralded by all quarters. A recent commission, sponsored by the American Bar Association, reported that whatever the exact number of crimes that comprise today's "federal criminal law," it is clear that the amount of individual citizen behavior now potentially subject to federal criminal control has increased in astonishing proportions in the last few decades.[8] And, that in the "face of serious and offensive incidents, it is becoming more and more frequent for citizens and legislators to simply urge that Congress should make the conduct a federal crime." The commission further asserted that "The important point that emerges from a review of the effects of the recent legislation is this: Increased federalization is rarely, if ever, likely to have any appreciable effect on the categories of violent crime that most concern Americans, because in practice federal law enforcement can only reach a small percent of such activity."[9]

IDEOLOGIES AND CRIMINAL JUSTICE POLICY

Some criminal justice scholars and pundits have argued that in recent years federal criminal justice policy has reflected a single "conservative" approach to the crime problem. That is, criminal justice proposals no longer reflect distinctively different Democratic and Republican or liberal and conservative approaches to crime. While this observation may or may not be true, it is important to understand ideological differences in criminal justice policies.

In his article, "Ideology and Criminal Justice Policy: Some Current Issues,"[10] criminal justice scholar, Walter B. Miller, lays out a framework for analyzing criminal justice policies from an ideological perspective. Miller asserts that ideology and its consequences exert a powerful influence on the policies and procedures of those who conduct the enterprise of criminal justice and that the degree and kinds of influence go largely unrecognized.[11] In this article, ideology is used to "refer to a set of general and abstract beliefs or assumptions about the correct or proper state of things, particularly with respect to the moral order and political arrangements, which serve to shape one's positions on specific issues."[12] Miller states that ideological assumptions are generally preconscious rather than explicit, and serve, under most circumstances, as unexamined presumptions underlying positions taken openly. In addition, they bear a strong emotional charge.[13] He presents the respective "crusading issues"—shorthand catchwords and rallying cries that furnish the basic impetus for action or change in the criminal justice field—that are derived from the "general assumptions"—deeper and more abstract set of propositions to desired states or outcomes—of criminal justice of the political right and left.[14]

The general assumptions of the left and right ideologies of criminal justice reflect different perspectives on who commits crime and why. Even within each perspective, however, there may be variations. The political right, typically identified with the Republican Party, may argue for increased criminalization of certain behavior, a "conservative position," while libertarians within the party may argue against federalizing the criminalization of such behavior on the grounds that government interference in the lives of individuals should be limited.

Criminal justice proposals and legislation, especially omnibus crime control initiatives, often include provisions reflecting different, even contradictory, perspectives on criminal justice. For example, while Congress included in the Anti-Drug Abuse Act of 1988, more funding for drug treatment programs—identified with a liberal or Democratic drug policy position—it also included Republican zero tolerance initiatives, providing for reductions in federal highway funds for states that did not enact "drugged driving laws." Such are the realities of the politics of compromise.

INCLUDED SELECTIONS

The first selection in this chapter, excerpted from a report prepared by the staff of the Congressional Research Service (CRS), describes the evolution of federal criminal justice legislation and summarizes the federal anti-crime and anti-drug legislation enacted since the 1960s.[15] This selection lays out the major provisions of the legislation, as well as identifying the source of these efforts. The article sets up issues that are examined in the later chapters of this text.

The second selection is excerpted from Walter B. Miller's article on ideology and criminal justice policy.[16] Although the article was published during the 1970s, Miller's conceptual framework still provides the tools to analyze the assumptions underlying specific proposals, legislation, and policy positions found in the subsequent chapters. The criminal justice policies articulated by presidents, legislators, bureaucrats, court justices, and interest groups may all be examined in terms of this ideological framework.

FOR DISCUSSION

From the selections in this chapter the reader should consider:

1. How the federal role in the criminal justice arena evolved.
2. The costs and benefits of the evolution of the federal criminal justice role.
3. How the various ideologies are reflected in criminal justice polices.
4. How the expansion of the federal criminal justice role has impacted state and local criminal justice systems.

RECOMMENDED READINGS AND OTHER SOURCES

Specific References

Cavanagh, Suzanne. *Crime Control: The Federal Response*. Congressional Research Service Issue Brief for Congress, May 26, 1999.
The Challenge of Crime in a Free Society: A Report of the President's Commission on Law Enforcement and Administration of Justice. New York: Avon Books, 1968.
Miller, Walter B. "Ideology and Criminal Justice Policy: Some Current Issues." *The Journal of Criminal Law and Criminology*, vol. 64, no. 2 (1973): 141–62.
Walker, Samuel. *Sense and Nonsense about Crime and Drugs*. 4th ed. Belmont, CA: Wadsworth Publishing, 1988.

General Sources

The Congressional Record. (Printed or online editions.)
Congressional Research Service, reports of.

Web Sites

Library of Congress <http://www.loc.gov>
Heritage Foundation <http://www.heritage.org>
American Civil Liberties Union <http://www.aclu.org>

CRIME CONTROL: THE FEDERAL RESPONSE

Suzanne Cavanagh

BACKGROUND AND ANALYSIS

Federal v. State Responsibility for Law Enforcement

Under the federal system in the United States, the states and localities traditionally have held the major responsibility for prevention and control of crime and maintenance of order. For most of the Republic's history, "police powers" in the broad sense were reserved to the states under the Tenth Amendment to the Constitution. Many still hold that view, but others see a string of court decisions in recent decades as providing the basis for a far more active federal role.

Perhaps the most significant factor behind the growth of federal police powers has been a broader interpretation of the Constitution's "commerce clause" (U.S. Constitution, Art. I, Section 8, C l. 2), which explicitly gives Congress power to regulate interstate and foreign commerce. A series of court decisions in this century has established that the impact of intrastate commerce on interstate commerce may justify a more inclusive approach. In addition, both Congress and the Court have shown an apparent willingness to view certain kinds of crime, or disorder on a large scale, as threats to commerce in and of themselves. The Supreme Court has established some limits on the power of Congress to regulate certain activity through the commerce clause of the Constitution. In *U.S. v. Lopez* (514 U.S. 549, 1995) the court, striking down a provision of the Gun Free Schools Act of 1990, held that the possession of a gun in a local school zone is not an economic activity that might have a substantial effect on interstate commerce.

Since the 1960s, the law and order issues that most often have generated debate over the appropriate limits of the federal role are financial assistance for state and local law enforcement and regulation of firearms. (For a discussion of firearm regulation, see CRS Issue Brief 97010, Gun Control.) In considering legislation that established the grant program administered by the Law Enforcement Assistance Administration (P.L. 90–351) and its forerunner, the Office of Enforcement Assistance (P.L. 89–197), some Members

Reprinted and excerpted from *Crime Control: The Federal Response*, by Suzanne Cavanagh, Congressional Research Service Issue Brief for Congress, May 26, 1999. This document is updated periodically by CRS staff. Updated versions may be found on the CRS web site.

of Congress and analysts expressed concern that the federal "power of the purse" would lead to a national police force.

The lack of significant opposition to local law enforcement assistance provisions in 1986 and 1988 anti-drug measures and the 1990 Crime Control Act suggests that such concern has diminished. This change in attitude might be explained by a widespread perception that the illicit traffic in dangerous drugs has become a national problem of overriding concern.

One indication of growth in federal involvement in crime control is the trend in annual spending under the budget category "administration of justice." Since 1965, it has risen from $535 million to an estimated $25.3 billion in FY1998. Congress appropriated approximately $18 billion for Department of Justice programs for FY1999.

Federal Assistance to State and Local Governments

During the 1960s the FBI Uniform Crime Reports showed that crime rates in the United States were increasing rapidly, and "law and order" and "crime in the streets" were key issues in the 1964 Presidential campaign. President Lyndon Johnson, in his first message to Congress in 1965, called for the establishment of a blue ribbon panel to probe "fully and deeply into the problems of crime in our nation." Johnson's requests led to the creation of the President's Commission on Law Enforcement and the Administration of Justice and to passage of the Law Enforcement Assistance Act of 1965 (P.L. 89-197; 79 Stat. 828). The latter established an Office of Law Enforcement Assistance in the Department of Justice and charged it with funding demonstration projects for the development of new methods of crime control and law enforcement.

In February 1967, the President's Commission issued its report, The Challenge of Crime in a Free Society, and recommended that the federal government provide more financial assistance to state and local governments for law enforcement purposes. The Commission found that "crime is a national, as well as a state and local phenomenon." Subsequently, President Johnson proposed an expanded program of grants to state and local governments, to be administered by the Department of Justice. In urging the passage of such legislation, he warned that "the federal government must never assume the role of the nation's policeman. True, the federal government has certain direct law enforcement responsibilities. But these are carefully limited to such matters as treason, espionage, counterfeiting, tax evasion and certain interstate crimes."

Congress responded in June of 1968 by passing the Omnibus Crime Control and Safe Streets Act of 1968 (P.L. 90–351; 82 Stat. 197). Title I of the Act established a Law Enforcement Assistance Administration (LEAA) to make grants to state and local governments for planning, recruitment, and training of law enforcement personnel; public education relating to crime prevention; building construction; education and training of special law enforcement units to combat organized crime; and the organization, education, and training of regular law enforcement officers, special units, and law enforcement reserve units for the prevention and detection of riots and other civil disorders. The Act also established a National Institute of Law Enforcement and Criminal Justice to make grants for training, education, research, and demonstration for the purpose of improving law enforcement and developing new methods for the prevention and reduction of crime.

The enactment of the Safe Streets Act and the creation of LEAA ushered in a new era of federal assistance to state and local governments for crime control. The grant programs significantly expanded the central government's involvement in local law enforcement. Although the program was criticized and ultimately phased out after a 12-year life and an expenditure of roughly $7.5 billion, support for the concept of direct federal aid for law enforcement and crime control resurfaced and grew during the 1980s as Congress sought solutions to the nation's drug problems.

LEAA's history is controversial. The block grant funding mechanism was criticized because it prevented the agency from exercising tight controls over the money sent to the states. Critics charged that funds were misused and that the program had no visible impact on crime. With the exception of one downturn in crime statistics in 1972, the reported violent crime rate continued to rise throughout the 1970s and 1980s. Although the program had been authorized through Fiscal Year 1983, budget reductions beginning in 1980 resulted in its virtual elimination. Four of its highly specialized functions remained to be administered by a successor agency, the Office of Justice Assistance, Research, and Statistics (OJARS).

Broader federal assistance was restored when the Reagan Administration requested authority, in 1983, to establish a more modest grant program. Additional expansion of the federal role occurred with congressional passage of four omnibus crime control bills. First was Chapter IV (the Justice Assistance Act) of the Comprehensive Crime Control Act of 1984 (P.L. 98-473). It created the Office of Justice Programs, headed by an assistant Attorney General, to coordinate the activities of the Bureau of Justice Assistance, the National Institute of Justice, the Bureau of Justice Statistics, and the Office of Juvenile Justice and Delinquency Prevention. The Anti-Drug Abuse Act of 1986 (P.L. 99-570) established matching formula grants to state and local law enforcement agencies; the Anti-Drug Abuse Act of 1988 expanded the program, the "Edward Byrne Memorial State and Local Law Enforcement Assistance Programs." Despite Reagan Administration opposition to such expansion, Congress appropriated $150 million for FY1989 for the programs. The Crime Control Act of 1990 (P.L. 101-647) authorized $900 million. Congress approved an appropriation of $552 million for the Byrne Programs for FY1999.

Major Enactments

Comprehensive Crime Control Act of 1984. In 1966, Congress created the National Commission on Reform of the Criminal Laws. Headed by California Governor Edmund G. Brown, Sr., the Commission issued a report that took the form of a new draft of the Federal Criminal Code. The Comprehensive Crime Control Act of 1984 was the culmination of a bipartisan effort to implement this report. The bill finally approved was somewhat limited, a compromise that overhauled the federal sentencing system, revised the bail statutes to permit pretrial detention of those considered dangerous to the community, tightened the legal definition of insanity, required mandatory minimum sentences for career criminals, increased the maximum fines for serious drug offenses, gave federal prosecutors new authority to seize the assets of drug traffickers, and established a victim compensation program in the Department of Justice. Controversial provisions related to the death penalty, federal exclusionary rule modification, and habeas corpus revision ultimately were dropped. Similar proposals have been reintroduced several times but continue to be a source of contention.

Anti-Drug Abuse Act of 1986. The Anti-Drug Abuse Act of 1986 (P.L. 99-570) was a far-ranging measure containing 15 titles and relating to almost every aspect of federal efforts to prevent and control the abuse of drugs. It stiffened penalties for violations of the Controlled Substances Act (P.L. 91-513), providing for mandatory minimum sentences in certain cases. It also contained provisions aimed at money laundering and expanded authority for seizure and forfeiture of assets derived from criminal activities. Other provisions related to international narcotics control and demand reduction efforts. It authorized $230 million annually for 3 years for state and local drug enforcement assistance. Overall, it raised existing authorization ceilings by $1.7 billion; final FY1987 appropriations for drug control were over $4 billion.

Anti-Drug Abuse Act of 1988. The Anti-Drug Abuse Act of 1988 (P.L. 100-690) was signed into law on November 18, 1988. This legislation built on the Anti-Drug Abuse Act of 1986 and, like its predecessor, contained provisions relating to virtually every facet of the federal effort to curb the abuse of narcotics and other dangerous drugs. The 10 main titles concerned (1) new and increased penalties for drug trafficking offenses (including the death penalty for killings committed by drug "kingpins" and for the drug-related killing of a law enforcement officer), and general increases in funding for drug law enforcement; (2) the organization and coordination of federal anti-drug efforts, including the creation of a new agency headed by a cabinet-level director (a so-called "drug czar"), subject to Senate confirmation; (3) the reduction of drug demand through increased treatment and prevention efforts; (4) the reduction of drug production abroad and of international trafficking in illicit drugs; and (5) sanctions designed to put added pressure on drug users ("user accountability"). The Act raised FY1989 authorization ceilings by $2.7 billion; actual appropriations brought the total federal anti-drug budget for FY1989 to approximately $6.5 billion.

Crime Control Act of 1990. The Crime Control Act of 1990 (P.L. 101-647) was an omnibus measure that, like some previous anti-crime proposals, was stripped of several of its more controversial provisions such as those pertaining to the federal death penalty, habeas corpus revision, federal exclusionary rule application, and firearms control. The legislation authorized $220 million in federal matching grants to assist states in establishing more effective prison programs, including alternatives to traditional incarceration. It established a grant program to develop and implement multidisciplinary child abuse investigation and prosecution programs and permitted alternatives to live-in-court testimony in a proceeding involving an alleged offense against a minor. The measure contained child pornography provisions requiring more stringent recordkeeping and enhanced penalties. It codified a Crime Victims' Bill of Rights in the federal justice system, and increased the funding level for victim compensation and assistance. Other provisions authorized a $20 million rural drug initiative, expanded the Public Safety Officers' Death Benefits program to include a one-time benefit for officers permanently disabled in the line of duty, authorized the hiring of additional FBI and Drug Enforcement Administration (DEA) agents, added 12 new chemicals to the list of precursor chemicals regulated under the Chemical Diversion and Trafficking Act, created a National Commission To Support Law Enforcement, and raised the authorization for the federal drug enforcement grant program to $900 million.

Violent Crime and Law Enforcement Act of 1994. The Violent Crime and Law Enforcement Act of 1994 (P.L. 103-322) authorized $30.2 billion for law enforcement and crime prevention measures. It increased to 60 the number of federal crimes punishable by death and established procedures whereby the death penalty may be carried out. It contained a "three strikes" provision requiring the imposition of a sentence of life imprisonment for violent three-time federal offenders. The Act authorized a total of $8.8 billion, from FY1995-2000, to states and localities for the expansion of law enforcement resources. It authorized a total of $1 billion for the Byrne program for FY1995-2000. In addition, it authorized, through new grant authorities, funds for additional correctional facilities, the expansion of alternative sanctions for non-violent young offenders, and the costs incurred by states incarcerating criminal aliens. The measure authorized $5.35 billion for crime prevention and violence against women programs. It prohibited the manufacture, for 10 years after enactment, of semiautomatic assault weapons and the possession or transfer of such firearms if they were not lawfully possessed on the date of enactment. It also authorized $150 million to implement the Brady Handgun Violence Prevention and the National Child Protection Acts. It included murder by international terrorists among the federal crimes punishable by death and increased the penalties for other terrorist crimes. It increased the penalties for repeat federal sex offenders and assaults against children within federal enclaves, and created a program for the registration of sexual predators with community notice. It also permitted the prosecution as adults of juvenile offenders 13 years of age and older who commit federal crimes of violence or federal crimes involving a firearm. The Act established a trust fund, subject to annual appropriation and financed by savings from reductions in the federal work force or in discretionary spending, to fund its programs. . . .

IDEOLOGY AND CRIMINAL JUSTICE POLICY: SOME CURRENT ISSUES

Walter B. Miller

IDEOLOGICAL POSITIONS

Right: Crusading Issues

Crusading issues of the right differ somewhat from those of the left; they generally do not carry as explicit a message of movement toward new forms, but imply instead that things should be reconstituted or restored. However, the component of the message that says, "Things should be different from the way they are now," comes through just as clearly as in the crusading issues of the left. Current crusading issues of the right with respect to crime and how to deal with it include the following:

1. *Excessive leniency toward lawbreakers.* This is a traditional complaint of the right, accentuated at present by the publicity given to reform programs in corrections and policing, as well as to judicial activity at various levels.

2. *Favoring the welfare and rights of lawbreakers over the welfare and rights of their victims, of law enforcement officials, and the law abiding citizen.* This persisting concern is currently activated by attention to prisoners' rights, rehabilitation programs, attacks on police officers by militants, and in particular by a series of well-publicized Supreme Court decisions aimed to enhance the application of due process.

3. *Erosion of discipline and of respect for constituted authority.* This ancient concern is currently manifested in connection with the general behavior of youth, educational policies, treatment of student dissidents by college officials, attitudes and behavior toward law-enforcement, particularly the police.

4. *The cost of crime.* Less likely to arouse the degree of passion evoked by other crusading issues, resentment over what is seen as the enormous and increasing cost of crime and dealing with criminals—a cost borne directly by the hard working and law abiding citizen—nevertheless remains active and persistent.

5. *Excessive permissiveness.* Related to excessive leniency, erosion of discipline, and the abdication of responsibility by authorities, this trend is seen as a fundamental defect in the contemporary social order, affecting many diverse areas such as sexual morality, discipline in the schools, educational philosophies,

Reprinted and excerpted from *The Journal of Criminal Law and Criminology*, vol. 64, no. 2, by Walter B. Miller, "Ideology and Criminal Justice Policy: Some Current Issues," pp. 141–62 (excerpted pp. 143–46), Copyright 1973 by Northwestern University School of Law, with permission from the author.

child-rearing, judicial handling of offenders, and media presentation of sexual materials.

Right: General Assumptions

These crusading issues, along with others of import, are not merely rit-ualized slogans, but reflect instead a more abstract set of assumptions about the nature of criminal behavior, the causes of criminality, responsibility for crime, appropriate ameliorative measures, and, on a broader level, the na-ture of man and of a proper kind of society. These general assumptions provide the basic charter for the ideological stance of the right as a whole, and a basis for distinguishing among the several subtypes along the points of ideological scale. Major general assumptions of the right may be phrased as follows:

1. The individual is directly responsible for his own behavior. He is not a passive pawn of external forces, but possesses the capacity to make choices between right and wrong—choices which he makes with an awareness of their consequences.

2. A central requirement of a healthy and well functioning society is a strong moral order which is explicit, well-defined, and widely adhered to. Preferably the tenets of this system of morality should be derived from and grounded in the basic pre-cepts of a major religious tradition. Threats to this moral order are threats to the very existence of the society. Within the moral order, two clusters are of particular importance:

    a. Tenets which sustain the family unit involve morally-derived restrictions on sexual behavior and obligations of parents to maintain consistent responsibility to their children and to one another.

    b. Tenets which pertain to valued personal qualities include: taking personal responsibility for one's behavior and its consequences; conducting one's affairs with the maximum degree of self-reliance and independence, and the minimum of dependency and reliance on others, particularly public agencies; loyalty, par-ticularly to one's country; achieving one's ends through hard work, responsi-bility to others, and self-discipline.

3. Of paramount importance is the security of the major arenas of one's customary activity—particularly those locations where the conduct of family life occurs. A fundamental personal and family right is safety from crime, violence, and attack, including the right of citizens to take necessary measures to secure their own safety, and the right to bear arms, particularly in cases where official agencies may appear ineffective in doing so.

4. Adherence to the legitimate directives of constituted authority is a primary means for achieving the goals of morality, correct individual behavior, security, and other valued life conditions. Authority in the service of social and institutional rules should be exercised fairly but firmly, and failure or refusal to accept or respect legitimate authority should be dealt with decisively and unequivocally.

5. A major device for ordering human relations in a large and heterogeneous so-ciety is that of maintaining distinctions among major categories of persons on the

basis of differences in age, sex, and so on, with differences in religion, national background, race, and social position of particular importance. While individuals in each of the general categories should be granted the rights and privileges appropriate thereto, social order in many circumstances is greatly facilitated by maintaining both conceptual and spatial separation among the categories.

Left: Crusading Issues

Crusading issues of the left generally reflect marked dissatisfaction with characteristics of the current social order, and carry an insistent message about the desired nature and direction of reform. Current issues of relevance to criminal justice include:

1. *Overcriminalization.* This reflects a conviction that a substantial number of offenses delineated under current law are wrongly or inappropriately included, and applies particularly to offenses such as gambling, prostitution, drug use, abortion, pornography, and homosexuality.

2. *Labeling and Stigmatization.* This issue is based on a conception that problems of crime are aggravated or even created by the ways in which actual or potential offenders are regarded and treated by persons in authority. To the degree a person is labelled as "criminal," "delinquent," or "deviant," will he be likely to so act.

3. *Overinstitutionalization.* This reflects a dissatisfaction over prevalent methods of dealing with suspected or convicted offenders whereby they are physically confined in large institutional facilities. Castigated as "warehousing," this practice is seen as having a wide range of detrimental consequences, many of which are implied by the ancient phrase "schools for crime." Signaled by a renewed interest in "incarceration," prison reform has become a major social cause of the left.

4. *Overcentralization.* This issue reflects dissatisfaction with the degree of centralized authority existing in organizations which deal with crime—including police departments, correctional systems, and crime-related services at all government levels. Terms which carry the thrust of the proposed remedy are local control, decentralization, community control, a new populism, and citizen power.

5. *Discriminatory Bias.* A particularly blameworthy feature of the present system lies in the widespread practice of conceiving and reacting to large categories of persons under class labels based on characteristics such as racial background, age, sex, income level, sexual practices, and involvement in criminality. Key terms here are racism, sexism, minority oppression and brutality.

Left: General Assumptions

As in the case of the rightist positions, these issues are surface manifestations of a set of more basic and general assumptions, which might be stated as follows:

1. Primary responsibility for criminal behavior lies in conditions of the social order rather than in the character of the individual. Crime is to a greater extent a product of external social pressures than of internally generated individual motives, and is more appropriately regarded as a symptom of social dysfunction than as a phenomenon in its own right. The correct objective of ameliorative efforts, therefore, lies in the attempt to alter the social conditions that engender crime rather than to rehabilitate the individual.

2. The system of behavioral regulation maintained in America is based on a type of social and political order that is deficient in meeting the fundamental needs of the majority of its citizens. This social order, and the official system of behavioral regulation that it includes, incorporates an obsolete morality not applicable to the conditions of a rapidly changing technological society, and disproportionately geared to sustain the special interests of restricted groups, but which still commands strong support among working class and lower middle class sectors of the population.

3. A fundamental defect in the political and social organization of the United States and in those components of the criminal justice enterprise that are part of this system is an inequitable and unjust distribution of power, privilege, and resources—particularly of power. This inequity pervades the entire system, but appears in its more pronounced forms in the excessive centralization of governmental functions and consequent powerlessness of the governed, the military-like, hierarchical authority systems found in police and correctional organization, and policies of systematic exclusion from positions of power and privilege for those who lack certain preferred social characteristics. The prime objective of reform must be to redistribute the decision-making power of the criminal justice enterprise rather than to alter the behavior of actual or potential offenders.

4. A further defect of the official system is its propensity to make distinctions among individuals based on major categories or classes within society such as age, sex, race, social class, criminal or noncriminal. Healthy societal adaptation for both the offender and the ordinary citizen depends on maintaining the minimum separation—conceptually and physically—between the community at large and those designated as "different" or "deviant." Reform efforts must be directed to bring this about.

5. Consistent with the capacity of external societal forces to engender crime, personnel of official agencies play a predominantly active role, and offenders a predominantly reactive role in situations where the two come in contact. Official agents of behavioral regulation possess the capacity to induce or enhance criminal behavior by the manner in which they deal with those who have or may have engaged in crime. These agents may define offenders as basically criminal, expose them to stigmatization, degrade them on the basis of social characteristics, and subject them to rigid and arbitrary control.

6. The sector of the total range of human behavior currently included under the system of criminal sanctions is excessively broad, including many forms of behavior (for example, marijuana use, gambling, homosexuality) which do not violate the new morality and forms which would be more effectively and hu-

manely dealt with outside the official system of criminal processing. Legal codes should be redrafted to remove many of the behavioral forms now proscribed, and to limit the discretionary prerogatives of local authorities over apprehension and disposition of violators.

NOTES

1. H. Scott Wallace, "When More Is Less: The Drive to Federalize is a Road to Ruin," *Criminal Justice*, vol. 8, no. 3 (fall 1993): 10, citing *Congressional Record* 45 (January 26, 1910), p. 1040.

2. David F. Musto, *The American Disease: Origins of Narcotic Control* (New York: Oxford University Press, 1987), p. 41.

3. Wallace, "When More Is Less," p. 11 and Musto, *American Disease*, p. 59.

4. Wallace, "When More Is Less," p. 12, citing 21 U.S.C. Sec. 801 (2), (4), and (5).

5. Ibid., p. 11, citing *Perez v. U.S.* (402 U.S. 146, 1971).

6. Ibid., "When More Is Less," p. 11.

7. Suzanne Cavanagh, *Crime Control: The Federal Response* (Congressional Research Service Issue Brief for Congress, May 26, 1999), p. 2, citing *U.S. v. Lopez* (514 U.S. 549, 1995).

8. *The Federalization of Criminal Law* (Washington, DC: The American Bar Association, 1998), p. 10.

9. Ibid., p. 18.

10. Walter B. Miller, "Ideology and Criminal Justice Policy: Some Current Issues," *The Journal of Criminal Law and Criminology*, vol. 64, no. 2 (1973): 141–62.

11. Ibid., p. 142.

12. Ibid., p. 141.

13. Ibid., p. 142.

14. Ibid., pp. 143–46.

15. Cavanagh, *Crime Control*, pp. 2–5, 7–8.

16. Miller, "Ideology and Criminal Justice Policy," pp. 143–46.

Chapter 3

Presidents and Criminal Justice Policy Making

INTRODUCTION

Recent U.S. presidents from Kennedy to Clinton have, to varying degrees, participated in criminal justice policy making. Although presidents are not often thought to be influential in regard to criminal justice policy,[1] recent presidents through their powers, both those formally enumerated in the Constitution (Article II, section 2) and those that have evolved over time, have influenced the nation's anti-crime agenda. Through their various roles—chief legislator, chief administrator, and chief communicator—presidents have affected Congress' anti-crime legislative agenda, the bureaucracies' criminal justice initiatives, and/or the public's awareness of crime. As chief administrator, some presidents have effected policy changes through executive orders or reorganizations. Some presidents have appointed commissions to address public concerns regarding crime and develop an anti-crime legislative agenda. Even presidential contenders, for example, 1964 Republican presidential candidate Barry Goldwater, have affected federal criminal justice policy making.[2] Through the appointment of federal judges, presidents also affect judicial criminal justice policy making.

This chapter focuses on the role of the president in criminal justice policy making. Specifically, it looks at President Lyndon Johnson's use of the 1965 Presidential Crime Commission to set a criminal justice agenda. Although any of the conceptual frameworks discussed in chapter 1 of this text—symbolic politics, interest groups, political culture, implementation of policy, and non–decision making—might be applied to the study of presidential criminal justice policy making, this chapter will focus on symbolic politics.

PRESIDENTS, ANTI-CRIME AGENDAS, AND PRESIDENTIAL COMMISSIONS

Since the 1960s, U.S. presidents have paid greater attention to crime, viewing it as not simply a state and a local matter, but also as a concern of the federal government. Although some federal anti-crime measures were enacted earlier,[3] beginning with the Kennedy administration federal measures were directed toward state crime control efforts.[4] The initiatives of the Kennedy administration concentrated on organized crime, juvenile justice, and the availability of legal counsel. It was, however, the 1964 presidential election that seems to have precipitated the expansion of the federal role in criminal justice. Although Goldwater lost the election, he raised the issue of crime to the national policy agenda; fear of crime was now on the minds of American voters and had the potential to affect the results of future elections. President Lyndon Johnson's subsequent response to the challenge raised by his political opponent laid the groundwork for carrying out an expanded role in federal criminal justice.[5]

On March 8, 1965, Lyndon Johnson sent to Congress his first message on law enforcement and the administration of justice.[6] As part of his message, President Johnson announced the establishment of a presidential commission comprised of men and women who "shared" his "belief that we need to know more about crime and prevention."[7] The commission was appointed in July 1965. The members and staff constituted a who's who in criminal justice research, then and now.

The President's Commission reported its findings and recommendations in 1967. In the view of many, the commission changed American thinking about crime and criminal justice. The commission's report (*Challenge of Crime in a Free Society*)[8] emphasized the need for citizen support of the criminal justice system, better training of criminal justice personnel, a wider range of correctional treatment, better information, and deeper and broader research; the importance of crime prevention; and the provision of federal resources to strengthen the criminal justice system. Special reports on corrections, juvenile delinquency, courts, police, and narcotics among other topics addressed a variety of criminal justice issues. The commission set forth more than two hundred recommendations.

Having announced in his 1967 State of the Union Message that he would recommend the Safe Streets and Crime Control Act of 1967 to Congress, President Johnson sent the proposal to Congress in February 1967,[9] just before the public release and distribution of his commission's final report.[10] The president recommended that Congress enact the legislation to provide planning and program grants to state and local governments; establish in the Department of Justice, a director of a new Office of Law Enforcement and Criminal Justice Assistance; authorize federal grants to states, cities, and regional and metropolitan bodies to assist them in developing plans to improve their police, courts, and correctional systems; authorize the attorney general to make research grants or contracts with public agencies, institutions of higher education, or other organizations; and address other anti-crime and anti-narcotics related matters.[11]

Congress ultimately enacted the Omnibus Crime Control and Safe Streets Act of 1968. The final legislation reflected the influence of Congress and the need for the White House to reach accommodation with conservative Democrats and Republicans to enact the legislation. For example, the president had proposed categorical grants, controlled by the federal government, to local governments; Congress, instead, legislated block grants to the states, giving discretion to the states as to how the funds would be spent. Key components of this legislation were the provisions authorizing federal grants[12] to states and localities to improve their police, courts, and correctional system, and for federally sponsored research programs. Moreover, programs funded through the legislation resulted in increased educational opportunities for criminal justice professionals; current and future criminal justice scholars; as well as the establishment in colleges and universities of new departments, schools, and specializations in criminal justice.

Since the Johnson administration, most U.S. presidents have articulated a crime agenda, although Democratic and Republican presidents have often pursued different substantive criminal justice policies. For example, Democratic presidents have tended to pursue measures expanding federal gun control initiatives, while Republican presidents have not.

PRESIDENTS, CRIME, AND SYMBOLIC POLITICS

Social policies, criminal justice among them, may be tangible or symbolic. That is, they may be directed toward distributing concrete rewards to various organized interests or they may seek to evoke a reaction from an audience, usually the general public—symbolic politics. Although a president's crime agenda may be tangible or symbolic, because of the limits of the federal government's criminal justice responsibility, presidential policies are often symbolic. According to political scientist Nancy Marion, such symbolic policies may be directed toward (1) enhancing the popularity of the officeholder with the public, (2) reassuring the public that the executive is taking steps to address the crime problem, (3) simplifying the complex problem of crime, (4) providing the states with models of good policy, (5) demonstrating acceptable and unacceptable behavior—a moral educative function, or (6) educating the public about a problem.[13]

President Johnson's anti-crime efforts were, at least in part, symbolic. In the language of symbolic politics, the presidential initiative was to reassure the public that the federal government was doing something about crime. Johnson's successors also undertook symbolic initiatives directed to calm the public's fears about crime and drugs. For example, although mandated by Congress in the Anti-Drug Abuse Act of 1986, the White House Conference for a Drug Free America, convened by President Reagan in 1988, proposed numerous anti-drug recommendations that were later included in the Anti-Drug Abuse Act of 1988. Many of these recommendations reflected the administration's "zero tolerance" perspective,[14] which was, at least in part, symbolic. By drawing a line between those who use drugs or those who just accept drug use and those who do not, the Reagan and Bush administrations sought to "morally educate" the public to the dangers and illegality of drug use, not just the selling of and trafficking in drugs.

Presidential involvement in criminal justice policy making has also been evidenced during the Clinton administration. Marion[15] laid out a preliminary analysis of the crime control policies put forth by the Clinton administration from the perspective of tangible and symbolic politics.[16] By analyzing President Clinton's speeches, press conferences, and party platforms between 1992 and June 1996, she sought to examine whether Clinton successfully used crime policies as symbolic issues to help him gather public support or to serve another function. Marion asserted that while the Clinton administration appeared to be creating tangible policies to address crime, it was in actuality successfully using crime as a symbolic issue for public support. She argued that while President Clinton has stated that crime is a state matter, some of his anti-crime measures have federalized crimes that have been handled traditionally by the states, that is, carjacking, drive-by shootings, and possessions of a handgun near a school.[17]

Although recent presidents may have played a more active role in criminal justice policy making, presidential influence on criminal justice and crime is still limited. At the federal level, presidential influence is limited because the presidency is one of three branches of power and it cannot act independently. As the experience of President Johnson suggests, presidential initiatives often cannot be effected without the support and influence of Congress. Moreover, since crime continues to remain primarily a state and local matter, the impact of presidential initiatives on crime is limited due to the federal nature of the American system. Despite these limitations, crime is likely to remain an issue on the presidential agenda.

INCLUDED SELECTIONS

The selections in this chapter provide insight into the role of the presidency in criminal justice policy making and how presidents have influenced the expansion of the federal government's involvement in criminal justice.

The excerpt from President Johnson's 1965 crime message[18] to Congress, announcing the creation of his crime commission, presents his mandate to the commission. The excerpt from President Johnson's 1967 crime message lays out the themes raised by the commission and the president's recommendations to Congress.[19] Since the commission's recommendations and the subsequent legislation have affected the organization and responsibilities of the federal criminal justice bureaucracy, which is discussed in chapter 5 of this text, a selection on the work of the commission thirty years later is included in that chapter. The third selection included in chapter 3 is an excerpt from Nancy Marion's article on the symbolic dimensions of President Clinton's crime control agenda. Although focused on the Clinton administration, Marion's article provides insight into how U.S. presidents may influence the federal crime agenda and federal criminal justice policy making

FOR DISCUSSION

From the selections in this chapter the reader should consider:

1. How presidents can influence the criminal justice policy-making process.
2. How the 1965 President's crime commission affected U.S. thinking about crime.
3. Which recommendations of the 1965 President's crime commission are reflected in current criminal justice policies and which remain issues.
4. The role of symbolic politics in presidential criminal justice policy making.
5. How the presidential federal criminal justice policy-making role may be affected by federalism and the separation of powers.
6. How state and local chief executives may use the same types of tools as presidents to influence state and local criminal justice policies.

RECOMMENDED READINGS AND OTHER SOURCES

Specific References

The Challenge of Crime in a Free Society: A Report of the President's Commission on Law Enforcement and Administration of Justice. New York: Avon Books, 1968.

Marion, Nancy E. A History of Federal Crime Control Initiatives, 1960–93. Westport, CT: Praeger, 1994.

Marion, Nancy E. A Primer in the Politics of Criminal Justice. Albany, NY: Harrow and Heston, 1995.

Marion, Nancy E. "Symbolic Policies in Clinton's Crime Control Agenda," Buffalo Criminal Law Review, vol. 1, no. 1 (1997): 67–108.

The White House Conference for a Drug Free America: Final Report. Washington, DC: U.S. Government Printing Office, June 1988.

Web Site

White House. <http://www.whitehouse.gov>

SPECIAL MESSAGE TO THE CONGRESS ON LAW ENFORCEMENT AND THE ADMINISTRATION OF JUSTICE

To the Congress of the United States:

. . .

PRESIDENTIAL COMMISSION

The proposals which I have discussed are promising immediate approaches to a number of the specific problems of controlling crime. In the longer run we must also deepen our understanding of the causes of crime and of how our society should respond to the challenge of our present levels of crime. Only with such understanding can we undertake more fundamental, far-reaching and imaginative programs.

As the first step, I am establishing the President's Commission on Law Enforcement and Administration of Justice. The Commission will be composed of men and women of distinction who share my belief that we need to know far more about the prevention and control of crime. I will ask the Commission to make a comprehensive report to me by the summer of 1966 and to make interim reports when early action on the basis of its recommendations may be possible.

No agency of government has ever in our history undertaken to probe so fully and deeply into the problems of crime in our nation. I do not underestimate the difficulty of the assignment. But the very difficulty which these problems present and the staggering cost of inaction make it imperative that this task be undertaken.

It is of the utmost importance that the people of this country understand what is at stake in controlling crime and its effects. I believe therefore that the Commission should disseminate information on its work and findings and build a broad base of public support for constructive action.

Typical of the examples of important and troubling questions on which I believe the Commission can furnish guidance are—

(1) How can law enforcement be organized to meet present needs?

In too many instances present divisions of responsibility for law enforcement reflect unexamined precedent rather than practical organization. In addition to exploring improved law enforcement and correctional tech-

Reprinted and excerpted from "Special Message to the Congress on Law Enforcement and the Administration of Justice, March 8, 1965," *Public Papers of the President of the United States: Lyndon B. Johnson, Book I May 1–May 31, 1965* (Washington, DC: United States Government Printing Office, 1966), pp. 263–71.

niques, the Commission can be helpful in suggesting possible reorganization of law enforcement functions and methods of achieving greater cooperation where there are separate responsibilities.

(2) What steps can be taken to create greater understanding by those involved in the administration of justice at the state and local level of the efforts of federal courts to ensure protection of individual rights?

The Commission should seek understanding of the needs of those responsible for carrying out our criminal laws and the relationship to these needs of the historic protections our Nation has accorded to the accused. The Commission may well serve as a bridge of understanding among all those involved in the fair and effective administration of criminal justice.

(3) Through what kinds of programs can the Federal Government be most effective in assisting state and local enforcement?

The Commission can recommend new and imaginative ways in which the Federal Government can render assistance—without infringing on the primary responsibility of states and localities.

(4) Is the nation as a whole providing adequate education and training opportunities for those who administer the criminal laws?

The Commission should evaluate the programs and institutions now available for law enforcement officers, correctional personnel and both prosecution and defense attorneys and make recommendations on necessary additions.

(5) What correctional programs are most promising in preventing a first offense from leading to a career in crime?

A large proportion of serious crimes is committed by persons who are previous offenders. Thus, reducing the total volume of crime is, to a large extent, a problem of reducing the rate of recidivism. The first offender's initial contact with our correctional system is often a turning point in his life. The Commission should consider how we can best insure that his first contact will be his last.

(6) What steps can be taken to increase public respect for law and law enforcement officers?

In a free land, order can never be achieved by police action alone, no matter how efficient. There must be a high level of voluntary observance of the law and cooperation with public authorities. Citizens too often shun their duty to report crimes, summon assistance, or cooperate with law enforcement in other ways. In the light of recent examples of what happens when private citizens remain bystanders at tragedy, I hope the Commission will suggest means of improving public attitudes toward the individual's sense of responsibility to his community and to his neighbor.

These questions only illustrate those which this Commission must put to itself. It must also:

—consider the problem of making our streets, homes and places of business safer;

—inquire into the special problems of juvenile crime;

—examine the administration of justice in our shockingly overcrowded lower courts through which so many citizens are herded wholesale;

—explore the means by which organized crime can be arrested by Federal and local authorities.

In its task, the Commission will not be working alone. In addition to its own staff and subpanels of experts in various fields and disciplines, it will have the close cooperation and support of representatives of the Federal Government.

I have directed the Attorney General, the Secretary of the Treasury, and the Secretary of Health, Education, and Welfare and the Director of the Office of Economic Opportunity to work closely with the Commission and to assist it in every possible way. Because of the importance of the Attorney General's responsibilities within the Federal Government for these problems—ranging from investigation and enforcement through administration of the Federal prison system—I anticipate that the Department of Justice and especially its newly created Office of Criminal Justice should take a particularly active role in assisting the work of the Commission.

The Commission also will work closely with representatives of state and local government; with such groups as the American Bar Association, the American Law Institute, state and local bar groups and appropriate law enforcement organizations; and with universities and other institutions and individuals engaged in important work in the social sciences, mental health and related areas.

The task before the Commission is one of consummate difficulty and complexity. But it could scarcely be more important. I hope and expect that its work will be a landmark to follow for many years to come.

Lyndon B. Johnson

The White House, March 8, 1965

SPECIAL MESSAGE TO THE CONGRESS ON CRIME IN AMERICA

To the Congress of the United States

. . .

THE NATIONAL CRIME COMMISSION REPORT

Two weeks ago I received the report of the National Crime Commission, which I appointed in July 1965, to make the most comprehensive study of crime in the history of our country. That report is now being printed and will be available shortly. . . .

Six principal themes run through the Crime Commission report:

1. *Crime prevention is of paramount importance.*

Prevention of crime means equipping police forces to respond quickly to emergency calls. It means reducing crime opportunities: from theft-proof ignition systems for cars, to stricter controls on the sale of guns, from better street lights and modern alarm systems to tactical deployment of police forces in high crime areas.

But crime prevention also means elimination of the conditions which breed crime. In the words of the Crime Commission,

"there is no doubt whatever that the most significant action, by far, that can be taken against crime is action designed to eliminate slums and ghettos, to improve education, to provide jobs, to make sure that every American is given the opportunities and the freedoms that will enable him to assume his responsibilities. We will not have dealt effectively with crime until we have alleviated the conditions that stimulate it. To speak of controlling crime only in terms of the work of the police, the courts and the correctional apparatus alone, is to refuse to face the fact that widespread crime implies a widespread failure by society as a whole."

2. *The system of criminal justice must itself be just and it must have the respect and cooperation of all citizens.*

So long as perfunctory, mass-production methods prevail in many lower courts, so long as scandalous conditions exist in many jails—where, in 1965, 100,000 children were held in adult jails, and where attempts to rehabilitate are almost non-existent—we cannot achieve full public confidence in the system of criminal justice.

Reprinted and excerpted from "Special Message to the Congress on Crime in America," February 6, 1967," *Public Papers of the President of the United States: Lyndon B. Johnson, Book I January 1–June 30, 1967* (Washington, DC: United States Government Printing Office, 1968), pp. 134–45.

What is required of that system is a profound self-analysis, the willingness to change, and a massive effort to:

—Improve the caliber and training of law enforcement, judicial and corrections officials.

—Strengthen the capability of police to detect crimes and apprehend those who commit them.

—Extend the range and quality of treatment services.

—Make full use of advanced scientific methods in the courtroom, to reduce frustrating and unfair delays and to make available to the sentencing judge all necessary information about the defendant.

—Provide better counsel for juveniles and for adults who cannot afford to provide their own.

—Improve communication and understanding between law enforcement authorities and the urban poor.

So long as we deny police, courts and correctional agencies the resources they need to provide fair and dignified public service, large elements of our population will challenge both the institutions of justice and the values they represent.

What is required of citizens in every community in America is an understanding, not only of the critical importance of first-rate law enforcement, but also of the difficulties under which their police, judges, and corrections officials labor today. If local citizens are prepared to cooperate with their own system of justice and to support it with the resources it needs to discharge its duty, those difficulties can be substantially reduced.

3. *Throughout the criminal justice system, better-trained people are desperately needed and they must be more effectively used.*

The Crime Commission found that current personnel practices in most jurisdictions often fail to attract high-caliber men and women. Requiring each new police officer to begin his career as a patrolman makes the lateral entry of better-qualified men almost impossible. There are today few means of tapping the special knowledge and skills of those brought up in slums. Today's single, rigid line of police promotion and service is inefficient. Critical shortages of specially trained policemen, probation and parole officers, teachers, caseworkers, vocational instructors, and group counselors are severely weakening the criminal justice system.

There are many ways to attack this problem. Some police chiefs suggested to the Crime Commission that many police forces could be restructured, to provide for:

—*Uniformed "community service officers,"* who would maintain close relations with people in their areas and be alert to potentially dangerous conditions that should be brought to the attention of other city agencies for prompt action. These officers might not meet conventional educational requirements. They might even have had minor encounters with the law as teenagers. But they would know their areas and the people who live in them.

—*Police officers*, who would perform the traditional police patrol duties. Typically these officers would have graduated from high school.

—*Police agents*, who would take on the most sensitive and complex police assignments—patrolling in the highest crime neighborhoods, staff duties, police-community relations, solving the most difficult serious criminal cases. Two years of college, and preferably a baccalaureate degree, might be required for assignment as an agent.

—Entrance into police service at any one of these three levels, or opportunities to work their way up through the different levels as basic education and other qualifications were met.

4. *A far broader—and more profound—range of treatment is needed than the present correctional system provides.*

This applies to offenders of all ages, but it is especially true—and particularly important for the young. Since the generation of children about to enter teen-age is the largest in our history, we can anticipate an even sharper rise in juvenile delinquency in the decade to come—unless we make drastic changes in the effectiveness of the criminal justice system, as well as in economic and social conditions.

Many offenders, the young most of all, stand a far better chance of being rehabilitated in their home communities than in ordinary confinement. Recently the California Youth Authority concluded a 5-year experiment with various methods of treatment. Convicted juvenile delinquents were assigned on a random basis either to an experimental group where they were returned to their communities for intensive personal and family counseling, or to the regular institutions of correction. The findings to date are dramatically impressive:

—Only 28 percent of the experimental group had their paroles revoked.

—More than half—52 percent—of those confined in regular institutions later had their paroles revoked.

Falling back into crime was almost twice as great for those treated in regular institutions, as for those treated in the community. And it appears that the community treatment program costs far less than institutional confinement.

On the basis of this California experiment and its other studies, the Crime Commission concludes that local institutions related to the community, each housing as few as 50 inmates, and supported by a wide range of treatment services, should be developed throughout the country.

This will require the commitment of new resources by most communities. In a recent survey of juvenile court judges, 33 percent said that no psychologist or psychiatrist was available to their courts. A full third had neither probation officers nor social workers. Further, if many young offenders are better handled by community agencies other than juvenile courts, the potential of those agencies must be enlarged and fully tapped.

5. *Access to better information and to deeper and broader research is vital to police and correctional agencies.*

The Crime Commission found little research being done on the fundamental issues of criminal justice—for example, on the effect of punishment in deterring crime, or on the effectiveness of various police and correctional procedures.

Private research can be valuable. More state and local operations research is essential. Regional institutes for research should be established. Improved collection, dissemination and analysis of criminal justice statistics is essential for deeper insights into the causes of crime, its prevention and control, and better probation and correction programs. State and city planning would benefit from sounder and more precise predictions of future crime levels and problems.

6. *Substantially greater resources must be devoted to improving the entire criminal justice system.*

The Federal government must not and will not try to dominate the system. It could not if it tried. Our system of law enforcement is essentially local-based upon local initiative, generated by local energies and controlled by local officials. But the Federal government must help to strengthen the system, and to encourage the kind of innovations needed to respond to the problem of crime in America.

THE SAFE STREETS AND CRIME CONTROL ACT OF 1967

I recommend that the Congress enact the Safe Streets and Crime Control Act of 1967 to:

—Provide planning and program grants to states and local governments.

—Establish, in the Department of Justice, a Director of a new Office of Law Enforcement and Criminal Justice Assistance. The agency he heads will be a cooperative link with state and local agencies of criminal justice. It will give us the practical means of assisting and encouraging modernization throughout the system. It will operate the grant program established under the Act, and focus research on the causes, prevention, and control of crime.

I am requesting $50 million in fiscal 1968 under the Safe Streets and Crime Control Act, largely for planning grants, research and pilot projects. Our best estimate is that the Federal investment under this Act in the second year will be approximately $300 million. The Federal investment beyond the second year will depend upon the effective response of state and local governments.

I recommend Federal grants of up to 90 percent to states, cities and regional and metropolitan bodies to assist them to develop plans to improve their police, courts, and correctional systems.

Through these grants, we intend to encourage comprehensive approaches to the problems of crime. The close inter-locking of every element in the criminal justice system makes comprehensive planning mandatory. . . .

Almost any reform of this nature will have significant secondary effects. Treating each reform as an isolated matter will create conflicts and loss of effectiveness throughout the system. Thus, the grants under this provision will require that comprehensive plans be developed that take into account the interrelationship among all aspects of law enforcement, courts and corrections, as well as closely related social programs.

I recommend Federal grants of up to 60 percent to support approved programs in action.

These grants would encourage innovative efforts against street crime, juvenile delinquency, and organized crime. To be eligible, the state or local governing body–or bodies–must show an increase in its own expenditures by an annual increment of 5 percent. The 60 percent grant would be applied against the cost of the program in excess of that increment. It must also show that it has adopted a comprehensive plan, containing clear priorities and balancing the needs of all parts of the criminal justice system. . . .

I recommend Federal grants of up to 50 percent for the construction of significant new types of physical facilities, on a regional or metropolitan basis, such as:

—crime laboratories,

—community correction centers,

—police academy-type centers.

RESEARCH AND SPECIAL PROJECTS

. . .

Under the Law Enforcement Assistance Act of 1965, we have conducted a program to improve the techniques of law enforcement through research and pilot projects. This program has proved its value. Research, along with pilot projects, must be vigorously supported if we are to improve the criminal justice system.

As part of a broader crime control program, I propose superseding the

Law Enforcement Assistance Act with a broader program of research, development and special pilot project grants.

I recommend that the Safe Streets and Crime Control Act authorize the Attorney General to make research grants or contracts, of up to 100 percent, with public agencies, institutions of higher education, or other organizations.

These grants could be used to:

—Support research and education projects of regional or national importance.

—Establish national or regional institutes for research and education in law enforcement and criminal justice.

[The president's message continues with proposals to foster federal, state, and local cooperation; establish a program for young Americans; fight narcotics and dangerous drugs; control firearms; establish a unified federal correctional system; establish a federal judicial center; extend federal efforts to root out organized crime; and protect the right of privacy by limiting the use of wiretaps.]

. . .

We can control crime if we will. We must act boldly, now, to treat ancient evils and to insure the public safety.

Lyndon B. Johnson

The White House, February 6, 1967

SYMBOLIC POLICIES IN CLINTON'S CRIME CONTROL AGENDA

Nancy E. Marion

Despite the accepted notion that crime control is primarily a state issue,[20] the federal government has been involved in regulating crime since the 1960s.[21] Every president since Kennedy has placed crime on his agenda, some placing it higher than others. Since then, crime has also been an issue addressed by Congress. Because crime control is primarily a state responsibility, both the president and members of Congress are limited as to how much effect they can have on crime in the nation. Thus, they often rely on symbolic policies when creating crime legislation.

President Clinton has placed crime control high on his agenda during each year he has served in office. This study is a preliminary analysis of Clinton's crime control agenda since the 1992 election to determine if Clinton's policies are tangible or symbolic. By analyzing statements made by Clinton in speeches, press conferences and party platforms since 1992, when he first ran for national office, through June 1996,[22] I will examine whether Clinton successfully uses crime policies as symbolic issues to help him gather public support or to serve another function. I hypothesize that President Clinton, like other presidents, relies on symbolic politics to get electoral support, and public support once in office.

I. 1992: ELECTION YEAR: BUSH v. CLINTON

Arkansas Governor Bill Clinton first ran for president in 1992 against incumbent George Bush. President Bush attempted to make crime control a key issue, hoping that it would work for him in 1992 as it did against Massachusetts Governor Michael Dukakis in 1988, when Bush successfully implied that his Democratic opponent was soft on criminals. Unfortunately for Bush, Clinton proved to be almost as conservative as himself when it came to crime control. Not only did Clinton support many of the same policies as Bush, but he also had the background to support his statements. Clinton presided over four executions while he was Governor of Arkansas, proving to the public that he was tough on crime; it put him on an even keel with President Bush in terms of voter confidence about his ability to deal with crime.[23]

Reprinted and excerpted from "Symbolic Politics in Clinton's Crime Control Agenda," *Buffalo Criminal Law Review*, vol. 1, no. 1 (1997), 67–108, by Nancy E. Marion, Copyright 1997, with the permission of the author and the *Buffalo Criminal Law Review*.

Clinton's crime control agenda started to form during the 1992 election, and can be seen in the Democratic platform and in his campaign speeches. The 1992 Democratic platform stated that crime was increasing in the U.S., particularly affecting the inner cities. The party promised to restore government as the upholder of basic law and order for these and all crime-ravaged communities. Clinton's long-term plans to reduce crime included better schools, Head Start programs for disadvantaged pre-schoolers, better health care, more jobs, more job training, equal opportunities, and revitalizing the cities—very similar to the 'Great Society' programs under the Johnson Administration.[24]

Clinton supported a more conservative approach than one would expect from a liberal candidate in the area of law enforcement. Clinton promised to put 100,000 new officers on the street, and to increase the presence of safety officers on the street through a "national service trust fund."[25] Clinton advocated community-based policing that involved cops walking beats and knowing the neighbors, as opposed to patrols only responding to 911 calls.[26]

Clinton also promised to provide increased law enforcement and judicial resources to fight the war on drugs,[27] and he also supported tougher penalties for certain crimes. Finally, Clinton emphasized his resistance to efforts to restrict weapons used for legitimate hunting and sporting purposes. But for those who violate the country's gun laws, Clinton thought there should be swift and certain punishment, as well as stronger sentences for criminals who use guns. Clinton supported legislation that included a ban on the possession, sale, importation and manufacture of the most deadly assault weapons as well as a reasonable waiting period for handgun purchases.

Clinton's anti-crime agenda also supported liberal ideas. He viewed illegal drug abuse primarily as a public health and education issue, and proposed to expand drug counseling treatment on demand for those who wanted it. Concerning corrections, Clinton supported non-incarcerative alternatives for non-violent, first-time, and youthful offenders, such as boot camps.[28] The Democrats also favored innovative sentencing and punishment options, including community service.

In addition to these ideas, Clinton spoke of a federal partnership between federal, state and local governments. He explained that since the state and local authorities are on the front lines and deal with crime each day, the federal government should provide resources, expertise, and leadership to help reduce crime. He supported what he thought was a more effective allocation of resources and responsibilities between the federal and state governments in controlling crime.

Other ideas were also proposed in the 1992 Democratic platform. The Democrats supported programs to reduce child and spousal abuse; they focused on white collar crime; victim-impact statements and restitution were proposed to ensure that crime victims would be recognized by the criminal justice system. Finally, initiatives to make our schools safe, including alternative schools for disruptive children, were included in the platform.

In sum, Clinton's agenda for crime control in 1992 was varied. It was both conservative and liberal, and included illicit drug abuse, law enforcement issues, victims, domestic violence, firearms, white collar crime, prisons, and safe schools. On the whole, Clinton's agenda was much more conservative than one would ordinarily expect from a liberal candidate for president. It encompassed many areas that were traditionally Republican strongholds but also included liberal approaches as well. This was a surprise to both the Republicans and the public, and helped to get Clinton elected into office that year.

II. CLINTON'S 1993 AGENDA

First and foremost, Clinton stated that the most effective control on criminal activity is strong communities and families.[29] Beyond this, however, there were concrete proposals for stopping crime. One agenda issue was stopping illicit drug use. Clinton supported shifting the federal approach to drug use from punishment to drug treatment and rehabilitation. The best approach, according to Clinton, is one that encompasses a "multifaceted offensive" that includes "more and better education, more treatment, more rehabilitation."[30] In addition, Clinton pledged "to work with other nations who have shown the courage and the political will to take on their own drug traffickers who destabilize their own societies and their own economies."[31]

In April 1993 Clinton chose Dr. Lee Brown as his first drug czar to coordinate the federal efforts to control drug trafficking. Brown was the first police official to head the agency, and had previous policing experience running the New York City, Houston and Atlanta police departments. Clinton also decided to restructure the Office of National Drug Control Policy by downsizing it from 146 employees to just 25, while concurrently raising it to cabinet status.[32] The Administration's drug control plan called for more treatment of hard-core drug users and for prevention programs for vulnerable populations such as children and pregnant women. The proposal provided money to state and local law enforcement agencies to improve their anti-drug programs and to develop juvenile justice and delinquency prevention programs. In his FY '94 budget, Clinton proposed a modest increase (about $300,000) in the "Weed and Seed" program that was intended to force drug dealers and criminals out of urban neighborhoods and provide residents new social service programs.

Another Clinton agenda issue was support for a strong law enforcement program to reduce crime. A key campaign issue was the promise to put

100,000 more officers on the streets who would focus on community policing techniques. Clinton believed in community policing

not only because it helps to prevent crime and to lower the crime rate but because
it cements better relationships between the people in law enforcement and the people that they're hired to protect. It reduces the chances of abusive action by police
officers and increases the chances of harmony and safe streets at the same time.[33]

Clinton continued to support the National Service Program to help increase police presence on the street. To further protect police officers, Clinton proposed an outright ban on so-called cop-killer, i.e., talon, bullets.
Despite these promises, Clinton's FY '94 budget included $206 million
in cuts in aid to local police agencies; approximately $40 million was cut
from the FBI budget. The outlays for federal law enforcement programs
dropped slightly and included $50 million to promote local community
policing efforts, $25 million to provide scholarships to students pursuing
law enforcement careers who promise to serve as police officers, and $25
million to upgrade federal criminal record-keeping systems.
Clinton's budget proposal did include grants to state and local governments to recruit officers, and to upgrade their criminal records and network
with federal law enforcement. Attorney General Reno announced that local
law enforcement agencies that wanted federal assistance to hire more officers could start applying for some of the $150 million Congress allocated
for that purpose. Applicants were required to show how additional officers
would lead to more community policing and how they would retain the
added positions after the three-year grant period ended.
The third agenda issue for Clinton was gun control. He wanted to limit
the types of weapons people could own. Assault weapons, according to the
President, should be banned. Clinton also supported the Brady Bill,[34] and
he wanted limits on gun dealers.[35]
Fourth, Clinton supported research into the causes and the most effective
policies to control crime. To assist him in this effort he appointed a group
of law enforcement leaders and academics to advise him on crime and law
enforcement issues. This included police executives, elected officials, and
leaders of professional associations.
Alternatives to incarceration for young first time, non-violent offenders
was the fifth issue on the Clinton agenda. Clinton supported boot camps
to give "young people the discipline, the training, the treatment they need
for a second chance to build a good life."[36] But his FY '94 budget proposal
demonstrates some inconsistencies in these promises. He proposed cuts of
$331 million for prison construction for the following five years, but al-
located $151 million to allow the Federal Prison System to build 4,620 new
beds. He also proposed three new federal prisons, creating approximately
4,600 new beds that would open in 1994. However, he also proposed

saving $331 million over four years by slowing the rate of prison construction.

Finally, the crime bill was an important agenda issue to Clinton, and he worked with enthusiasm to see it passed. When he took office, Clinton said he was going to get a crime bill passed quickly, but was sidetracked by budget fights with Congress and a delay in appointing the Attorney General. Clinton finally proposed a crime bill on August 11, 1993.[37]

Clinton called for strong bipartisan support to make the bill an effective anti-crime measure that was based on fact, not on party politics.[38] Clinton promised to do what he could to get the bill passed stating, "I pledge to you my best and strongest efforts to pass this bill at the earliest possible time. There are good things in it. It will make our people safer. It will shore up our police officers. It will move America in the right direction."[39]

Overall, Clinton gave forty-three speeches that either focused solely on crime control or mentioned it in 1993 (see Table 3.1). This agenda list is far more detailed than the one from 1992, when Clinton was just a candidate. It shows his apparent commitment and concern about crime in the nation, and his willingness to work to reduce it.

III. 1994: CLINTON'S SECOND YEAR IN OFFICE: 103RD CONGRESS

Since the 1960s, crime had been a solidly Republican issue in presidential politics, with voters viewing Republicans as tougher on crime than Democrats.[40] Since then, Democrats have fought the reputation of being soft on crime, and under the Clinton administration, have finally begun making inroads into those stereotypes. In 1994, both the President and Democratic members of Congress wanted to continue fighting the liberal image on crime control. But at the same time, Republicans wanted to get the issue back in their court and remain as the party known as being hard on crime.

In his first State of the Union, President Clinton acknowledged the problem of violent crime by citing the case[s] of Polly Klaas, where a young girl was kidnapped and killed; the Long Island train shooting, where a man opened fire on a commuter train; the murder of Florida tourists; and a murder in Washington, D.C. Clinton stated that crime was the result of the "breakdown of community, family and work" and that the fear of violent crime was "crippling our society" by placing limits on personal freedom and breaking apart community ties. Clinton acknowledged that Congress passed the Brady Bill and the National Service Program, but noted that more needed to be done. However, he also acknowledged that "most laws, criminal laws, are State laws, and most criminal law enforcement is done by local police officials."[41] Despite this, Clinton created a clear agenda for crime control. Clinton's agenda was similar to that of the previous year, with some minor changes. In 1994 he spent more time discussing correc-

Table 3.1
Clinton's 1993 Agenda

Topic	Number of Mentions
Crime Bill Passage	19
Gun Controls	
Brady Bill/Waiting Period	23
Purchase only One Gun/Month	2
Regulations on Gun Dealers	4
Assault Weapons Ban	15
Ban Ownership by Juveniles	6
Gun Imports Ban	2
Right to Own Guns	5
Safe Schools	6
Law Enforcement	
More Police/100,000 Officers	26
Community Policing	18
National Service Program	7
Community/Family Involvement	11
Drug Policy	
International Cooperation	4
Counseling and Treatment	8
Education	6
Rehabilitation	2
Drug Czar	2
Boot Camps/Alternatives	10
Capital Punishment	2
Youth Crime/Gangs	3
Parental Kidnapping	1

tions, grants to states, crime in public housing, domestic violence, and others (see Table 3.2).

The primary issue on Clinton's 1994 agenda was the prompt passage of the proposed anti-crime bill. Clinton was very forward in indicating what he wanted in that bill including a "three strikes you're out" provision where, upon conviction of a repeated violent offense, the offender would be sentenced to life in prison; more police officers and more community policing; a national police corps; more money for drug treatment; boot camps for youthful offenders that include programs for the youth to get off drugs and to stay off drugs; provisions for tougher sentences for violent criminals and more prisons to house them; and provisions for prevention

Table 3.2
Clinton's 1994 Agenda

Topic	Number of Mentions
Law Enforcement	
More Police/100,000 Officers	39
Community Policing	21
National Service Program	4
Gun Controls	
Brady Bill/Waiting Period	10
Ban Ownership by Juveniles	17
Assault Weapons Ban	29
Regulations on Gun Dealers	1
Gun Imports Ban	1
Right to Own Guns	4
Corrections	
More Prisons	19
No Parole	1
3 Strikes-You're-Out	26
Boot Camps/Alternatives	9
Community/Family Involvement	11
Youth Crime/Gangs	17
Drug Policy	
Counseling and Treatment	8
Education	3
Drug Courts	1
International Cooperation	2
Crime Bill Passage	41
Grants to States	6
Public Housing	9
Capital Punishment	8
Crime Prevention	14
Safe Schools	8
Domestic Violence	3
Health Care	3
TV/Music/Movie Violence	2
Child Sexual Predators	2
Abortion Clinic Access	1
Mediation	1
Neighborhood Watch	1
Violence against Women	1

programs for at-risk youth. Clinton also repeated the need for bipartisan support of the anti-crime bill.[42] Clinton called for legislation banning assault weapons and handgun ownership by minors while at the same time allowing hunters and law-abiding citizens to own guns.[43] Clinton continued to reiterate the importance of community and family in reducing criminal activity.[44] The President also continued his support for safe and drug-free schools. He said we need to "make our schools gun-free, drug-free, and violence-free. If kids can't go to school safe, this country cannot move into the 21st century in good shape."[45]

One of the new agenda issues for the President was a proposal for "three strikes and you're out." The President said "if you commit three violent crimes, you shouldn't be paroled ever."[46] To stop crime in public housing, Clinton proposed a "policy allowing police to sweep public housing so that criminals cannot find shelter in the places they terrorize."[47] A third new agenda issue for Clinton was violence against women and children, who would find greater protection under the proposed crime bill that imposed "tougher penalties on those who prey on them."[48] Finally, Clinton also proposed grants to states "to put new police on the street in 150 more cities and towns,"[49] and to make available "more funds for prisons to house serious offenders."[50]

Clinton's FY '95 budget proposed allocating $17.3 billion for fighting crime and related law and judicial activities. Of that, $698 million went to finance the proposed anti-crime package and to put 100,000 new officers on the street. Clinton allocated $100 million to implement the Brady Bill.[51] Under the proposed budget, spending for federal prisons would increase 17% to a total of $2.6 billion. The final appropriations for the Justice Department provided $2.3 billion in funding for anti-crime initiatives in the proposed crime bill. This actually reduced the administration's requests by $767 million. Of the $2.3 billion, $1.3 billion was slated for community policing programs.[52]

Clinton's drug policy included $76 million to cut the production of cocaine in countries like Colombia and Peru. The emphasis of the program was not on more police but rather treatment of addicts. To carry out his program Clinton asked Congress for an increase of $355 million aimed at heavy drug users. When Congress appropriated funds for Clinton's budget they gave approximately $80 million of the $355 million the President requested, providing, instead, more money for law enforcement.

IV. 1995: CLINTON'S THIRD YEAR IN OFFICE/104TH CONGRESS

For the first time in many years, the Republicans won the majority in both the House and Senate. They immediately announced their *Contract with America*,[53] which identified areas in which the Republicans wanted to see action, and gave themselves 100 days to address the issues. The second point in the contract was crime.[54] The GOP promised to rewrite the 1994 crime bill to add new mandatory minimum sentences,[55] make it easier to impose the death penalty,[56] and transfer money from crime prevention to prison construction.[57] The Republicans also wanted stronger "truth-in-sentencing,"[58] "good faith" exclusionary rule exceptions,[59] and additional law enforcement officers to keep people secure in their neighborhoods and children safe in their schools.[60]

Clinton was very concerned that the new Republican majority would succeed in rewriting the bill which he had worked on so hard and in which he had so much faith. During 1995 Clinton gave ninety speeches about crime or some aspect of it (see Table 3.3), and many of those speeches dealt with the importance of the 1994 anti-crime bill.[61] Of the Republican plan, Clinton said, "[t]hey want to replace an initiative guaranteed to put 100,000 police on the street with a block grant program that has no guarantees at all."[62] Clinton continued to acknowledge the importance of family and communities in reducing crime. "The first line of defense, of course, has to be in our communities, with our parents and teachers and our neighbors, other role models in law enforcement and the religious community, telling our young people in no uncertain terms that drugs and violence are wrong."[63] Many issues kept arising in Clinton's speeches, including the crime bill, law enforcement issues, assault weapons, and his anti-drug strategy. Clinton's agenda continued to expand to include new issues such as drug testing of student athletes,[64] enforcement of child support laws, anti-terrorism legislation, zero tolerance for guns in schools,[65] and the V-chip to help parents monitor television violence.[66]

Maintaining the assault weapons ban continued to be a primary concern for Clinton. He said,

we should not repeal the assault weapons ban. We should not do that. This issue . . . is not a Republican-Democratic issue, it is not a liberal-conservative issue; it is overwhelmingly an urban-non-urban issue. And what we have to do is to convince people . . . that . . . we don't want to fool with anybody's hunting rifles. . . . We don't want to interfere with anybody's legitimate pursuit of happiness in the exercise of their right to keep and bear arms. But there is nothing in the Constitution that prevents us from exercising common sense.[67]

Additionally, the importance of maintaining the Brady Bill was repeated by Clinton. He said, "over 40,000 convicted felons, fugitives, drug dealers, gang members, stalkers, were prevented from purchasing handguns in the Brady law's first 11 months."[68] Clinton continued to support law enforcement this year, with calls for increased police on the street and community policing. He also called for a ban on talon bullets. "If a bullet can rip

Table 3.3
Clinton's 1995 Agenda

Topic	Number of Mentions
Law Enforcement	
More Police/100,000 Officers	38
Community Policing	18
Talon Bullet Ban	3
Gun Controls	
Brady Bill/Waiting Period	15
Ban on Assault Weapons	26
Increase Penalties	1
Right to Own Guns	4
Corrections	
More Prisons	10
Increased Punishments	8
3 Strikes-You're-Out	12
Community/Family Involvement	15
Youth Crime/Gangs	11
Drug Policy	26
Counseling and Treatment	7
Education	10
International Cooperation	11
Testing/Student Athletes	4
Crime Bill	36
Grants to States	13
Capital Punishment	8
Crime Prevention	14
Safe Schools	16
Zero Tolerance	4
Domestic Violence	9
Abortion Clinic Access	1
Republican Plan	9
Terrorism	23
Oklahoma City Bombing	26
World Trade Center Bombing	2
Child Support	12
V-chip	1

through a bulletproof vest like a knife through hot butter, then it ought to be history."[69]

Another important agenda issue for Clinton was drug use, especially since reports showed that drug use among youth was on the rise. Clinton supported working with other nations to reduce drugs coming into the U.S.,[70] as well as supporting treatment of drug users.[71]

Terrorism became an agenda issue after the Oklahoma City bombing. He wanted legislation that would increase federal investigative powers to combat terroristic acts, add an additional 1,000 new federal law enforcement employees to track terrorism threats and prosecute offenders, create an interagency center on domestic counterterrorism to be headed by the FBI, provide a broader federal wiretap authority under court order for terrorism cases, allow the military to assist federal law enforcement in cases involving chemical and biological weapons, and impose a mandatory minimum prison sentence of ten years for transferring a firearm or explosive with the knowledge that it will be used in a violent or drug trafficking crime.[72]

Despite all these proposals, Clinton continued to acknowledge that crime is a state issue. He said, "most laws that deter crime are passed in the State level, by the State legislature. And most laws then have to be implemented as a matter of policy by local police organizations."[73]

V. 1996: CLINTON'S FOURTH YEAR IN OFFICE/ 104TH CONGRESS/ ELECTION YEAR

In his State of the Union address, Clinton reported that violent crime was decreasing in the U.S., which, according to the 1996 Democratic Platform, was due to the new crime bill that put new officers on the streets and the "three-strikes-you're-out" legislation. Clinton's anti-crime agenda for the first half of 1996 included many issues already discussed: the crime bill; assault weapons ban; drug policy; the television V-chip.[74] But he added some new issues, including tracking dangerous sexual predators, neighborhood watch programs,[75] curfews, and a "one-strike-you're-out" program for people found to have drugs in public housing (see Table 3.4).

Law enforcement was still a priority on Clinton's agenda. Of course, he still supported his program to increase the number of officers on the street by 100,000 and a ban on cop-killer bullets, he also asked citizens to respect the police so community policing would work. On May 15, Clinton announced $604 million in federal grants to hire nearly 9,000 police officers across the country. The money was slated to hire 8,646 full time and 472 part-time officers in more than 2,500 communities in forty-six states, Puerto Rico and American Samoa to work in community policing programs. The Justice Department reported that this would bring the number of new officers hired or funded under the program to 43,000.

Table 3.4
Clinton's 1996 Agenda (Through June)

Topic	Number of Mentions
Law Enforcement	
More Police/100,000 Officers	22
Community Policing	8
Talon Bullet Ban	2
Gun Controls	
Brady Bill/Waiting Period	15
Ban on Assault Weapons	12
Corrections	
3 Strikes-You're-Out	3
Community/Family Involvement	10
Youth Crime/Gangs	19
Drug Policy	9
Counseling and Treatment	2
Education	7
International Cooperation	5
Prevention	2
Public Housing	1
Crime Bill	14
Grants to States	3
Capital Punishment	2
Crime Prevention	4
Republican Plan	2
Safe Schools	5
Zero Tolerance	3
Domestic Violence	3
Terrorism	11
Oklahoma City Bombing	7
World Trade Center Bombing	4
V-chip	4
Neighborhood Watch Programs	7
Curfews	2
Church Burnings	3
Megan's Law	4

In May, Clinton announced a plan to attack gang and youth violence. He asked the FBI to take on gangs the way it had taken on the mob, and proposed legislation designed to produce tougher prosecution of juvenile offenders and to keep guns and drugs away from young people. This would make it easier for prosecutors to try more juveniles as adults and give judges more flexibility to impose longer sentences on youthful offenders.

Clinton asked the states to have truth-in-sentencing and have serious violent offenders serve at least 85% of their sentence. Under his administration, Clinton asked states to guarantee that violent criminals serve at least 85% of their sentence. To help them do this, Clinton promised to provide $8 billion in new funding to help states build new prison cells.

Drugs also received more attention from Clinton. He nominated Barry McCaffrey as the new drug czar to cut the flow of drugs into America. McCaffrey was a hero of the Persian Gulf, commander-in-chief of the U.S. Military's Southern Command, as well as the recipient of three purple hearts and two silver stars. The new drug czar presented a $15.1 billion anti-drug strategy to the Senate in May 1996 that had anti-drug education as its first priority. Clinton challenged Congress to not cut support for drug-free schools. He also signed a directive requiring drug testing of anyone arrested for a federal crime, and he challenged states to do the same for state offenders. To help control drug use in inner cities, Clinton backed Operation Safe Home, which was designed to protect the law-abiding residents of public housing from violent criminals and drug dealers who use their homes as a base for illegal activities. Finally, Clinton supported a "one-strike-and-you're-out" policy for those found with drugs in public housing.[76]

Clinton signed Megan's law[77] on May 17 to require that states tell a community whenever a dangerous sexual predator enters its midst. In June, Clinton endorsed legislation that would create a national registry to track sex offenders and child molesters. Now, every state in the country must compile a registry of sex offenders. In another attempt to help children, Clinton signed an executive order requiring that missing children posters be allowed to be posted in courthouses and other facilities. The order was the result of the experience of a family in Florida whose child was missing, and who put up posters that were torn down.

Gun control continued to be on Clinton's agenda. He wanted to make it a federal crime for any person under eighteen to possess a handgun except when supervised by an adult. He also supported a zero tolerance for guns in schools, requiring schools to expel for one year any student who brings a gun to school. Clinton announced a program to trace weapons seized from juveniles to identify and arrest those who supply weapons to kids.

Clinton also supported victims rights by advocating on behalf of a Constitutional amendment to protect the victims of crime. As a country, he said, we must guarantee that the victims of violent crimes are treated with the respect and the dignity they deserve. The amendment was proposed on May 22 to mark National Crime Victims' Rights Week. It would give victims of violent crime the right to speak at the sentencing of their attacker and would be protected from intimidation, and would also be informed of any release or escape of the criminal. Very little was done with the proposal.

VI. 1996 PRESIDENTIAL ELECTION: CLINTON v. DOLE

The 1996 presidential election was interesting because the question of crime was reminiscent of the 1992 election. The Republican nominee, Bob Dole, attacked Clinton as being a soft-on-crime liberal, and Clinton, of course, responded with his own attacks on Dole, whom he accused as talking tough on crime but not acting tough. The election was similar to 1992 because the Republican nominee attempted to make crime an issue, but was unsuccessful because Clinton is more conservative on crime than previous Democrats. In addition, national polls indicate that crime and drugs were ranked far below other issues such as the economy and health care by voters.

To beat the image that he is soft on crime, Clinton continued to emphasize his accomplishments in office geared at stopping crime: 43,000 new officers on the street (with intentions to hire up to 100,000), the Brady Bill, the assault weapons ban, and anti-gang proposals. He claimed to have increased the number of crimes that carry the death penalty, widen[ed] the use of wiretaps, and propose[ed] legislation to make methamphetamine sentences the same as crack sentences. Clinton also cut aid to Columbia, and has received cooperation with Mexico to track down billionaire drug traffickers. He gave public housing authorities the power to evict tenants found with drugs. Additionally, Clinton repeated that he did not commute the sentences of any prisoners during his four years in office, and has overseen the highest level of incarceration in this country's history. The Administration reported that as a result of Clinton's policies, violent crime went down across the nation each year during his presidency.

Republican challenger Bob Dole pointed out that President Clinton coddles criminals, especially because he supported education rather than punishment for drugs and he called for the abolition of parole for violent offenders. He accused Clinton of talking like Dirty Harry but acting like Barney Fife. Dole promised that if elected, he would lead the nation in a "real war" to punish criminals. Dole promised to appoint judges who will protect the rights of crime victims, and not expand the rights of the criminals. He said he would make sure violent criminals serve more than a fraction of their sentences, make prisoners work to offset incarceration costs, and vigorously prosecute those who use guns in criminal acts.

Clinton and Dole were similar on many issues. They both supported "truth in sentencing" legislation that forces offenders to serve their entire sentence. Neither candidate supported early release or parole for violent offenders, but both supported federal money that would help states build more prisons. Both candidates also supported similar policies for drug control: international interdiction, and money for safe schools and drug education in schools. Both candidates supported treating juveniles as adults when they commit serious violent offenses, and both candidates came out in favor of a proposal to prohibit those convicted of domestic violence (or that are under a restraining order from the court) from buying a handgun.

However, there were some significant differences between the two candidates. One area where there were distinct differences was drug control. Dole pointed to many indicators that Clinton was not effective at reducing drug use, and even accused Clinton of "wink-and-a-nod" policies toward drug use. For example, he said that a president should convey a message that drug use is morally repugnant, and that Clinton, since he used drugs before, could not fill that role. One of Dole's campaign ads showed Clinton, during a 1992 interview on MTV, saying that if he could relive his college days, he would probably inhale while smoking marijuana. Dole also pointed to Clinton's reduction in the Office of Drug Control Policy as an indication that Clinton does not care about drug use. Dole called on the entertainment industry to halt movies and music that glamorize drug use, and coined the phrase "just don't do it" to emphasize his commitment to educating youth about the dangers of drug abuse. Dole claimed to be able to cut drug use by 50 percent if elected.

Clinton responded by saying that it was wrong to have tried drugs, and that he regrets it. He wants to see treatment upon request for those addicted to drugs, as well as more emphasis on education as a prevention to drug use. He claimed that Dole voted against creating the drug policy director's office, and that he voted against money for school anti-drug programs. There were also distinct differences between the two candidates with regard to law enforcement. Clinton wanted to continue to put additional officers on the street that would emphasize community policing. Dole, on the other hand, wanted to replace the 100,000 officer program with grants to allow local officials to choose their own programs to suit their needs. Dole was opposed to the Brady Bill, instead supporting an instant check system, and he wanted to repeal the assault weapons ban, but later backed away from that promise. Dole also supported the concealed weapons policies enacted in many states across the country. Clinton disagreed with Dole, and continued to support the Brady Bill, the assault weapons ban, and the ban on cop-killer bullets. On September 16, Dole unveiled an anti-crime program that would double federal spending on state prison construction (currently at $405 million a year), and would require all able-bodied federal prisoners to work no less than forty hours per week to help compensate the victims of their crimes. Part of the proposal also included a Constitutional amendment guaranteeing crime victims certain rights, including the right to be heard at sentencing.

Despite the rhetoric, Clinton was reelected to office in November. Crime played only a minor role in the campaign.

VII. SUMMARY/CONCLUSION

Although it appears as if President Clinton has created tangible policies to combat crime and drug use in the country, an analysis of those policies actually shows otherwise. Clinton successfully uses crime as a symbolic issue for public support.

Clinton repeatedly says that crime is an issue that belongs to the individual states. However, he continues to propose anti-crime legislation on the federal level. The federal government, however, is Constitutionally limited as to which areas it can become involved in, and crime control is one of those areas. This means that the majority of anti-crime legislation must come from the states, and that federal legislation should be minimal. Any anti-crime legislation is therefore symbolic since it is not a product of the primary crime-control body in the country.

Despite the fact that Clinton agrees that crime control belongs in the state arena, his anti-crime legislation actually federalized many crimes that were traditionally state issues such as carjacking, drive-by shootings, possession of a handgun near a school, possession of a handgun by a juvenile, embezzlement from an insurance company, theft of "major artwork", and murder of a state official assisting a federal law enforcement agent. Since many of these crimes are already outlawed by the states, they have become symbolic gestures for Congress. "Clearly, a major cause of the federalization of criminal law is the desire of some members of Congress to appear tough on crime, though they know well that crime is fought most effectively at the local level."[78] By passing these laws, Congress and the President appear to be doing something when indeed they are not.

The federalization of crimes may have little effect on the U.S. crime rate. Since most crimes are still under the jurisdiction of the states, new federal sentences or regulations may have little impact. "The fact is that, for all the politicians' promises and the voters' frustration, the federal criminal justice system has precious little to do with fighting the kind of crime that Americans fear. Ninety-five percent of the criminal prosecutions in America are brought at the state and local level."[79] Since only six percent of those behind bars in the U.S. are federal prisoners, federal legislation is going to affect very few inmates.

The anti-crime legislation passed in 1994, first proposed by Clinton and including many of Clinton's agenda issues, is symbolic in and of itself. The bill received a lot of attention during debate and for a long time after passage. Politicians who supported it also received a lot of attention and credit for "doing something" about the crime problem in the nation. However, when each item is examined more closely, it can be seen that the bill offers no real solutions to the crime problem.

Although Clinton supports the death penalty and even used it as Governor, the inclusion of capital punishment in the 1994 crime bill was purely symbolic. This is simply because the death penalty, as it is now implemented, does not reduce crime on either the state or federal level. The literature on these studies is overwhelming. "There is no correlation between the frequency of crime and the presence or absence of the death penalty in the various states."[80] In addition, the death penalty has not been used on the federal level for many years. The obvious question emerges: how can capital punishment reduce crime when it is not used? The death penalty makes it appear as if Clinton is tough on crime, but it is more or less meaningless when it comes to actually reducing violent crime. "Politicians have found that it is easier to reaffirm their support for the death penalty during a political campaign by using a thirty-second sound bite than to offer a meaningful program that seriously addresses the crime problem in America."[81]

The handgun legislation passed during the Clinton administration also has elements of symbolism. All in all, the Brady law "is not expected to make much of a dent in the epidemic of gun violence."[82] Those people who want guns can get them, legally or not. Overall, there is no evidence that increased gun control laws can reduce violent crime.[83] Despite this, many Americans support Clinton in his battle to keep the Brady law on the books. "A new nationwide survey of 1,479 people showed growing public support for Clinton's efforts to control the use of handguns—57 percent approved, 29 percent disapproved, and the rest expressed no opinion."[84] The survey also showed that "51 percent opposed a ban on handgun sales, while 45 percent favored one."[85] This means that the issue of gun control as a symbolic policy for Clinton is providing Clinton with public support while making no tangible changes in the national crime rate.

Boot camps, as an alternative to prison, have received a lot of attention from the public because of their claims of rehabilitation and low recidivism rates. However, most boot camp populations are comprised of volunteers who choose this option over prison. This population of volunteers may have had low recidivism rates had they gone through a boot camp or a prison term. Marvin Wolfgang, of the University of Pennsylvania, says that "the research on boot camps shows they're not effective . . . but they sound good and tough."[86] For a politician such as Clinton, supporting boot camps gives the impression of being tough on young criminals, but at the same time understanding that young, first time offenders will not be put through the horrors of a correctional facility.

The Clinton Administration can argue that it has a tough anti-drug policy, but chances are its drug policy will do little to stop illicit drug use in the nation. One anti-drug strategy involves working with other countries to arrest leaders of drug cartels, and to reduce the flow of drugs into our country. It has been recognized that "federal agents can no more stop drugs from crossing our borders than they can stop illegal aliens."[87] Others have noted that "[u]nless and until there is a dramatic reduction in demand, supply will continue to outstrip law enforcement's ability to deal with it."[88] "Public policies and criminal justice system efforts to reduce supplies of narcotics have been more symbolic than effective."[89] Requiring drug testing of all federal prisoners and making it easier to kick drug dealers and their families out of public housing will also do little to reduce drug use by youth across the country.

Clinton's approach to halting illicit drug use is not terribly different from those policies supported by earlier presidents, liberal or conservative. They all involve some mix of treatment and punishment. "Despite the President's announcement that the national drug strategy would change, despite the change in the country's drug users, the tactics coming from Washington are essentially the same, and these tactics come not just from a Congress acutely aware of the crime issue, but from an administration with similar instincts."[90] Drug use under previous administrations did not go down significantly, as it failed to do under the Clinton administration.

Many people doubt that the curfew program supported by Clinton will do much to reduce crime in our nation. Most cities already impose curfews—three-quarters of the nation's largest 200 municipalities have some sort of law that orders teens indoors after dark. Curfews have done nearly as much good as they are likely to do at this point.

Overall, it is doubtful that the 1994 anti-crime legislation will do much to combat the crime problem in the U.S. According to Epstein, "[m]any outside experts doubt that . . . [the bill] . . . would do little to reduce the muggings, robberies, rapes and murders that infest high-crime areas daily."[91] In addition, James Fyfe of Temple University said that no legislation from the federal government will reduce violence on the streets of cities.[92] But the bill does serve an important purpose: it makes the President appear as if he cares about people, and that he is working to protect them. Obviously this is especially important to a first-term president seeking re-election.

An important question to ask is if any president can solve the problem of crime in our country. Many reply "no." Since crime is primarily a state issue, the federal government can have very little impact on the crime problem. In addition, the separation of powers prohibits the president from making laws by himself. Laws have to be made with the agreement of Congress (and the Courts). This means that the president cannot take all the blame, nor the credit, for laws that do or do not work. Additionally, our government changes every other year, and people in office need to pass laws quickly to portray the image of working on the problem. Unfortu-

nately, quick fixes do not work to solve the problems related to crime in
our country.

The danger inherent in these symbolic policies lies in the fact that the
public may perceive the crime problem to be much less complicated than
it really is. When Clinton suggests that crime has gone down in the past
four years as a result of the 1994 anti-crime legislation, and the shift towards community policing, he suggests that a complex societal problem
such as crime can be solved very simply. Long-term solutions are not created by the politicians—only quick, short-term changes are sought. Most
politicians would find it difficult, if not impossible, to publicly state that
crime control must involve long-term solutions based on fact rather than
the need for immediate and possibly misleading changes. Of course, long-
term solutions may be impossible in our political system where lawmakers
may come and go every other year. The need for immediate results becomes
necessary for these individuals who are concerned with maintaining public
support for a possible reelection bid.

NOTES

1. Nancy E. Marion, *A Primer in the Politics of Criminal Justice* (Albany, NY:
Harrow and Heston, 1995), p. 28.

2. Thomas E. Cronin, Tania Z. Cronin, and Michael E. Milakovich, *U.S. v.
Crime in the Streets* (Bloomington: Indiana University Press, 1981), p. 18.

3. James Calder asserts that reform of federal law enforcement, courts, and
corrections agencies from 1929 to 1933, during the administration of President
Herbert Hoover, is a piece of crime policy history largely unrecognized by crimi-
nologists, criminal justicians, and social historians. See James D. Calder, *The Origins and Development of Federal Crime Control Policy: Herbert Hoover's
Initiatives* (Westport, CT: Praeger, 1993).

4. Marion, *Primer*, pp. 32–33.

5. The selection by Suzanne Cavanaugh included in chapter 2 of this text provides a detailed summary of the anti-crime initiatives introduced early in President
Lyndon Johnson's administration.

6. "Special Message to the Congress on Law Enforcement and the Administration of Justice," *Public Papers of the President of the United States: Lyndon B.
Johnson, Book I May 1–May 31, 1965* (Washington, DC: United States Government Printing Office, 1966), pp. 263–71 and Cronin, Cronin, and Milakovich, *U.S.
v. Crime in the Streets*, p. 27.

7. President Johnson was not the first president to appoint a crime commission.
In May 1929, President Herbert Hoover established the eleven-member National
Commission on Law Observance and Enforcement, chaired by George W. Wickersham who had served as President Taft's attorney general. The commission's report identified problems in the criminal justice system and called for major law
enforcement and judicial reforms (Cronin, Cronin, and Milakovich, *U.S. v. Crime
in the Streets*, p. 28).

8. *The Challenge of Crime in a Free Society: A Report of the President's Com-*

mission on Law Enforcement and Administration of Justice (New York: Avon Books, 1968).

9. "Special Message to the Congress on Crime in America February 6, 1967," *Public Papers of the President of the United States: Lyndon B. Johnson, Book I January 1–June 30, 1967* (Washington, DC: United States Government Printing Office, 1968), pp. 134–45.

10. Cronin, Cronin, and Milakovich, *U.S. v. Crime in the Streets*, p. 45.

11. "Special Message to the Congress on Crime in America February 6, 1967," pp. 135–45.

12. Federal funds were provided through block grants, distributed through the states to law enforcement agencies rather than being distributed by federal bureaucracies through categorical grants. The former is considered a Republican and conservative Democratic approach to disbursing federal funds, supporting state interests. The latter is viewed as a liberal Democratic approach, supporting greater federal involvement at the state and local levels.

13. Nancy E. Marion, "Symbolic Policies in Clinton's Crime Control Agenda," *Buffalo Criminal Law Review*, vol. 1, no. 1 (1997): 67–108.

14. *The White House Conference for a Drug Free America: Final Report* (Washington, DC: U.S. Government Printing Office, June 1988).

15. Marion, "Symbolic Policies."

16. Ibid.

17. Ibid., p. 103.

18. "Special Message to the Congress on Law Enforcement and the Administration of Justice," pp. 269–71.

19. "Special Message to the Congress on Crime in America," pp. 135–45.

20. Herbert Jacob et al., *Governmental Responses to Crime: Crime on Urban Agendas* (Washington, DC: U.S. Department of Justice, National Institute of Justice, 1982).

21. Nancy E. Marion, *A History of Federal Criminal Initiatives, 1960–93* (Westport, CT: Praeger, 1994); Joel Rosch, "Crime as an Issue in American Politics," in Erika S. Fairchild and Vincent J. Webb, eds., *The Politics of Crime and Criminal Justice* (Beverly Hills, CA: Sage Publications, 1985); Cronin, Cronin, and Milakovich, *U.S. vs. Crime in the Streets*; Stuart A. Scheingold, *The Politics of Law and Order* (New York: Longman, 1984).

22. These data were gathered from *Public Papers of the President and Presidential Documents.*

23. Henry Scott Wallace, "Clinton's Real Plan on Crime," *National Law Journal*, vol. 15 (1992): 12.

24. Ibid.

25. Jill Zuckman, "The President's Call to Serve Is Clear but Undefined," *Congressional Quarterly Weekly Report*, vol. 51 (January 30, 1993): 218. Under this program, also known as the Police Corps, students could borrow money from the fund to cover the cost of either a college or job training program, and then repay the debt in the usual fashion by paying a percentage of their earnings over the next years, or by serving their communities doing work such as helping state or local police agencies. Ibid.

26. Morton Kondracke, "Clinton, Congress Must Tackle Crime in the First 100 Days," *Roll Call* (December 10, 1992), p. 6.

27. Wallace, "Clinton's Real Plan," 22.

28. Ibid.; Kondracke, "Clinton."

29. The President's News Conference, *Public Papers* (November 10, 1993), pp. 1942, 1947.

30. Remarks on the Swearing-In of National Drug Control Policy Director Lee Brown, *Public Papers* (July 1, 1993), p. 967.

31. Ibid. p. 968.

32. Holly Idelson, "Downsizing of Drug Czar Office Draws Mixed Reviews," *Congressional Quarterly Weekly Report*, vol. 51 (1993): p. 320.

33. Remarks to Law Enforcement Organizations and an Exchange with Reporters, *Public Papers* (April 15, 1993), pp. 435, 436.

34. Remarks Announcing the Anticrime Initiative and an Exchange with Reporters, *Public Papers* (August 11, 1993) p. 1361 (hereinafter Remarks Announcing the Anticrime Initiative).

35. The President's Radio Address, *Public Papers* (October 23, 1993), pp. 1811, 1818.

36. Remarks Announcing the Anticrime Initiative.

37. The proposal included billions in federal dollars to put more police officers on the streets, to build ten regional prisons for drug offenders and aid other state law enforcement programs such as those for juvenile offenders; restrictions on the ability of inmates who seek to challenge their death sentences in federal court with habeas corpus petitions; an expanded list of about fifty federal offenses that would carry the death penalty (such as killing a federal law enforcement officer); federal gun control initiatives such as a waiting period for handgun purchases (Brady Bill); $3.4 billion over five years to help communities put up to 50,000 more police officers on the streets; limits on the number of appeals after the Supreme Court has refused to review the case; and limits on the time in which death row inmates have to file one appeal for federal court review of their state court convictions.

38. Remarks Announcing the Anticrime Initiative.

39. Ibid.

40. Wallace, "Clinton's Real Plan."

41. Remarks to the Law Enforcement Community in London, Ohio, *Public Papers* (February 15, 1994), p. 257 (hereinafter Remarks in London, Ohio).

42. Ibid.

43. Interview with Larry King, *Public Papers* (January 20, 1994), pp. 106, 113.

44. Remarks in London, Ohio.

45. Ibid.

46. Remarks to General Motors Employees in Shreveport, Louisiana, *Public Papers* (February 8, 1994), pp. 202, 203.

47. The President's Radio Address, *Public Papers* (April 9, 1994), pp. 658, 659.

48. The President's Radio Address, *Public Papers* (August 27, 1994), pp. 1510, 1511.

49. Remarks on Signing the Violent Crime Control and Law Enforcement Act of 1994, *Public Papers* (September 13, 1994), pp. 1539, 1540.

50. Remarks on the National Association of Police Organizations in Minneapolis, Minnesota, *Public Papers* (August 12, 1994), pp. 1463, 1464.

51. *See* 18 U.S.C. § 922 note (Supp. V 1993).

52. Carroll Doherty, "Funding for Crime Program Heads to President," *Con-*

gressional Quarterly Weekly Report, vol. 51 (1994): 2455. Clinton had originally proposed $1.7 billion for this program.

53. See Ed Gillespie and Bob Schellhas, eds., *Contract with America: The Bold Plan by Rep. Newt Gingrich, Rep. Dick Armey and the House Republicans to Change the Nation* (New York: Times Books, 1994) [Hereinafter *Contract with America*]. The *Contract with America* was announced on September 27, 1994. Ibid., p. 6. The Republican signatories to the *Contract* pledged to introduce ten pieces of major legislation within the first 100 days of Congress including: a vote on congressional term limits, a balanced budget amendment, welfare reform, tax cuts for families, and national defense measures. Ibid., p. 15.

54. See ibid., pp. 37–64.

55. Ibid., pp. 46–47. According to the *Contract with America*, mandatory minimum sentences send a message to criminals and aid prosecutors in building cases against "criminal crime bosses." Ibid., p. 46.

56. Ibid., pp. 45–46. The *Contract* proposed that funding be provided to states in order to lessen the burden of prosecuting capital cases. Ibid., p. 45. The Republican plan also sought to modify jury instructions in capital cases, Ibid., as well as limit federal habeas corpus proceedings. Ibid., pp. 43–44.

57. Ibid. pp. 51–53.

58. Ibid.

59. Ibid., pp. 52–53.

60. Ibid., pp. 49–51.

61. Remarks to the U.S. Conference of Mayors, *Presidential Documents*, vol. 31 (January 27, 1995), p. 131.

62. The President's Radio Address, *Presidential Documents*, vol. 31 (February 11, 1995), p. 231.

63. The President's Radio Address, *Presidential Documents*, vol. 31 (March 4, 1995), p. 362.

64. Remarks on Receiving the Abraham Lincoln Courage Award in Chicago, *Presidential Documents*, vol. 31 (June 30, 1995), pp. 1171, 1174.

65. Remarks at the National Education Association School Safety Summit in Los Angeles, California, *Presidential Documents*, vol. 31 (April 8, 1995), pp. 596, 598; The President's Radio Address, *Presidential Documents*, vol. 31 (May 5, 1995), p. 735. Even though the Supreme Court struck down the law, Clinton continued his support of the policy, asking the Attorney General to report back on how such a policy could be legally created.

66. Remarks to the American Federation of Teachers, *Presidential Documents*, vol. 31 (July 28, 1995), pp. 1321, 1324.

67. Remarks to the U.S. Conference of Mayors.

68. Remarks Commemorating the First Anniversary of the Brady Law and an Exchange with Reporters, *Presdential Documents*, vol. 31 (February 28, 1995), p. 326.

69. Ibid.

70. Remarks Announcing Community Policing Grants, *Presidential Documents*, vol. 31 (February 8, 1995), pp. 206, 208.

71. Ibid. p. 209. Clinton summarized his drug policy when he said: "It involves cutting off drugs at the source, stiffer punishments for drug dealers, more education and prevention, and more treatment. But perhaps the most important part of this

strategy will be to boost efforts to educate our young people about the dangers and penalties of drug use. Our children need a constant drumbeat reminding them that drugs are not safe, drugs are illegal, drugs can put you in jail, and drugs may cost you your life." The President's Radio Address, *Presidential Documents*, vol. 31 (February 11, 1995), pp. 231, 232.

72. Holly Idelson, "Details of Anti-Terrorism Proposals," *Congressional Quarterly Weekly Report*, vol. 53 (1995): 1178.

73. Remarks and a Question-and-Answer Session with the Mayor's Youth Council in Boston, Massachusetts, *Presidential Documents*, vol. 31 (January 31, 1995), pp. 158, 159.

74. The President's Radio Address, *Presidential Documents*, vol. 32 (February 10, 1996), pp. 240, 242.

75. Remarks at the Pennsylvania State University Graduate School Commencement in State College, Pennsylvania, *Presidential Documents*, vol. 32 (May 10, 1996), pp. 835, 840.

76. Remarks to the Community in Louisville, *Presidential Documents*, vol. 32 (January 24, 1996), pp. 102, 107.

77. Public Law No. 104–145, 110 Stat. 1345 (codified as amended at 42 U.S.C. §§ 13701, 14071).

78. Edwin Meese III and Rhett DeHart, "How Washington Subverts Your Local Sheriff," *Policy Review*, vol. 75 (1996): 48.

79. Wallace, "Clinton's Real Plan," p. 13.

80. Reo Christenson, *Challenge and Decision*, 3rd ed. (New York: Harper & Row, 1970), p. 216.

81. Victor E. Kappeler, Martin Blumberg, and Gary W. Potter, *The Mythology of Crime and Criminal Justice* (Prospect Heights, IL: Waveland Press, 1993), p. 214.

82. Wallace, "Clinton's Real Plan," p. 14.

83. Thomas R. Dye, *Understanding Public Policy* (Englewood Cliffs, NJ: Prentice-Hall Inc., 1987).

84. Robert A. Rankin, "Clinton Says U.S. is Fed Up with Crime," *Beacon Journal* (Akron, Ohio) (December 10, 1993), p. Al.

85. Ibid.

86. Aaron Epstein, "Experts Doubt Crime Bill Value," *Beacon Journal* (November 28, 1993), p. A8.

87. John C. McWilliams, "Through the Past Darkly: Politics and Policies of America's Drug War," *Journal of Political History*, vol. 3 (1991): 356, 357.

88. Magnus J. Seng and Thomas M. Frost, "Crime in the 1990s: A Federal Perspective," in Chris Eskridge, ed., *Criminal Justice: Concepts and Issues* (Los Angeles: Roxbury Publishing, Co., 1993), p. 15.

89. David J. Bellis, *Heroin and Politicians: The Failure of Public Policy to Control Addiction in America* (Westport, CT: Greenwood Press, 1981), p. 25.

90. National Public Radio broadcast, September 13, 1994 (transcript on file with the *Buffalo Criminal Law Review*).

91. Epstein, "Experts Doubt Crime Bill Value," p. A8.

92. Ibid.

Chapter 4

Congress and the Legislating of Criminal Justice Policy Making

INTRODUCTION

By enacting laws through the legislative process, Congress can influence criminal justice policy and by so doing has played a key role in expanding federal involvement in criminal justice. On occasion, Congress has responded to presidential initiatives and, at other times, Congress has initiated criminal justice legislation. As indicated in chapter 2 of this text, in the early twentieth century Congress enacted laws to prohibit the interstate transportation of a woman or girl for immoral purposes and to regulate narcotics. During the past three decades, through various legislative initiatives, Congress has facilitated the expansion of the federal criminal justice role by federalizing crimes that traditionally had been state and local matters and by using the "power of the purse" to provide grants to states and localities to institute certain criminal justice policies and programs. These initiatives reflected both liberal and conservative ideological perspectives.

Federal criminal justice legislation is enacted through the formal congressional structures and law-making process. Accordingly, comprehending how Congress is organized to do its work and how our laws are made is a prerequisite to understanding Congress's role in criminal justice policy making. The formal structures and process, however, depict only one dimension of legislative policy making. In fact, several omnibus crime packages enacted by Congress skipped one or more of the steps in the formal law-making process, thereby enabling Congress to respond swiftly to public concerns about drugs and crime—symbolic politics.[1] Even when the formal legislative process is followed, interest groups attempt to influence Congress to support criminal justice policies of benefit to the groups. Therefore, to understand congressional criminal justice policy making, it is necessary to understand not only the formal, but also the informal structures and processes that affect legislation. This chapter examines the formal and informal structures and processes through which Congress makes criminal justice policy from the perspectives of symbolic politics and interest groups.

THE FORMAL PROCESS AND STRUCTURES OF CONGRESSIONAL CRIMINAL JUSTICE POLICY MAKING

In Congress, the House and Senate Judiciary Committees and their respective subcommittees typically handle criminal justice legislation. These committees and subcommittees consider legislation that authorizes or reauthorizes criminal justice agencies, programs, and policies. The Appropriations Committees and their subcommittees can also affect criminal justice policies by providing funding for agencies and programs. In addition, congressional oversight committees—the House Committee on Government Reform and Senate Committee on Governmental Affairs—can review programs in justice agencies and by so doing affect policies. On occasion, Congress also creates a special select committee to study all aspects of an issue. For example, for more than twenty years, the Select Committee on Narcotics Abuse and Control (SNAC) held hearings and examined all aspects of the drug issue, but it could not process legislation. Traditionally, select committees have had broader jurisdiction over a particular problem, for example, drugs, poverty, or aging, than a legislative standing committee, but could only propose but not process legislation. Usually, only standing/permanent legislative committees can process legislation. (An exception, for example, is the Senate Select Committee on Intelligence, which has broad jurisdiction over intelligence matters and can process legislation.)[2]

The formal congressional legislative process is typically depicted in a flow chart that begins with the introduction of a bill in one or both houses of Congress.[3] The bill is sent to and moves through the appropriate subcommittee, where hearings are held, and then to committee where members make changes to the bill, a process referred to as "mark up." The bill, with the changes made by the subcommittee and/or committee, is considered by the total house where it may be amended. Passed by one house, the bill is then sent to the other house, where it follows the same process. If there are differences in the versions enacted by each house, a conference committee, comprised of members from the relevant committee(s) of each house, is appointed and then a conference is held to resolve the differences. Each house must agree to the conference committee's report or the legislation dies. Once both houses of Congress agree on legislation, it is sent to the president for signature or veto. Most bills, criminal justice or otherwise, do not complete the windy road of the legislative process; some bills are reintroduced from one Congress to the next and may be enacted in the end. Some measures become parts of omnibus bills. In short, the history of a particular bill, generally, follows the previous description, but may include variations in the formal script.

ANALYZING CONGRESSIONAL CRIMINAL JUSTICE POLICY MAKING

The history of recent criminal justice legislation demonstrates that legislation does not always follow the formal process. Understanding the informal aspects of congressional criminal justice policy making involves an examination of particular legislation through the formal process to determine (1) whether and which steps in the formal process may have been skipped and (2) the informal influences affecting legislation, including symbolic politics and interest groups.

The 1984 omnibus anti-crime legislation was enacted after being amended to an unrelated appropriations bill. Accordingly, the legislation skipped the process of floor discussions. Despite the fact that the crime bill was hundreds of pages long, negotiations over differences between the House and Senate versions were resolved in a conference committee comprised of Appropriations not Judiciary Committee members, because the primary legislation to which the crime bill was added as an amendment was an appropriations bill. Some of the provisions debated during the consideration of the criminal code revision efforts appeared to be of concern primarily because of their symbolic significance to the public. For example, efforts to revise and develop new federal death penalty provisions, in order to respond to Supreme Court decisions in the 1970s laying out constitutionally required procedures for imposing the penalty, were perceived as symbolic efforts rather than meeting interest groups' needs.[4] Symbolic politics—political acts are directed toward the public and serve to reassure or to threaten the onlooker, perform a moral educative and/or an educative function, and provide models to the states—also helped to explain why certain ineffective policies were retained federal law, for example, the Logan Act[5] and no decisions are made on other issues. Some members believed that removing laws, even those that had never been enforced, such as the Logan Act, would send to the public a message that Congress was redrawing the line between right and wrong and now believed that that behavior, previously defined as unlawful, was acceptable.[6]

The "Anti-Drug Abuse Act of 1986" also did not follow the congressional legislative flow chart. The legislation, in its entirety, was not processed through the relevant subcommittees and/or committees. Although hearings were held by the responsible subcommittee or committee on some of the provisions in this omnibus crime legislation, many provisions were not reviewed through the formal process. In addition, the history of this legislation supports the assertion that symbolic politics play a role in criminal justice policy making. Congressional action on the drug legislation has been depicted as a response to the death of University of Maryland basketball player and Boston Celtics draftee, Len Bias, due to an overdose of cocaine, on June 19, 1986. Upon returning from the July 4 congressional recess, then House Speaker Thomas P. O'Neill convened committee chairs with the purpose of developing a comprehensive drug initiative before the end of the 99th Congress. The death of Bias had focused the nation's attention on the drug issue and the enactment of the 1986 anti-drug legislation is most readily explained by symbolic politics. That is, by enacting the legislation, Congress sought to reassure the public that it was (1) doing something about the drug/crime, (2) providing a model for the states of a "good" anti-drug policy, and (3) carrying out a moral educative function—communicating the line between right and wrong with respect to drug trafficking and abuse.[7]

The role of interest groups in criminal justice policy making has been sporadically and unsystematically considered in the criminal justice literature.[8] At the federal level, research indicates that interest groups have played a role in Congress's consideration of criminal justice legislation.[9] For example, between 1990 and 1994 at Senate Judiciary Committee hearings on domestic violence legislation, women's groups and victims of domestic violence testified to communicate the message that domestic violence was not a family matter, but a crime; Congress enacted domestic violence legislation in 1994 as part of an omnibus crime bill.[10]

The literature indicates that interest groups participating in the congressional criminal justice policy-making process exhibit diverse types of goals, including broad, narrow, concrete,[11] solidary,[12] or purposive.[13] The nature of its goals affected each group's ability to influence the process. For example, during the debates on the criminal code revisions in the 1980s, the Justice Department and American Civil Liberties Union had broad criminal justice interests and articulated concerns regarding numerous provisions in the legislation. These groups were also found to have used a variety of techniques, at different points in the legislative process, in order to influence the legislative outcome. While many groups testified at congressional hearings, internal access to staff and members seemed be essential if a group were to influence legislative provisions successfully. At the same time some groups were able to block legislation even for a time, and in so doing affected the criminal justice issues that were subject to congressional consideration.[14]

INCLUDED SELECTIONS

The readings in this section introduce the reader to the formal and informal structures and processes of congressional criminal justice policy making. The first section enumerates the congressional committees and sub-committees involved in criminal justice policy making during the 106th Congress. Updated information may be found on the House and Senate web sites. The second selection is a legislative history of the "Anti-Drug Abuse Act of 1986," from the U.S. House of Representatives Select Committee on Narcotics Abuse and Control's annual report. The third section is excerpted from an article by Barbara Stolz in which she describes the roles played by interest groups and symbolic politics in the congressional deliberations on omnibus crime legislation that was ultimately enacted in 1984. The final selections are excerpts from interest group testimony on the death penalty, during Senate hearings on criminal code reform. These excerpts reflect conservative and liberal perspectives, respectively, with the former emphasizing crime as a matter of choice and deliberation and the latter focusing on the fairness of the system. Although some of the facts have changed, the rationales for and against the death penalty, articulated in the 1980s, are the same as those heard today.

FOR DISCUSSION

In this chapter, the reader should consider:

1. The formal structures of Congress through which criminal justice policy is made and how these structures affect policy.
2. The formal congressional law-making process through which criminal justice policy is made and how these processes affect policy.
3. The role of symbolic politics in congressional criminal justice policy making.
4. The role of interest groups in congressional criminal justice policy making.
5. The role of state and local legislative bodies, for example, legislatures and city councils, in criminal justice policy making.
6. How interest groups seek to influence state and local criminal justice policy making.

RECOMMENDED READINGS AND SOURCES

Specific References

Marion, Nancy E. *A Primer in the Politics of Criminal Justice.* Albany, NY: Harrow and Heston, 1995.
Roby, Pamela. "Politics and Criminal Law: Revision of the New York State Penal Law on Prostitution." *Social Problems*, vol. 17 (summer 1969): 83–109.
Stolz, Barbara Ann. "Interest Groups and Criminal Law: The Case of Federal Criminal Code Revision." *Crime and Delinquency*, vol. 30, no. 1 (1984): 91–106.
Stolz, Barbara Ann. "Congress, Symbolic Politics and the Evolution of 1994 'Vio-

lence Against Women Act.' " *Criminal Justice Policy Review*, vol. 10, no. 3 (1999): 401–28.

Weatherford, J. McIver. *Tribes on the Hill*. New York: Bergin & Garvey, Publishers, Inc., 1985.

General Sources

Congressional Quarterly Weekly.
The National Journal.
Various directories of Congress, published periodically, e.g.,
  Congressional Directory. Washington, DC: U.S. Government Printing Office.
  Congressional Yellow Book. Washington, D. C.: Leadership Directories, Inc.
  Congressional Staff Directory. Washington, DC: C.Q. Staff Directories, Inc.

Web Sites

Congressional Quarterly <*http://www.cq.com*>
Library of Congress Congressional <*http://thomas.loc.gov*>
U.S. House of Representatives <*http://www.house.gov*>
U.S. Senate <http://www.senate.gov>

STRUCTURE OF CONGRESSIONAL CRIMINAL JUSTICE POLICY MAKING

U.S. SENATE STANDING COMMITTEES WITH CRIMINAL JUSTICE AS A PRIMARY RESPONSIBILITY

Appropriations Committee
  Subcommittee on Commerce, Justice, State, and Judiciary

Governmental Affairs Committee

Judiciary Committee
  Administrative Oversight and the Courts Subcommittee
  Antitrust, Business Rights and Competition Subcommittee
  Constitution, Federalism and Property Rights Subcommittee
  Criminal Justice Oversight Subcommittee
  Immigration Subcommittee
  Technology, Terrorism and Government Information Subcommittee
  Youth Violence Subcommittee

U.S. HOUSE OF REPRESENTATIVES STANDING COMMITTEES WITH CRIMINAL JUSTICE AS A PRIMARY RESPONSIBILITY

Appropriations Committee
  Subcommittee on Commerce, Justice, State, and Judiciary

Governmental Reform Committee
  Subcommittee on Criminal Justice, Drug Policy, and Human Resources

Judiciary Committee
  Subcommittee on Commercial and Administrative Law
  Subcommittee on the Constitution
  Subcommittee on Courts and Intellectual Property
  Subcommittee on Crime
  Subcommittee on Immigration and Claims

Other Senate and House committees and subcommittees may also consider criminal justice–related concerns as part of their responsibility.[15]

ANTI-DRUG ABUSE ACT OF 1986:
A LEGISLATIVE HISTORY

1986 was a significant year for legislative efforts to control drug abuse and drug trafficking. The passage of H.R. 5484, the Anti-Drug Abuse Act of 1986, marks the first time the Congress enacted legislation to address all aspects of our Nation's drug problem—international narcotics control, interdiction, drug law enforcement, treatment, prevention, and education.

President Reagan signed H.R. 5484 into law on October 27, 1986 (P.L. 99–570). The enactment of the Anti-Drug Abuse Act of 1986 is a tribute to the bipartisan leadership in the House of Representatives whose initiatives led to the drafting of the new drug law. The Select Committee on Narcotics Abuse and Control was given a unique role to play in this process. It served as a resource to the standing committees of the House and individual members during the development of the bill, and directly assisted the House leadership when H.R. 5484 came up for consideration on the House floor.

During the Select Committee's field hearings and investigations in 1986, the members of the committee observed increased public concern over the growing nature and extent of drug abuse in America. Practically every community has been affected by drug abuse and drug–related crime. Yet, at the same time, governmental and private efforts to come to grips with these twin problems seemed to always fall short of success.

A national tragedy then occurred. Len Bias a young, talented basketball star at the University of Maryland who had recently been drafted by the Boston Celtics of the National Basketball Association, died of an overdose of cocaine on June 19, 1986. The Bias death touched off an outpouring of national concern and frustration over the direction of Federal drug abuse policy. When Members of Congress returned home for the 4th of July recess, drug abuse emerged as the major topic of concern among constituents.

On July 23, 1986, House Speaker Thomas P. O'Neill convened a meeting of all committee chairmen with jurisdiction over drug abuse and drug trafficking issues. The objective of the meeting was to develop a comprehensive drug initiative before the 99th Congress adjourned.

At this meeting the Speaker stated, "The drug trade needs to be hit, and hit hard, at both ends; where these poisons are produced, and at the demand end, on the streets and in the suburbs, where the drugs are being

Reprinted from *Annual Report for the Year 1986 of the Select Committee on Narcotics Abuse and Control 99th Congress Second Session* (Report 99–1039). Washington, DC: U.S. Government Printing Office, 1987.

consumed." The Speaker appointed House Majority Leader Jim Wright to serve as the coordinator of the standing committees' efforts to bring a comprehensive drug bill to the House for a vote by September 10, 1986.

On July 24, 1986, Majority Leader Wright hosted a luncheon meeting of committee chairman and other key members who had been active on drug abuse issues. House Minority Leader Robert Michel co-hosted this luncheon. A joint statement on bipartisan strategy on drug abuse issued by the Leadership after the luncheon stated, "Democratic and Republican leaders are in total agreement on the need to prepare comprehensive legislation on the growing problem of drug abuse in the United States." The leaders went on to state that in addition to working with the standing committees they would, "enlist the support of the Reagan Administration in the preparation of a legislative initiative."

Between July 24 and the August recess the standing committees began hearings and markup on various items of drug legislation that had been pending before them. In addition, the committees sought out new ideas and initiatives for inclusion in the omnibus proposal.

The Select Committee is pleased to note that several of its legislative initiatives were included in the omnibus bill fashioned by the bipartisan steering committee. During the course of the deliberations by the standing committees on these and other initiatives, Chairman Rangel, Ranking Minority Member Gilman, as well as other members of the Select Committee testified on these measures in committee or participated in their deliberations through their standing committee assignments.

In the first session of the 99th Congress members of the Select Committee introduced H.R. 526, the "State and Local Narcotics Control Assistance Act." This measure authorized $750 million per year for fiscal years to assist State and local governments in drug law enforcement and drug abuse treatment and prevention efforts. On August 7, 1986, the Subcommittee on Crime of the Judiciary Committee held a hearing on this bill and received testimony from Mr. Rangel and Mr. Gilman.

The Judiciary Committee also reported out the "Designer Drug Enforcement Act of 1986" on July 29, 1986. This bill, which was strongly supported by members of the Select Committee, proscribes the manufacturing and trafficking in controlled substance analogs, so called "designer drugs."

On February 6, 1986, members of the Select Committee introduced H.R. 4155, the "Drug Abuse Education Act." This bill authorized $100 million for fiscal years 1987 through 1991 for a program of Federal grants to States to establish drug abuse education programs in elementary and secondary schools. The program would be administered by the Secretary of Education. On August 6, Chairman Rangel testified in support of this measure for inclusion in the omnibus bill before the House Committee on Education and Labor.

On May 8, 1986, Chairman Peter W. Rodino of the Judiciary Committee was joined by Mr. Rangel, Mr. Gilman, Mr. Guarini, and Mr. Hughes in introducing H.J.Res. 631, the "White House Conference on Drug Abuse Resolution." This resolution calls on the President to convene a White House Conference on Drug Abuse and drug trafficking within six months of its enactment. The objective of the conference is to call together the best minds in the country to assess the Nation's war on drugs. On July 24 the Judiciary Subcommittee on Crime held a hearing on this resolution and proceeded into markup. The full Judiciary Committee reported the bill on July 29, 1986.

On September 20, 1985, Chairman Rangel and Mr. Gilman introduced H.R. 3404, the "Narcotics Control Trade Act." This bill stipulated that any country that is a direct or indirect source of illegal drugs significantly affecting the United States shall not be granted most-favored-nation-trade status if the President determines that the nation is not cooperating with the United States to restrict the cultivation, production, and traffic in illicit drugs. This bill was co-sponsored by the following members of the Select Committee: Representatives Rodino, Scheuer, Stark, Ortiz, Collins, Akaka, Matsui, Fauntroy, Towns, Levine, Chappie, Strang and DioGuardi.

On August 5, 1986, Mr. Rangel testified in support of H.R. 3404 before the Subcommittee on Trade of the Committee on Ways and Means. Mr. Rangel urged that the sanctions contained in the Narcotics Control Trade Act be included in the omnibus drug bill and stated his support of other measures pending before the Trade Subcommittee to enhance the role of the Customs Service in drug interdiction. Mr. Fascell, as Chairman of the House Foreign Affairs Committee, and Mr. Gilman and Mr. Smith, as co-chairmen of the Foreign Affairs Task Force on International Narcotics Control, were instrumental in the development of the provisions contained in H.R. 5352, the International Narcotics Control Act of 1986. This bill became the international drug control section of the omnibus bill, contained many provisions to improve the management of existing international narcotics control programs, provided additional funds if the President requests and justifies the need for them, encouraged a regional response to narcotics control in Latin America, and urged increased international cooperation in this area.

On September 10, 1986, the House began floor consideration of H.R. 5484, the omnibus drug control act. The bill was managed by House Majority Leader Wright assisted by Select Committee Chairman Rangel. During the course of the floor debate, the following members of the Select Committee offered amendments to the bill:

Mr. Rangel, to raise the level of Federal assistance to state and local law enforcement to the amounts proposed in H.R. 526.

Mr. Levine, to ban the sale of hard core drug paraphernalia in the mails or in interstate commerce.

Mr. Hunter, to significantly expand the role of the military in drug interdiction.

Mr. Smith, to establish a reward for information leading to the arrest or conviction of Jorge Luis Ochoa Vasquez for narcotics offenses, and to make a portion of narcotics assistance to Mexico contingent on the full investigation of the murder of DEA Agent Camarena and the detention and torture of DEA Agent Cortez.

Mr. Towns, to require the Department of Health and Human Services to conduct a study of the nature and effectiveness of drug treatment programs.

Mr. Coughlin, to widely disseminate audio-visual and other curricular materials for drug abuse education.

H.R. 5484 achieved final passage in the House, with amendments, on September 11, 1986, and the bill was sent to the Senate where it was passed with amendments. In lieu of a formal conference the difference[s] between the two versions were resolved through a series of amendments passed by the House and the Senate. H.R. 5484 was passed in final form as the "Anti-Drug Abuse Act of 1986" by both the House and Senate on October 17, 1986. The bill was signed into law by President Reagan on October 27, 1986.

During debate on the bill many members of Congress expressed the view that H.R. 5484 should be seen as a first step in developing a comprehensive national drug abuse policy. The Select Committee believes that the Congress must exercise careful oversight of the legislation to assure that it is implemented effectively and expeditiously, and to assure that additional resources are provided to solidify and expand the gains that this legislation will make possible. . . .

CONGRESS AND CRIMINAL JUSTICE POLICY MAKING: THE IMPACT OF INTEREST GROUPS AND SYMBOLIC POLITICS

Barbara Ann Stolz

Although criminal justice administration in the United States is primarily a state and local, rather than a federal, function, Congress does make criminal justice policy. Little attention, however, has been paid to how it does so. This article examines congressional criminal justice policy making in the context of efforts toward federal criminal-code revision and capital punishment. Repeatedly, Congress has tried and failed to pass legislation in these two areas. Specifically, the article focuses on how interest groups and symbolic politics have affected these policy efforts. Such an analysis contributes to our understanding of the political realities of criminal justice policy making. . . .

POLITICAL ANALYSIS, CONGRESS, AND CRIMINAL LAW

Political science has emphasized the necessity for political analysis on two levels—the tangible and the symbolic. The former level focuses on how political acts provide people with tangible rewards and the latter on what political acts mean to the public.[16] One of the foremost writers on symbolic politics[17] has postulated that every instance of policy formulation involves a "mix" of both symbolic effect and the rational reflection of interests in resources, although one may be dominant in a particular case. Since understanding any political act requires analysis on both levels, it follows that criminal justice policy making must be so examined.

Tangible benefits tend to be distributed to well-organized groups, called interest groups. Political interest groups are defined as groups whose shared activities include attempts to influence decisions made within the public policy-making system.[18] The role of these groups in policy formation at the state and national level has been well documented in the political science literature.[19] How to measure their effect, or their influence, however, has been debated without resolution.[20]

For this study, the congressional staff interviewed were asked to define influence. They emphasized a group's ability to have its concerns given serious consideration by congressional members. This could mean ensuring that specific legislative provisions reflected the group's interest, but it could also mean stopping legislation. Congressional staff were primarily concerned with the former type of influence.

Symbolic rewards tend to be distributed to the less-organized public. They are the means by which those unable to analyze a complex situation rationally may adjust to it through stereotyping, oversimplification, and reassurance.[21] Symbols, thus, derive their meaning from an audience's response rather than from the act itself. The case study of federal capital-punishment legislation indicates that a symbolic component of congressional death penalty legislation exists and encompasses three functions: a "model" for the states, reassurance, and moral education.[22]

METHODS

The case method[23] was used to investigate the legislative process surrounding efforts toward federal capital-punishment legislation between 1972 and 1982[24] and toward criminal-code revision between 1971 and 1982.[25] In each case, hearing records and other congressional records were employed in the analysis. Between 1976 and 1982, the author also observed numerous hearings and mark-up sessions on each piece of legislation. Interviews with members of Congress and congressional staff clarified and expanded the information gathered from written sources.

The capital-punishment hearings provided the basis for determining which members of Congress had been most actively involved in the issue. Sixteen members were identified as activists between 1972 and 1982, having introduced capital-punishment legislation, been involved intensively in hearings, or been recognized by other members as active on the issue. These activists were asked to respond to a questionnaire; nine (six House members and three Senate members) did. Five were pro-capital punishment; four were against.

A semi-structured questionnaire, a technique used effectively by political scientists,[26] was used. Questions were designed to evoke information regarding the rationale for the member's interest in the issue, explanations for general congressional interest, interest-group participation and influence, and perceptions of the effect of the legislation. Several staff members who had worked extensively on the issue were also interviewed.

In the case of criminal-code revision, written records underscored the prevalence of interest-group participation but not the significance of that involvement. To determine interest-group influence, a reputational technique was used. Staff members were asked, first, to define influence. They were then asked to identify the groups they felt had influenced the reform process and to describe how the groups had accomplished this. The same groups were named repeatedly. Representatives of most of these groups were subsequently interviewed. All interviewees concurred on how the groups influenced the substance of the criminal-code legislation and, for the most part, on who was influential. To further investigate symbolic concerns, interviews were conducted with key House, Senate, and Justice Department staff.

THE ROLE OF INTEREST GROUPS IN THE CRIMINAL JUSTICE POLICY-MAKING PROCESS

The hearing records on criminal-code revision and capital-punishment legislation in the House and Senate indicate that diverse groups testify on criminal justice legislation.[27] These include legal and criminal justice professional associations (e.g., the American Bar Association, the National Black Police Association, the International Association of Chiefs of Police, the National Legal Aid and Defender Association); reform groups (e.g., the National Council on Crime and Delinquency); representatives from state agencies (e.g., state attorney generals); civil liberties organizations (e.g., the American Civil Liberties Union and the National Committee Against Repressive Legislation); and issue-related organizations (e.g., the National Coalition to Ban Handguns and the National Coalition against the Death Penalty). Organizations whose primary interest is not criminal justice, such as church, media, labor, and business groups also testified and lobbied on criminal-code revision and capital punishment. Although government agencies are not usually classified as interest groups, they do articulate their interest in criminal justice legislation. In this article, therefore, governmental agencies, whether executive or judicial, are categorized as interest groups. The Justice Department and the Judicial Conference testified on the criminal code repeatedly.

Criminal-code revision addressed the concerns of numerous groups. Both House and Senate staff felt that many of these groups had had their interests met, but only a few were designated as influential. These included: the U.S. Justice Department, the American Bar Association, the American Civil Liberties Union, the Business Round Table, the National Association of Manufacturers, the Association of General Contractors, the National Committee Against Repressive Legislation, and the AFL-CIO. Representatives of interest groups, when interviewed, concurred with the assessment of congressional staff.

In contrast, although various groups testified in the death penalty deliberation, they were not perceived as influencing the process. Thus the following two sections focus on the groups involved in criminal-code revision efforts; specifically, on their goals and techniques.

Goals

The groups participating in the process of criminal-code revision exhibited different types of goals. Interests were broad, narrow, concrete, solidary, or purposive. The nature of their goals affected each group's ability to influence the process.

The three groups with the broadest criminal justice interests were the Justice Department, the American Civil Liberties Union (ACLU), and the American Bar Association (ABA). Since the Justice Department is generally responsible for implementing federal criminal justice legislation and is thus the primary constituency concerned about criminal-code revision, the breadth of its interest is not surprising. The Department also purports to speak for the public interest. Both publicly and privately, the Department was the most active participant in the revision process and, according to many, the most influential, particularly in the Senate. The description of the ACLU by some interviewees as a "shadow Justice Department" with a liberal persuasion indicates the breadth of the ACLU's involvement. The basis for their involvement in the code and other criminal justice legislation is, according to organizational sources, the ACLU's view that criminal law is the most fundamental type of legislation because it sets limits on people's behavior. The American Bar Association was primarily concerned with encouraging, for the "public good," modernization and rationality in the criminal justice system. These three groups—the Justice Department, the ACLU, and the ABA—supported the concepts of modernization and comprehensive reform but opposed and sought changes in a broad range of specific provisions. The ACLU, in particular, was a vocal critic of many sections of the criminal-code revision.

A fourth group exhibiting a broad interest in the bill was the National Committee against Repressive Legislation (NCARL). Unlike the ABA, the ACLU, and the Justice Department, the NCARL opposed the omnibus approach of the bill as well as specific provisions. They argued that an omnibus bill forced members of Congress to vote for provisions they did not like.

Most groups, however, expressed only narrow interests, seeking action on a few specific provisions that affected them directly. The AFL-CIO was concerned with issues such as labor extortion. The Judicial Conference, the body governing the administration of the federal judiciary, testified on provisions establishing sentencing guidelines and a sentencing commission.[28] Prison-reform groups and church groups sought alternatives to incarceration. The press was concerned about first amendment rights. Business groups lobbied for or against provisions affecting corporate interests. During the decade of legislative debate, more groups became aware that the legislation could potentially affect them and entered the process in support of specific interests. Interviewees did not perceive the specific and limited nature of those concerned or the diversity of groups interested to be unusual in this policy area. Moreover, they did not feel that the narrowness of a group's interest made it less influential.

Among the groups designated by staff and other groups as influential were not only the Justice Department and legal organizations, but groups whose primary concern is not criminal justice. Criminal justice reform groups or representatives of specific minority interests were not considered influential (although one might argue that the ACLU represents such concerns). Business groups, however, were viewed as highly successful in having their demands met. Yet their interests were not only narrow, but parochial. While the pursuit of their interests affected the criminal justice system, these groups were not primarily concerned with good criminal justice policy, but with protecting business interests—a parochial concern.

Goals may also be concrete (e.g., monetary), solidary (e.g., psychological, ideological rewards), or purposive or altruistic (e.g., civil liberties).[29] The groups participating in criminal-code revision varied along this dimension as well. Church groups, the Moral Majority, and criminal justice reform groups articulated purposive concerns, such as the abolition or retention of capital punishment or the abolition of prisons. The goals of the Moral Majority were also solidary; they hoped to move others in society toward their ideological position. Another example: the Business Round Table, an association of business executives from 180 companies, opposed sentencing reforms that would permit novel sanctions, particularly restitution, arguing that the ineffectiveness of traditional punishment (e.g., fines and prison) had not been proven. The concern of this organization appeared to reflect a fear of the potential effects of novel sanctions on its members, since providing restitution for the victim of a crime means that the complaining witness has a direct economic stake in the outcome of a criminal trial. This could prove expensive in cases of corporate crimes.[30]

Staff indicated that the practicality of a group's goals was most important to them. If a group presented its position as non-negotiable, that group was considered impractical and would be written off. Similarly, if congressional members perceived a group's goals as unattainable, then the group was viewed as impractical and received less attention. Clearly, concrete goals are more likely to be practical than are solidary or purposive goals. Those groups identified as having practical goals that could be negotiated were perceived by staff to be influential. The Justice Department, the ACLU, the ABA, the Business Round Table, the Chamber of Commerce, the Association of General Contractors, the National Association of Manufacturers, and the AFL-CIO had such goals.

The list of influential groups did not include the Judicial Conference, although this organization spoke for the federal judges and testified more than most other groups. They would not, however, compromise; therefore, their demands were not viewed as practical. The Moral Majority's interests, similarly, could not be negotiated. The National Council on Crime and Delinquency, perhaps the most notable national criminal-justice-reform group, was also perceived as having impractical interests.

Groups having impractical goals did appear to be influential in stopping legislation. Most interviewees attributed the failure of S.1630 of 1983 to the Moral Majority. Many of the positions of this group—for example, the inclusion of the death penalty—were viewed as impractical. Other complaints of the group were vague—for example, they claimed the bill was "soft on crime"—and in their vagueness, non-negotiable and impractical. The blocking of S.1 of 1973 and 1975 was attributed by several interviewees to the National Committee Against Repressive Legislation. Their goals, too, were perceived as impractical.

Techniques

Staff also indicated that the techniques used by a group affected its ability to influence criminal justice policy. Many groups testify at hearings. While hearings provide a forum for airing issues publicly and sometimes attract the press, both congressional staff and the representatives of interest groups agreed that testifying, no matter how often, does not signify that a group is influential. Rather, a group's ability to influence policy was believed to be affected by the use of other techniques and informal mechanisms. These were categorized as: internal access, expertise, group membership, and external influences. The criminal-code case indicates that the utility of a specific technique depends on whether a group wants to amend or block passage of a bill.

Internal access means that some groups seek access to congressional members who serve as spokespersons for their interests. The Moral Majority had the support of Senators Helms, McClure, and Denton during the 97th Congress. The ACLU had advocates in both the House and Senate.

Expertise is a resource that groups can use to aid congressional members and staff. Influential groups, including the ABA, the ACLU, and the Justice Department, as well as business groups, indicated that they prepared written recommendations and documentation to support their position. Such efforts were viewed as assisting staff. Interviewees also indicated that follow-up discussions with congressional staff and members were essential. The failure of groups such as the Judicial Conference to achieve their goals was attributed, in part, to their not having followed up testimony with informal meetings.

Organizations with a membership barraged members of Congress with letters, an approach political scientists have labeled the shotgun method.[31] They also asked some of their more influential members to contact specific congressional members; this is known as the rifle approach.[32] The National

Committee Against Repressive Legislation used the shotgun approach, mustering strong grassroots opposition to S.1 of 1973 and 1975. The Business Round Table provided written statements from members' companies for specific congresspeople, a rifle approach, to support their concerns.

Groups also use external influences, including other organizations and the press. Coalitions have existed on both sides of the criminal-code issue at various times. On the left, the National Committee Against Repressive Legislation informed other groups how their interests were affected by the bill, often garnering the support of those organizations. During the 96th and 97th Congress, a coalition emerged on the right. The "Library Court" held meetings at which representatives of various conservative groups were told how the bill affected their interests. It is unclear how influential these coalitions were. Such efforts may create the impression of possible grassroots opposition, convincing some congressional members that voting on such controversial legislation may not be wise; consequently, coalition activities may explain inaction on legislation.

Groups use the media to draw attention to their concerns. Jack Landau of the Reporters Committee publicized First Amendment concerns in S.1. The Moral Majority used the press to focus attention on S.1630. Supporters of criminal-code-revision bills also used the press. Editorials chastizing the House for its slow deliberations appeared after the Senate passed S.1437 in 1978.

In summary, on the level of interest-group politics, the case material on the criminal code indicates that a variety of groups with different types of goals participate in criminal justice policy making. Not all participants are influential. Influence depends on the practicality of goals and the ability to use certain informal techniques successfully. However, simply examining criminal justice policy from the perspective of interest groups does not fully explain the criminal justice policy making process.

SYMBOLIC POLITICS[33]

The second level of political analysis is the symbolic. In the criminal-code-revision efforts, certain issues appeared to be of concern primarily because of their symbolic significance to the public. Federal death penalty provisions, both within the code and in separate legislation, were perceived as symbolic efforts rather than as being directed toward meeting interest-group needs. Interviews indicated further that legislation could perform one or more symbolic functions: as a model for the states, as reassurance, or as moral education.

Model for the States

Both supporters and opponents of capital punishment, when interviewed, asserted that federal capital-punishment legislation was important because it provided a model for the states. With respect to federal criminal justice agencies, this role of the federal government has been acknowledged by policy makers. For example, the development of the Federal Bureau of Prisons as a model for the states was supported by the National Advisory Commission on Criminal Justice Standards and Goals,[34] and the Law Enforcement Assistance Administration and the Office of Juvenile Justice and Delinquency Prevention were created to promote change by providing monies for programs in states and communities, based on federal notions of good policy.[35] What the interviews indicated was that this perception of the federal government as a model did not refer simply to federal agencies, but also extended to federal criminal law in general. Such legislation was intended to demonstrate, by example, what a criminal law and penal system should include. Since capital punishment is the most extreme form of punishment, it was perceived to be a significant component of the model.

While agreeing on the importance of federal capital-punishment legislation as a model, opponents and proponents disagreed on the substantive content of that model. Supporters believed that the ultimate crime deserves the ultimate punishment. The death penalty should be part of the federal system because it is an essential component of any good penal system. In contrast, opponents felt the federal government would be setting an enlightened example by not imposing this sanction. Both sides perceived the content and function of the model as important because the legislation was thought to exemplify good criminal justice policy.

Moreover, by creating the impression that Congress is attempting to deal with the problem and can demonstrate how to do so, Congress may, at least symbolically, enhance its power position vis-à-vis the states. The need for the federal government to generate such an impression of power may explain why some proponents interviewed expressed concern over the failure of Congress to act on the death penalty. They suggested that inaction created an image of the federal government as "behind" the states. Similarly, the failure of Congress to pass criminal-code-revision legislation, when many of the states have revised their codes, diminishes Congress' symbolic position as a leader.[36]

The Reassurance Function

A second symbolic function is public reassurance. Edelman explores the general concept of the *reassurance function* and postulates that symbolization induces a feeling of well being and reduces tension. Using the example of regulatory statutes (and their administration), he explains that political activities can convey a sense of well being to the onlooker because they suggest vigorous activity, although there may be, in fact, inactivity.[37] In the criminal justice area, "getting tough" efforts, i.e., increasing penalties, are purportedly the last hope of crime control because of their perceived deterrent effect,[38] but they may also perform a reassurance function.

That is, they suggest that "something" is being done about crime, whether or not that "something" is an effective deterrent. The audience to be reassured is that segment of the public who see and think in terms of stereotypes, personalization, and oversimplification and who cannot tolerate ambiguous, complex situations.[39]

A statement by the current chairman (1979) of the Senate Judiciary Committee provides an excellent example of belief in the dual function of the "getting tough" position as it relates to capital punishment:

The death penalty must be restored if our criminal justice system is to effectively control the increasing number of violent crimes of terror. The confidence of the American people in our criminal justice system must also be reclaimed and the imposition of the death penalty can restore such confidence.[40]

Supporting capital punishment is an example of the "getting tough" posture. The first sentence quoted above implies that the intended audience is those who would commit violent acts but who would be deterred by the death penalty. The second sentence indicates a belief that reinstituting capital punishment would restore public confidence in the criminal justice system because it would reassure people that something is being done about crime.

Congressional opponents of capital punishment also recognize the significance of the reassurance function. This point was illustrated by the interviewees' descriptions of what they felt would happen if death penalty legislation were to come to the Senate floor during the 97th Congress. Opponents were expected to introduce an amendment to substitute "life imprisonment without parole" for the death sentence in the proposed bill, rather than to try to kill the bill outright, because of a perceived need to reassure the public that Congress was dealing with crime.

The interviews also indicated a public misconception about federal law that might enhance the reassurance effect of a federal death penalty as well as a misconception about federal criminal law in general. A segment of the public perceives federal law as nationalizing policy. According to this misconception, a federal death penalty statute would result in the nationalizing of the death penalty for any murder, when in fact, such a statute would apply only to certain federal cases. As a consequence of this misconception, the passage of federal death penalty legislation could ensure a greater sense of well being.

In the context of criminal-code revision, opposition to the repeal of the Logan Act[41] reflected symbolic concerns directed toward public reassurance. Proponents of the repeal argued that the act reflected symbolic concerns directed toward public reassurance and that the act was a useless appendage, since it had never been enforced. Opponents of the repeal emphasized that, although the law was unenforceable, it was perceived as a public policy statement. Maintaining the law reassured the public (particularly in the midst of international crises such as the Iranian hostage situation) that the conduct of international affairs was vested in the executive branch of government rather than in the private citizen.[42]

Both the death penalty and the Logan Act underscore the significance that the need to reassure the public may have in maintaining or repealing a statute.

The Moral Educative Function

While criminal justice scholars debate whether or not the criminal law performs a moral educative function,[43] the case studies of both the death penalty and criminal-code revision indicate that members of Congress act as if it does. Perceiving criminal law as performing a moral educative function reflects a belief that criminal law communicates a message to the public, socializes, and, in the case of federal law, indicates a national moral consensus.

Interviewees, both proponents and opponents, concurred that a federal death penalty law performed this function, but did not agree on the message communicated. Proponents of capital punishment believed the death penalty communicates society's ultimate disapproval. By associating "the ultimate punishment" with a crime, the death penalty emphasizes the distinctiveness of the acts for which it is imposed. Moreover, a federal death penalty statute carries particular weight because of the perception that it reflects a national consensus.

A message is not only communicated to offenders, but also to "law-abiding" citizens. The death penalty is believed to reassure "those who do right," by distinguishing them from "the criminals." In the words of one congressional proponent, it is a "catharsis for the law abiding." This view has been articulated by Berns,[44] who argues that criminal law works by praising as well as by blaming.

The opponents of the death penalty who were interviewed, while agreeing that federal capital-punishment legislation communicates a message, reached different conclusions. Capital punishment was felt to "legitimize the taking of life under certain circumstances." In so doing, capital punishment contributes to the level of violence in society. Some opponents were also concerned about the message communicated when the wrong person is executed. The tangible consequence of such an act to the individual executed is evident, but the miscarriage of justice also communicates a message to the "law-abiding citizen" that obeying the law does not necessarily protect the individual from unjust punishment.

Opponents believed abolition of federal capital punishment would communicate a complex message, but they preferred this message. First, abolition was perceived as a statement against violence. Second, abolition would transmit the notion that economic and social injustice are partially responsible for crime and that, therefore, society must bear a share of the responsibility.

A related question is whether or not the law has to be enforced in order to communicate a message. In the case of capital punishment, the proponents interviewed indicated it did, but they did not suggest how frequently. If, however, one considers the debates that can ensue over laws that have never been enforced, implementation of the law appears to be a lesser concern. Some legislators interviewed believed that tinkering with existing laws indicates that policy has changed, thereby communicating approval where there has once been disapproval. These legislators, therefore, opposed changing even those laws that have never been and may never be enforced. The aforementioned debates over the repeal of the Logan Act illustrate this point clearly.

SUMMARY AND IMPLICATIONS

Examining congressional criminal-code revision and capital-punishment efforts from the perspectives of interest-group involvement and symbolic politics suggests a complex policy-making process. It indicates that criminal justice policy may be influenced by pressure from groups or by the need to respond to public concerns rather than by rational, comprehensive policy making.

With respect to interest-group politics, it was found that the groups most influential in having their interests incorporated in legislation included not only the Justice Department and the American Civil Liberties Union, but organizations with parochial concerns who had no interest in general criminal justice policy. These influential groups had practical, negotiable goals.

Moreover, a group's use of various techniques affects its ability to influence policy. Giving formal testimony rarely influences legislative outcomes; using informal techniques effectively, can. Those seeking specific changes, such as the ACLU and Justice Department, relied on internal access and expertise. These techniques meshed well with "practical" goals. Those wishing to stop bills—groups such as National Committee Against Repressive Legislation and the Moral Majority—relied heavily on grass-roots–oriented techniques. These techniques, used in conjunction with "impractical" goals, were effective. Groups identified by interviewees as non-influential even though they testified often (e.g., the Judicial Conference and the National Conference on Crime and Delinquency) had impractical goals and did not use informal techniques to follow up their testimony.

Ultimately, the breadth of criminal-code legislation and the diversity of narrow interests concerned has ensured a steady flow of groups whose interests have had to be considered by congressional staff and members. This suggests that criminal justice policy may be the result of brokering interests rather than of conscious planning.

On the symbolic level, three functions of legislation were described: a model for the states, reassurance, and moral education. These functions are primarily directed toward the public. In trying to reassure the public, to provide a model, or to educate, Congress may focus on policy issues that have little importance in the actual functioning of the criminal justice system, and even less in crime reduction, but that communicate to the public or to the states (1) what good policy is and (2) that the federal government is in control and is working on the problem. With respect to policy outcomes, analysis on the symbolic level helps explain why ineffective policies, e.g., the Logan Act, are maintained; why no decision is made on certain issues, e.g., capital punishment; and why policy makers may advocate seemingly unacceptable policies, e.g., why capital punishment opponents accept life imprisonment.

Together, the findings on both levels of analysis further suggest that it is easier to block policy than to effect policy changes. Neither the death penalty bills nor the federal-code bills have passed both houses of Congress. Criminal justice legislation may be blocked because of demands from an overwhelming variety of narrow interests. Or, interest groups with "impractical" concerns not included in the legislation may thwart the legislative process using grass-roots techniques. The symbolic component may make a particular criminal justice policy the subject of intense public concern. Since congressional members dislike controversy, the legislation of such a policy may be avoided or limited in scope. A possible exception to this scenario might occur in a case where the public reaction to an issue is strong and where most legislators agree with that reaction. Congressional efforts to reform the federal insanity defense in response to the Hinckley verdict may prove to be a case in point.

The potential for blocking comprehensive criminal justice policy (omnibus legislation) is even greater. The scope of such legislation, i.e., the number of issues included, means that such legislation affects more interested parties. Symbolic issues (even those having little significant impact on the criminal justice system) incorporated in such legislation may be sufficiently volatile to preclude passage of the total package. Over the last decade, numerous symbolic issues have been removed from the proposed criminal-code legislation, with the agreement of both liberals and conservatives, on the grounds that leaving these issues in would jeopardize the entire package. . . .

CONCLUSION

This article is a beginning in the study of the process of federal criminal justice policy making. It examines this process from two perspectives, that of interest-group influence and that of symbolic politics. Certain groups do influence the making of federal criminal justice policy, but the most effective groups may be less concerned with criminal justice policy than with parochial concerns. Symbolic concerns may focus more attention on issues of interest to the public but may have less bearing on the substance and operation of the criminal justice system. The process seems more likely to produce either no legislation or limited compromises than to produce well-planned policies. . . .

Further research on Congress and criminal justice policy is needed. There is a broad range of federal criminal justice concerns that may reflect different types of politics. With respect to the process of policy making, the role of congressional staff and the relationship of congressional members' goals to public policy should be examined, as they have been in other policy areas. As a beginning, however, applying the findings and recommendations presented in this article should enhance the quality of criminal-justice-policy advocates' participation in the highly political, criminal justice policy-making process by increasing awareness of what that process is rather than of what it should be.

IMPOSITION OF CAPITAL PUNISHMENT: HEARINGS BEFORE THE SUBCOMMITTEE ON CRIMINAL LAW AND CRIMINAL PROCEDURES OF THE COMMITTEE ON THE JUDICIARY, UNITED STATES SENATE (93RD CONGRESS, FIRST SESSION)

TESTIMONY OF EDWARD J. KIERNAN, PRESIDENT, INTERNATIONAL CONFERENCE OF POLICE ASSOCIATIONS

Mr. Chairman and Members of the Committee:

I want to thank you for the opportunity to testify on the legislation being considered by you which is probably one of the most important pieces of legislation to be considered during this session.

My name Is Edward J. Kiernan and I am the President of the International Conference of Police Associations, representing more than 150,000 officers from every section of our country. I formerly served as the President of the Patrolmen's Benevolent Association of the City of New York and recently retired after thirty years of service as a patrolmen. I feel that I can qualify as a spokesman for our police officers from both a personal as well as an observer's point of view.

On April 19, 1972, Mr. Robert D. Gordon, Executive Director of ICPA, testified before the House Judiciary Subcommittee #3 opposing the enactment of several bills that would have abolished the death penalty under all laws of the United States, authorizing the imposition of life imprisonment in lieu thereof.

The problem of capital punishment has absorbed the people of this country for many years. Through various stages, imposition of the death penalty has been gradually abolished and this process has been accompanied by a great deal of speculation concerning its true deterrent ability. No definitive analysis has been possible, for in recent years the rate of serious crime has been soaring at an incredible pace.

How many murders would not have occurred if the threat of execution were present? How many murderers were deterred from that final act under the old system? None of us can really known the answers; we can only

Reprinted from *Imposition of Capital Punishment*, Hearings Before Subcommittee on Criminal Law and Criminal Procedures of the Committee on the Judiciary, United States Senate (93rd Congress, First Session), pp. 156–58.

shudder at the mounting totals and seek solutions with growing desperation.

Over the last several years present statistics have shown a frightening increase in crimes against the person, crimes that either involved the taking of a life or that occurred in circumstances which might easily have resulted in the taking of a life. In that period of time, the same statistics show us the horrible offshoot of such a breakdown in the morals of our society. In 1966, 57 police officers were killed in the performance of their duties; in 1967, there were 76; 1968, 64; 1969, 86; 1970, 100; 1971, 126; 1972, 112; and already in 1973, January to May, there have been 56, 10 more than the comparable period last year. As you can see, the number of police officers killed in the performance of their duty has doubled in the last eight years. Just last week I attended the funerals of two policemen in the City of New York who gave their lives and during that same period of time, there were seven other attempts to murder policemen in the City of New York. Multiply this by the number of Police Departments we have in this country and you come up with a figure that is almost astronomical.

In Philadelphia recently, two wardens were killed in cold blood by prisoners who had been sent to jail as a result of previous killings of law enforcement people. It is a fact of life that our present laws only protect the killers while the police officer is forced to try to do his job knowing that society is playing Russian roulette with his life. How long are you going to gamble with the families of police officers as the chips in this no limit game? How long do you think you can last in the jungle that is being created without having the policeman to pull your chestnuts out of the fire? The primary duty of the policeman is enforcement of laws enacted by you as legislators. In that role the police walk constantly among criminals, some of whom are chronic repeaters and some of whom are the toughest, most hardened miscreants in our society. Police officers are trained to weight the motives of such men, and soon come to understand some of the character, some of the drives and above all some of the fears which are prevalent among this criminal element. They know, from the synthesis of their total experience, that lurking behind the toughest facade is often a deep-seated fear of that terrifying punishment and they know that sometimes the specter of that fear will stay a trigger finger at the critical moment.

In a recent bank holdup in New York City, the perpetrators held several hostages inside a bank and threatened to kill them if their demands were not met. When they were questioned about their threatened assassinations, retorted, "What do we have to worry about? Even if we kill them, we can't get the chair." Recollect if you will, the murders of our political leaders, John and Robert Kennedy, the attempted assassination of Presidential candidate Governor Wallace, the ambushing of policemen under the guise of political or racial injustices, the hijacking of airplanes loaded with innocent passengers and the resulting death of crew or law officers attempting to prevent the crime. Think of the correctional officers who have been killed in the riots inside our penitentiaries; killed by murderers who were sentenced to jail rather than the gas chamber.

We are not talking here about the so-called crimes of passion, the family fights or drunken brawls, or the actions of the mentally unbalanced. In the past, attempts to mandate the death penalty were opposed by the so-called bleeding hearts because of their reluctance to take a life. Their obvious lack of concern for the police officer who gave his life was excused by the theory that this is a part of the job of being a policeman. What they fail to take into consideration is their responsibility to do everything possible to make the job of being a policeman as safe as they possible can. They worry about the families of the killer, but shed no tears for the families of the dead officer. In a survey consulted by UMCA in the City of New York in February 1972, relative to capital punishment more than 2 to 1 [were] in favor of capital punishment.

There is much that needs to be done if we, as a people, are to be freed at last from the age-old scourge of crime. From the past, we may draw upon the values that once were transmitted to each new generation of Americans as a matter of counsel; the doctrine which decreed responsibility for one's self and respect for one's fellow man. With it, went a profound respect for the ideals of law and order and justice—propositions which are much maligned today. We must not jeopardize our future by ignoring the harsh realities of today's world in a vain attempt to put off our responsibilities to the next generation. The structure of this nation was built upon a solid foundation of individual responsibility, common effort and adherence to law. Unless that foundation is bettered now, the goals of tomorrow will be shaped on a bed of ashes. We urge this committee to weigh the human factor most bravely and recommend positive consideration of legislation that will restore society's ultimate sanction. We have tried the easy way out and it obviously has not worked. Please, before it is too late, try our way.

Thank you.

STATEMENT OF DOUGLAS B. LYONS, EXECUTIVE DIRECTOR, CITIZENS AGAINST LEGALIZED MURDER

I will limit my remarks today to one recommendation made by the Commission's Report: the abolition of the death penalty.[45]

Reprinted from *Imposition of Capital Punishment*, Hearings Before Subcommittee on Criminal Law and Criminal Procedures of the Committee on the Judiciary, United States Senate (93rd Congress, First Session), pp. 162–65.

Death Penalty Abandoned

The real question facing the Judiciary Committee and the Congress is not whether to abolish the death penalty, but when. For as the Commission found in its working papers ". . . while de jure abolition has ebbed and flowed, a de facto abolition has practically become a reality in the United States."[46] Executions in this country have declined dramatically in the last generation. In 1935 there were a record hundred and ninety-nine (199) executions. In 1966 there was one, and in 1967 there were two executions. The last execution in the United States was on June 2, 1967—almost five years ago.

Since 1930 (when the U.S. Department of Justice started keeping accurate statistics), the Federal government has carried out only thirty-three (33) executions—an average of less than one per year. The last Federal execution was—nearly a decade ago.[47] Outside the District of Columbia, there are no Federal prisoners now awaiting execution. As a practical matter, it seems to me the Federal government no longer executes people. But courts and state legislatures point to the retention of the death penalty by the Federal government; an example of the widespread acceptance of capital punishment. They thus justify and support the existence of capital punishment in their own states.

The death penalty is enforced only on an incredibly selective basis. Since 1965 there have been approximately 78,000 homicides in this country. During the same period roughly 600 men were sentenced to death for murder. Yet there have been only three executions since 1965.[48] In other words, in the last six years, we have executed only one two hundred and fiftieth of one percent.

677 men and 7 women are now on death row in our nation. Yet, as we have seen, it is inconceivable that more than an arbitrary handful of these prisoners will ever be put to death.

The selectivity with which the death penalty is enforced is best exemplified [by the] case of Eddie Slovik. During World War II, 40,000 American soldiers deserted. Theoretically, they all could have been executed. In fact, however, only Slovik faced the firing squad—the only American soldier executed for desertion since the Civil War.[49]

The Supreme Court of the United States is now considering whether the death penalty, as selectively enforced, is "cruel and unusual punishment," prohibited by the Eighth Amendment. But the Congress need not await the Court's decision to decide for itself that human life is sacred, and that the Federal government should not be in the business of killing people.

Deterrence

The major argument used to support capital punishment is that it is a deterrent to serious crimes, especially to murder. But the death penalty is not a deterrent to murder.[50] The President's Commission on Law Enforcement and Administration of Justice examined the death penalty with particular reference to its alleged value as a deterrent. The Commission concluded:

It is impossible to say with certainty, whether capital punishment significantly reduces the incidence of heinous crimes. The most complete study on [the] subject, based on a comparison of homicide rates in capital and non-capital jurisdictions concluded that there is no discernible correlation between the availability of the death penalty and the homicide rate. This study also revealed that there was no significant difference between the two kinds of States in the safety of policemen. Another study of 27 States indicated that availability of the death sentence had no effect on the rate of assaults and murders of prison guards."[51]

In fact, virtually every study which has been conducted on the question of deterrence has concluded that capital punishment is not a deterrent to murder.[52]

If the death penalty were a deterrent to murder, it would follow that those states which have and use the death penalty would have lower murder rates than the states which have abolished it. But just the opposite is true. In 1970 the death penalty states had an average of 7.7 homicides per 100,000 population, while the abolition states had an average murder rate of only 4.6. Furthermore, in 1970 the states which had the three highest murder rates were all states which have and use the death penalty: Georgia, South Carolina, and Florida. On the other hand, the states with the three lowest murder rates in 1970 were all abolition states: Maine, Vermont, and North Dakota. If the death penalty were a deterrent to murder the situation would be reversed. That is, the abolition states would have the highest murder rates, and the states which have capital punishment would have the lowest murder rates. This is not the case.[53]

Discussing the problem of murder, J. Edgar Hoover, a supporter of the death penalty pointed out that:

". . . police are powerless to prevent a large number of these crimes, which is made readily apparent from the circumstances or motives which surround criminal homicide. The significant fact emerges that most murders are committed by relatives of the victim or persons acquainted with the victim. It follows, therefore, that criminal homicide is, to a major extent, a national social problem beyond police prevention."[54]

I agree.

Far from deterring murder, the continued existence of the death penalty is a serious danger to society. Capital punishment may in fact encourage murder. Three of the last four men executed in this country wanted to be executed, and they committed their crimes so that they would be executed.[55]

The question is often asked: What about the victims? Our history is clear—capital punishment has done nothing for the victims. We are told that capital punishment will prevent the murderer from killing again. But we know that murderers have the lowest recidivism rate of any criminal group.[56]

Capital punishment serves no legitimate social end. The criminal law should do more for the victim than seek revenge. To protect society, we must not rely upon the ineffective weapon of capital punishment.

We must, I believe, seek new means to rid our society of the plague of murder. I suggest a national campaign to seek out and study the factors which lead to and cause murder. Such a study might begin with an examination of the murderers now on death row, and of the thousands of murderers who are imprisoned under lesser sentences. Another aspect of the homicide problem which might be studied is the glaring fact that each year over half of all homicides are carried out with guns.[57]

The facts are clear. Capital punishment does not stop murder. If we wish to deal with the problem of murder we must seek out its causes.

Worldwide Abolition of Capital Punishment[58]

By abolishing the death penalty, the Federal government will not only demonstrate that it rejects the notion that grave social problems can be solved only through the use of force: this country will take the civilizing step of joining the long list of nations throughout the world which have already abolished the death penalty.

Only France and Spain among the Western European nations outside the Soviet bloc still prescribe death for murder and other peacetime crimes. In the Western Hemisphere, this country stands virtually alone in keeping the death penalty. Capital punishment for murder, rape, and kidnapping has been almost completely abandoned in the Anglo-American world—except for the United States.

Executing the Innocent

In 1966 Queen Elizabeth issued a royal pardon to Timothy John Evans. Unfortunately, Evans had been hanged in 1950—for a murder he did not commit. The Evans case, in which England discovered that it had hanged an innocent man, led to the abolition of the death penalty in Great Britain.[59]

I hope that the United States will do away with this form of legalized murder before we discover that we too have executed an innocent man and are forced to issue a posthumous pardon—the ultimate absurdity in a society which calls itself civilized.

Conclusion

The comments of the Archbishop of Canterbury after the abolition of capital punishment in England in 1969 are equally applicable to this nation. He said:

"Abolition of capital punishment, once and for all, will help create a more civilized society in which to continue the search for the causes of crime. . . . I am certain it will redound in very many ways to the advantage and honor of the nation."[60]

The abolition of the death penalty by the Federal government will demonstrate to the entire world that we believe, in act as well as word, that killing is wrong.

I speak for millions of Americans Mr. Chairman in urging you to adopt the Commission Report's recommendation that the Federal death penalty be abolished.

NOTES

1. Barbara Stolz, "Congress and the War on Drugs: An Exercise in Symbolic Politics," *Journal of Crime and Justice*, vol. 15, no. 1 (1992): 119–36.

2. From time to time, Congress has reorganized its committee and subcommittee structure. A major reorganization occurred in the 1970s, which produced a decentralization of committee powers into the subcommittees. More recently there have been a few instances of changes in committee or subcommittee names or reordering of responsibilities, particularly among subcommittees.

3. For a more detailed description of the legislative process, go the Library of Congress congressional web site <http://thomas.loc.gov> to the note Legislative Process.

4. Barbara Ann Stolz, "Congress and Criminal Justice Policy Making: The Impact of Interest Groups and Symbolic Politics," *Journal of Criminal Justice*, vol. 13, no. 4 (1985): 307–19, and Barbara Ann Stolz, "Congress and Capital Punishment: An Exercise in Symbolic Politics," *Law and Policy Quarterly* 5 (April 1983) 157–79.

5. The Logan Act of 1789 (18 U.S. Code 953) forbids private citizens undertaking diplomatic correspondence or intercourse with a foreign power with intent to influence conduct in relation to controversies with the United States. See Stolz, "Congress and Criminal Justice Policy Making," p. 317.

6. Ibid., p. 315.

7. Stolz, "Congress and the War on Drugs."

8. Erika S. Fairchild, "Interest Groups in the Criminal Justice Process," *Journal of Criminal Justice*, vol. 9 (1981): 181–94; Albert P. Melone and Robert Slatger, "Interest Group Politics and the Reform of the Federal Criminal Code," in Stuart Nagel, Erika Fairchild, and Anthony Champagne, eds., *The Political Science of Criminal Justice* (Springfield, IL: Charles C. Thomas Publishers, 1983), pp. 41–55; and Barbara Ann Stolz, "Interest Groups and Criminal Law: The Case of Federal Criminal Code Revision," *Crime and Delinquency*, vol. 30, no. 1 (1984): 91–106.

9. Stolz, "Interest Groups and Criminal Law"; Melone and Slatger, "Interest Group Politics."

10. Barbara A. Stolz, "Congress, Symbolic Politics, and the Evolution of 1994 'Violence Against Women Act,' " *Criminal Justice Policy Review*, vol. 10, no. 3 (1999): 401–28.

11. Carole S. Greenwald, *Group Power: Lobbying and Public Policy* (New York: Praeger, 1977), p. 52 refers to concrete goals (e.g., monetary).

12. Ibid., refers to solidary goals (e.g., psychological, ideological rewards).

13. Ibid., refers to purposive or altruistic goals (e.g., civil liberties).

14. Stolz, "Congress and Criminal Justice Policy Making," p. 309.

15. See committee web pages of the U.S. House of Representatives and U.S. Senate web sites, respectively <http://www.house.gov> and <http://www.senate.gov>.

16. T. Anton, "Roles and Symbols in the Determination of State Expenditures" *Midwest Journal of Political Science*, vol. 11 (1967): 27–43; T. Arnold, *The Symbols of Government* (New Haven, CT: Yale University Press, 1935); Murray Edelman, *The Symbolic Uses of Politics* (Chicago: University of Illinois Press, 1964); Murray Edelman, *Politics As Symbolic Action: Mass Arousal and Quiesence* (New York: Academic Press, 1971); H. Lasswell and A. Kaplan, *Power and Society: A Framework for Political Inquiry* (London: Routledge and Kegan Paul, 1952).

17. Edelman, *The Symbolic Uses of Politics*, p. 42.

18. Greenwald, *Group Power*, p. 15.

19. A. Bentley, *The Process of Government* (1908; reprint, Cambridge, MA: Belknap Press, 1967); B. Gross, *The Legislative Struggle: A Study in Social Combat* (New York: McGraw-Hill, 1953); R. Huitt and R. Peabody, *Congress: Two Decades of Analysis* (New York: Harper and Row, 1969); D. Truman, *The Governmental Process* (New York: Knopf, 1951); Greenwald, *Group Power*.

20. Robert A. Dahl, *Who Governs?* (New Haven, CT: Yale University Press, 1961); L. Milbrath, *The Washington Lobbyist* (Chicago: Rand McNally, 1963); and Greenwald, *Group Power*.

21. Edelman, *The Symbolic Uses of Politics*, p. 40.

22. Stolz, "Congress and Capital Punishment."

23. A detailed presentation of the capital-punishment study is found in Stolz, "Congress and Capital Punishment" and of the criminal code revision in Stolz, "Interest Groups and Criminal Law."

24. The time period 1972–1982 was chosen because both legislation to abolish and to reinstitute capital punishment were considered; thus both pro and con forces introduced legislation and dominated the process.

25. The time period includes the entire recent congressional criminal-code revision effort.

26. Huitt and Peabody, *Congress: Two Decades of Analysis*, p. 28.

27. U.S. Congress, Senate, Committee on Judiciary, *Hearings on Reform of the Federal Criminal Law before the Subcommittee on Criminal Law and Procedures*, 92nd Congress, 2d sess., 1972; U.S. Congress, House, House Committee on Judiciary, *Sentencing in Capital Cases*. Hearings before Subcommittee on Criminal Justice of the House Committee on Judiciary on H.R. 13360, 95th Congress, 2d sess., 1978; U.S. Congress, House, Committee on Judiciary, *Legislation to Revise and Recodify Federal Criminal Laws*, Hearings before Subcommittee on Criminal Justice of the House Committee on Judiciary on H.R. 6869, 95th Congress, 1st and 2d sess., 1977–1978. Parts 1–3. U.S. Congress, Senate, Committee on Judiciary, *To Establish Constitutional Procedures for the Imposition of Capital Punishment*, Hearings before Subcommittee on Criminal Laws and Procedures of the Senate Committee on the Judiciary on S.1382, 95th Congress, 1st sess., 1977; U.S. Congress, Senate, Committee on Judiciary, *To Establish Rational Criteria for Imposition of Capital Punishment*, Hearings before Senate Committee on Judiciary on S. 1382, 95th Congress, 2d sess., 1978; among others. See also appendix in Stolz, "Congress and Criminal Justice Policy Making," pp. 317–18.

28. Congressional Quarterly Service, "Criminal Code Revision," *Congressional Quarterly Almanac* (Washington, DC: Congressional Quarterly Service, 1977), p. 603.

29. Greenwald, *Group Power*, p. 52.

30. *Hearings before Subcommittee on Criminal Justice on H.R. 6869*, 1978: vol. 3, 2602–3.

31. V. O. Key, *Politics, Parties, and Pressure Groups*, 5th ed. (New York: Thomas Y. Crowell, 1964), p. 135.

32. Ibid., p. 134.

33. Because of space limitations, this section is organized according to the categories of analysis. A more formal case-study presentation and a detailed discussion of the symbolic functions are found in Stolz, "Congress and Capital Punishment."

34. National Advisory Commission on Criminal Justice Standards and Goals, *Corrections* (Washington, DC: U.S. Government Printing Office, 1973), pp. 602–3.

35. U.S. Congress, House, *Conference Report on Juvenile Justice and Delinquency Prevention Act of 1974 to Accompany S.821*, 93rd Congress, 2d sess., 1974: No. 93–1298, pp. 40–44; Juvenile Justice and Delinquency Prevention Act of 1974: PL 93–415; Juvenile Justice Amendments of 1977: PL 95–115; Omnibus Crime Control and Safe Streets Act of 1968: PL 90-351; D. C. Gibbons et al., *Criminal Justice Planning* (Englewood Cliffs, NJ: Prentice Hall, 1977), p. 3; D. T. Shanahan and P. Whisenand, *The Dimensions of Criminal Justice Planning* (Boston: Allyn and Bacon, 1980), p. 55.

36. A limited crime bill did pass Congress in 1984. While its passage supports the arguments presented in this article, the bill passed too late to be included in the analysis.

37. Edelman, *The Symbolic Uses of Politics*, p. 38.

38. F. Zimring and G. Hawkins, *Deterrence: The Legal Threat in Crime Control* (Chicago: University of Chicago Press, 1973), pp. 18–19.

39. Edelman, *The Symbolic Uses of Politics*, p. 31.

40. U.S. Congress, Debate on Capital Punishment, *Congressional Record* (January 23, 1979 [daily ed.]) p. S.419.

41. The Logan Act of 1979 (18 U.S. Code 953) forbids private citizens undertaking diplomatic correspondence or intercourse with a foreign power with intent to influence conduct in relation to controversies with the United States.

42. U.S. Congress, House, Committee on Judiciary, *Criminal Code Pending Matters*, Mark-up before House Committee on Judiciary, 96th Congress, 2d sess., July 2, 1982. (Observed)

43. J. Andanaes, *Punishment and Deterrence* (Ann Arbor: University of Michigan Press, 1974); Zimring and Hawkins, *Deterrence*; and Arnold, *The Symbols of Government*.

44. Walter Berns, *For Capital Punishment* (New York: Basic Books, 1979).

45. See Chapter 36, "Final Report of the National Commission on Reform of Federal Criminal Laws."

46. National Commission on Reform of Federal Criminal Laws, "Working Papers," pp. 1350–51.

47. Fifteen of these executions were for murder; six were for kidnapping. (Under the Federal kidnapping statute, the death penalty provision of which was ruled unconstitutional by the U.S. Supreme Court in *United States v. Jackson*, 390 U.S. 750 (1968), kidnapping is a capital crime only if the victim is not released unharmed. In five of the six cases, the victims were killed by the kidnappers); six were executed for sabotage. (All in the District of Columbia in 1942); two for rape on a federal reservation; two for bank robbery with murder; and two for conspiracy to commit espionage. Source: U.S. Department of Justice, Bureau of Prisons, "Capital Punishment 1930–1968," *National Prisoner Statistics Bulletin* 45 (August 1969) (hereafter *NPS*), p. 29.

48. *NPS*, p. 7

49. See Huie, "The Execution of Private Slovik."

50. See the attached memorandum on deterrence, and the excerpts from "The Case Against Capital Punishment" (this hearing, pp. 166–71).

51. "The Challenge of Crime in a Free Society: A Report by the President's Commission on Law Enforcement and Administration of Justice" (1967), p. 143.

52. See T. Sellin in *To Abolish the Death Penalty*, Hearings Before the Subcommittee on Criminal Laws and Procedures of the Senate Judiciary Committee, 90th Cong., 2nd sess. (1968) (hereinafter Hearings), p. 80.

53. Source: *Crime in the United States, Uniform Crime Reports—1970* (U.S. Department of Justice, FBI, 1971) (hereinafter *UCR*) pp. 72–81. See the attached list (in this hearing, p. 165) of all states in descending order of homicide rate.

54. *UCR*, p. 9.

55. See the attached synopsis of these cases (this hearing, p. 166). Also see L. West in Hearing, p. 126.

56. See attached excerpts (this hearing pp. 166–71) from "The Case Against Capital Punishment" on recidivism.

57. *UCR*, p. 9.

58. See the attached memorandum (this hearing p. 171) on worldwide abolition.

59. See Kennedy, "Ten Rillington Place."

60. *New York Times*, December 19, 1969, p. 9.

Chapter 5

The Bureaucracy: Affecting Criminal Justice Policy through Information

INTRODUCTION

Among the ways that bureaucracies can influence public policies, in general, and criminal justice policies, in particular, is by providing information to policymakers and implementing policies. This chapter focuses on bureaucracies, information, and policy making; chapter 6 examines how bureaucracies can affect policy through implementation. The information that agencies disseminate may help to define a problem for policymakers, indicate how programs and policies are working, or identify new problems. In so doing, bureaucracies may influence policymakers to continue, terminate, or initiate programs and policies.

At the federal level, the president appoints top officials within the bureaucracy. Although members of the president's cabinet are the most prominent of these appointments, presidential appointments reach farther down into an agency's organizational structure. Through the power of appointment (Constitution, Article II) the president can influence the policy direction taken by an agency and the bureaucracy, in general. Congress, through the "advise and consent" powers of the Senate, can affect those presidential appointments subject to confirmation by confirming or refusing to confirm a presidential nominee. With respect to executive appointments, Congress usually gives deference to the president's choice. A majority of agency employees are, however, permanent civil servants who remain employed despite changes in the presidential administration and ensure continuity of policies and programs.

Despite changes in administration, the federal criminal justice information bureaucracy has grown, since the 1965 President's Crime Commission made its recommendations. The number of bureaus, offices, and grants programs has increased. This chapter examines the primary federal criminal justice bureaucracies that provide crime and criminal justice information to Congress and the public. It includes a description of the organization and programs of the Office of Justice Programs, which is the primary source of federal criminal justice research and publications. In addition, it includes a discussion of the U.S. General Accounting Office, Congress's watchdog agency, which audits and reviews federal criminal justice policies, programs, and agency operations.

FEDERAL CRIMINAL JUSTICE AGENCIES: INFORMATION BUREAUCRACY

The Department of Justice, the primary federal agency for criminal justice, and the agencies within it gather and provide to Congress and the public information on criminal justice activities. Since 1930, the FBI has collected and compiled crime statistics, voluntarily submitted by many law enforcement agencies across the country, and then published those data in the *Uniform Crime Reports*. The Drug Enforcement Administration (DEA) in more recent years has published information on drug trafficking trends.

Since the 1960s, the Justice Department has taken a more active role in supporting and sponsoring criminal justice research and in gathering information on criminal justice policies and programs, thereby changing the landscape of criminal justice research and the information available to policymakers. As reported in chapters 2 and 3 of this text, the 1965 President's Crime Commission identified the need for criminal justice research to inform public policy making. Even before the commission issued its report in 1967, President Johnson sent to Congress and it enacted legislation, creating the Office of Law Enforcement Assistance (OLEA) to fund demonstration projects to develop new methods of crime control and law enforcement. The Law Enforcement Assistance Administration (LEAA) succeeded OLEA in 1968. LEAA was established to make grants to state and local governments for a variety of criminal justice administrative, educational, and enforcement activities. LEAA was eliminated effectively in the 1980s, but some of its specialized functions were continued by its successor agency, the Office of Justice Assistance, Research, and Statistics (OJARS). In 1984, the Office of Justice Programs (OJP) was established as an umbrella agency over a number of bureaus and offices, which have continued to grow in number. OJP and its component agencies provide information to Congress and the public on a wide range of criminal justice issues.

Other federal agencies, not part of the Department of Justice, also provide information on various aspects of criminal justice policy and administration. These agencies include the Office of National Drug Control Policy, the United States General Accounting Office, and the Congressional Research Service, among others.

OJP

In 1984, Congress enacted legislation establishing the OJP, headed by an assistant attorney general, a presidential appointee. OJP is the umbrella for five bureaus and several offices that carry out a wide range of criminal justice programs and initiatives. The five bureaus, each headed by a presidential appointee, include the National Institute of Justice (NIJ), the Bureau of Justice Statistics (BJS), the Bureau of Justice Assistance (BJA),[1] the Office of Juvenile Justice and Delinquency Prevention (OJJDP), and the Office for Victims of Crime (OVC). The program offices focus on violence against women, drug courts, and police and law enforcement education.

The OJP bureaus and offices award grants and contracts, implement programs, provide technical assistance, conduct research and evaluation, and collect and analyze data. NIJ is authorized to support research and development programs, conduct demonstrations of innovative approaches to improve criminal justice, develop new criminal justice technologies, and evaluate the effectiveness of OJP-supported and other justice programs. BJS, the primary source for criminal justice statistics, collects, analyzes, publishes, and disseminates information on crime, criminal offenders, victims of crime, and the operation of the criminal justice system at all levels of government. BJA provides funding, training, and technical assistance to state and local governments to combat violent and drug-related crime and to help improve the criminal justice system. OJJDP provides national leadership, coordination, and resources to prevent and respond to juvenile delinquency and victimization. OVC was established in 1984 to oversee diverse programs that benefit victims of crime.

The OJP agencies award grants in two forms—formula and discretionary. Formula grants are awarded to states or units of local government, which in turn determine how the funds are distributed to state, local, and nonprofit organizations. The formulas used (e.g., population, crime rates, or juvenile population) vary with each program. Discretionary awards are made directly by OJP bureaus and offices to state and local agencies and private organizations.[2]

Congress authorizes and appropriates funds for OJP, and during that process Congress may also "earmark"—designate specifically, from either formula or discretionary grants programs—how funds are to be spent or to whom they are to be distributed. For example, in 1996, Congress required the attorney general to provide a "comprehensive evaluation of the effectiveness" of over $3 billion annually in grants to assist state and local law enforcement and communities in preventing crime. Congress mandated that the research be "independent in nature" and "employ rigorous and scientifically recognized standards and methodologies." The assistant attorney general for OJP asked NIJ to commission an independent review. That review resulted in a report on what was found to work, not work, or was promising in crime prevention based on a review of more than 500 prevention program evalutions.[3] In other instances, Congress specifically has identified the organizations to which program funds were to go. For example, from the Local Law Enforcement Block Grant Program, overseen by BJA, Congress earmarked $50 million for the Boys and Girls Clubs in OJP's fiscal year 2000 appropriation. OJP's annual plan and web site are excellent sources of information regarding OJP's programs and the types of criminal justice information available.

Other Federal Agencies

Other federal agencies develop and/or disseminate to Congress and the executive branch data on various aspects of crime and provide them with information on how well criminal justice programs and policies are being carried out. The Office of National Drug Control Policy (ONDCP) focuses on all aspects of the drug problem and provides information on drug use and abuse, trafficking, and even on new illicit drugs. Agencies in the U.S. Department of the Treasury, including the U.S. Customs Service and the Bureau of Alcohol, Tobacco, and Firearms, gather information on crime problems that fall under their jurisdiction. The Congressional Research Service prepares reports to Congress on criminal justice policies, programs, as well as pending anti-crime legislation In addition, Congress has its own watchdog—the U.S. General Accounting Office (GAO)—to audit and evaluate federal policies, agencies, and programs, including criminal justice policies, agency administration, and programs. GAO was established in 1921 as part of the "Budget and Accounting Act," but over the years its authority has been expanded. The agency is headed by the Comptroller General of the United States, who is appointed for a fifteen-year term. With approximately 3,000 employees, GAO staff are located in its Washington, D.C., headquarters and in several field office. GAO's mission is to (1) assist Congress, committees, and members in their oversight role; (2) audit and evaluate programs, activities, and financial operation of federal departments and agencies and make recommendations to improve effectiveness and efficiency; and (3) ensure financial controls.

To fulfill the agency's mission, staff carry out various types of reviews—descriptive (what is, e.g., How many prisoners are served by the Federal Bureau of Prisons [BOP]?), compliance (what is as compared to what should be, e.g., Are BOP's medical programs in compliance with applicable laws?), economy and efficiency (what is versus what should be the effect, e.g., Is BOP making optimal use of bed space?), program impact (what is the condition with or without a program, e.g., What has been the impact of the drug courts?), and prospective options analysis (what is the best approach, e.g., What is the best approach to reduce the number of crack babies?). Whether the studies are requested by members of Congress, mandated by legislation, or initiated by agency staff, the objective is primarily to provide information to Congress. As illustrated in its 1997 report on the drug courts, GAO may provide recommendations to Congress on programs, policy, and administration.[4]

INFORMATION AND THE CRIMINAL JUSTICE BUREAUCRACY: COMMENT

The Federal Criminal Justice Information Bureaucracy Performs Symbolic Functions

Drawing on the discussion of symbolic politics in the previous chapters, it is possible to posit how criminal justice information agencies may perform several symbolic functions. In particular, these agencies, through the various programs they carry out and the information they disseminate may perform an educative function or model for the states function. OJP's publications provide information that may educate policymakers, practitioners, academics, and the public about criminal justice issues. That information may be statistical or provide case study information on programs that work. Through demonstration programs, grants-in-aid, and training and technical assistance, the OJP agencies provide funding to establish programs that the federal government believes to be good policy. In so doing, the federal information bureaucracy has further expanded and continues to expand the federal criminal justice role, as it relates to state and local criminal justice policy making.

The Federal Criminal Justice Information Bureaucracy Has Its Critics

The criminal justice information provided by federal agencies is not without its critics, however. The agencies that provide grants for research or community groups have been criticized for repeatedly awarding grants to the same researchers or programs and not supporting new initiatives. Some have criticized the agencies for limiting their focus to certain criminal justice issues. Still others have criticized the quality of agency data or how those data are used. Still other criticisms are a matter of program administration. For example, the paneling process used to select discretionary grantees may need to be expanded to include different reviewers.

For some of these criticisms remedies may be easy. For example, the assertion that federal grants programs fail to support new initiatives may be addressed by such measures as setting aside funds for new initiatives. Other criticisms may be more difficult to address, since OJP's research agenda is not entirely independent, due to its source of funding, from the perspectives of Congress, the attorney general, and the White House. Some academics have suggested that NIJ, perhaps with BJS, be established as an independent institute, similar to the National Institutes of Health. Alternatively, the limits of a government funded criminal justice agenda underscore the need for continued private funding of criminal justice research.

For the Future

For better or worse, Congress and other policymakers have access to more information about criminal justice problems and issues than they did in the 1960s. What the federal criminal justice research and information agenda should be for the next decade and new century, as well as what structures are needed to provide that information, is subject to continued discussion. OJP and its agencies are not only subject to the annual appropriations process and program authorization establishing new programs under OJP's jurisdiction, but also to periodic reauthorizations by Congress, subjecting the agency, itself, to the possibility of reorganization and change. One can expect that under the new Bush administration there will be changes in programs, if not in the structure of OJP and its component agencies. To keep abreast of the changes, the reader may wish to view OJP's web page from time to time.

INCLUDED SELECTIONS

The first selection in this chapter links the efforts of the 1965 President's Crime Commission to the current federal criminal justice information bureaucracy that oversees criminal justice research, grants programs, and state and local initiatives. The second describes that bureaucracy—the Office of Justice Programs and its components within the U.S. Department of Justice. The United States General Accounting Office has the responsibility for providing Congress with information on how federal agencies, including the Department of Justice, operate and carry out government programs; the third selection in this chapter provides a description of that agency. The final selection is the executive summary from a GAO report on drug courts, which was mandated by the Congress.[5] Title V of the Violent Crime Control and Law Enforcement Act of 1994 (P.L. 103–322) authorized federal grants for drug court programs that include court-supervised drug treatment and required that GAO assess the effectiveness and impact of these grants.

FOR DISCUSSION

From the selections in this chapter the reader should consider:

1. Why the 1965 President's Crime Commission believed that criminal justice research and information were important.
2. The structure and organization of the federal criminal justice information bureaucracy.
3. The types of information now available to policymakers.
4. The criticisms of criminal justice information available through the federal criminal justice information bureaucracies.
5. The role that information may play in federal criminal justice policy making.
6. Which state and local agencies provide criminal justice information and in so doing affect state and local criminal justice policy making.

RECOMMENDED READINGS AND OTHER SOURCES

Specific References

The Challenge of Crime in a Free Society Looking Back . . . Looking Forward. Washington, DC: U.S. Department of Justice, Office of Justice Programs, May 1998.

Drug Courts: Overview of Growth, Characteristics, and Results (GAO/GGD-97-106). Washington, DC: U.S. General Accounting Office, 1997.

McGee, Jim, and Duffy, Brian. *Main Justice.* New York: A Touchstone Book, Simon and Schuster, 1996.

Office of Justice Programs. *Fiscal Year 1999 Program Plan.* Washington, DC: U.S. Department of Justice, Office of Justice Programs.

Web Sites

OJP Agencies <http://www.ojp.usdoj.gov>
　　　　　　　<http://www.ojp.usdoj.gov/bjs>
　　　　　　　<http://www.ojp.usdoj.gov/nij>
　　　　　　　<http://www.ojp.usdoj.gov/bja>
　　　　　　　<http://www.ojp.usdoj.gov/ojjdp>
Department of Justice <http://www.usdoj.gov>
FBI <http://www.fbi.gov>
Office of National Drug Control Policy (ONDCP) <http://www.whitehouse.drugpolicy.gov>
U.S. General Accounting Office <http://www.gao.gov>
Other OJP agency sites may be found through the OJP web page.

THE CHALLENGE OF CRIME IN A FREE SOCIETY LOOKING BACK ... LOOKING FORWARD

In a dramatic statement to the American people in 1967, the President's Commission on Law Enforcement and Administration of Justice called for a "revolution in the way America thinks about crime." It set forth seven goals that remain challenging today: prevent crime, adopt new ways of dealing with offenders, eliminate injustice and unfairness, upgrade personnel, conduct research to find new and effective ways to control crime, put up the money necessary to do the job, [and] involve all elements of society in planning and executing changes in the criminal justice system.

The President's Commission urged the Nation to view law enforcement and criminal justice as a system and to upgrade it to be more effective in preventing and reducing crime. It called for the use of new technologies developed by Space Age science. It advocated basing policy on fact and not on myth, and maintaining American democratic values of fairness and respect for the individual. . . .

This paper is not a formal research document. It makes no pretense to be a definitive analysis of outcomes 30 years later. Rather, it uses reflections and insights of some of those who were there to examine briefly what the Commission set out to do, what it accomplished, and how those efforts help to inform policy debate on crime and criminal justice today.

SUCCESSES OF THE COMMISSION

Here are the views of Commission members, the executive director, senior staff, and one of the heads of the Law Enforcement Assistance Administration (LEAA) about what the Commission contributed.

Propounding a Criminal Justice "System"

In many jurisdictions in 1967, police, courts, and corrections operated independently of one another. The Commission viewed this situation as ineffective and envisioned one comprehensive system devoted to enforcing law and administering justice. Commission Chairman Nicholas deB. Katzenbach says, "I would give particular emphasis to the Commission's ap-

Reprinted and excerpted from *The Challenge of Crime in a Free Society Looking Back . . . Looking Forward: Research Forum, June 19–21, 1997,* "The Challenge of Crime in a Free Society Looking Back . . . Looking Forward," by Joseph Foote, prepared for the Office of Justice Programs and Office of Community Oriented Policing Services, May 1998.

proach of seeing criminal justice as having several parts that have to work together, or it cannot be effective. This is a lesson that has not been learned, it seems to me, by the general public, or by Congress or State legislatures."

"The idea of a criminal justice system," adds Deputy Director Henry S. Ruth, Jr., "has its roots in the writings of Roscoe Pound and the Wickersham Commission.[6] The work of Frank Remington and others also focused on the interactions of elements of the criminal justice system."

"The matter of discretion at every step of the criminal justice process is critical to understanding how the system works," Ruth adds. "The police have discretion as to whom they arrest, the prosecutor as to whom to prosecute, the jury as to whom to convict, and the judge as to how to sentence. Thus, 100,000 crimes come down to 3,000 people in prison."

"Practically no data on the criminal justice system existed when the Commission began work," Ruth notes. "Not much police data existed. Court data were a mess."

Much credit for developing the concept of a criminal justice system goes to Alfred Blumstein, chairman of the Commission's Task Force on Science and Technology. He produced a flow chart of the criminal justice system that attracted wide attention and is used today. The data were so scanty, however, that Blumstein "had to stretch to estimate the numbers for his famous chart," Ruth says.

The Commission sparked change: "The criminal justice system today is less brutal and takes advantage of modern technology," says Commission Executive Director James Vorenberg. In addition, says Commission member Herbert Wechsler, "The Commission launched something important in this country—objectivity in government with respect to crime." Policy would be based on reality and facts.

Laying the Foundation for Federal Efforts

An enduring contribution of the Commission has been, in the eyes of Chairman Katzenbach and his colleagues, to lay the foundation for the appropriate role and most useful direction and scope of Federal efforts in State and local law enforcement and administration of justice. A direct line runs from the Commission to LEAA to the Office of Justice Assistance, Research, and Statistics (OJARS) to today's Office of Justice Programs (OJP).

Office of Justice Programs

OJP operates under the leadership of Assistant Attorney General [then] Laurie Robinson, who also directly administers Corrections, Drug Court, and Violence Against Women Act grant programs and the Executive Office for Weed and Seed. OJP also includes the Bureau of Justice Assistance (BJA), Bureau of Justice Statistics (BJS), National Institute of Justice (NIJ), Office of Juvenile Justice and Delinquency Prevention (OJJDP), and Office for Victims of Crime (OVC). Close to 700 employees work in OJP, fewer than the high of 800 who worked at LEAA but more than the 300 who were in OJP just 3 years ago.

Even as the Commission conducted its work, the Office of Law Enforcement Assistance was founded in 1966. The Commission reported in 1967, drawing significant attention because of the growing public concern about crime, the prestige of its members, and the controversy expressed in the report by the sharp division between the majority and the dissenters. Congress, sensing the need to respond but ever careful of the then prevalent view of limited Federal responsibility for crime control, enacted the landmark Omnibus Crime Control and Safe Streets Act of 1968. That act created LEAA, the first comprehensive Federal programmatic response to State and local crime control by providing to the States—in part through block grants and in part through categorical grants—funds to reduce crime by improving local criminal justice systems—police, courts, and corrections. An LEAA administrator, Donald Santarelli, says, "The creation of LEAA was a direct response to the Commission's report. Its creation signaled the makings of a significant change in the Federal Government's attitude towards crime, avoiding the federalization of State and local crime and assumption of operational responsibility, and with great respect for the dual federalism of government responsibility, it sought to strengthen the States rather than assume Federal enforcement responsibility." LEAA ran its program for 14 years.

In the Justice Assistance Act of 1984, Congress created the separate OJARS agencies to perform many of the functions of LEAA, which were later organized under OJP. When Congress enacted the Violent Crime Control and Law Enforcement Act of 1994, it accelerated the momentum of Federal support for local jurisdictions. Federal funding for State and local crime control came more than full circle as Congress authorized a record $2.7 billion in 1996 and $3.2 billion in 1997.

Today, OJP carries on the work begun and nurtured by many people of both political parties who labored in Congress and the Department to build a Federal presence that is useful to State and local law enforcement and criminal justice agencies.

"The Commission believed that the proper Federal role is to be supportive," Katzenbach says, "supportive in dollars, in ideas, and in encouraging and coordinating the exchange of information." The Commission wanted to stimulate creativity at every level of government, he says, and to urge everyone in the criminal justice system to find ways of doing things more

effectively and economically. Those notions guide Federal thinking and policymaking today.

The COPS Program

Title I of the Violent Crime Control and Law Enforcement Act of 1994
provides Federal grants to States and units of local government to enable
them to hire additional police officers. The program is administered by the
Office of Community Oriented Policing Services (COPS), established in the
Department of Justice in 1994. The Office reports to [then] Acting Associate
Attorney General John C. Dwyer. By February 1997, grants had been
awarded to hire or redeploy 54,000 police officers and sheriffs' deputies, who
will serve more than 87 percent of the American population.

Advocating Federal Money and Standards

"Money was the single most useful idea that the Commission dwelt on,"
says Wechsler. "More money was absolutely essential for the enlargement
of personnel and the authorization of new programs, both nationally and
locally."

"Perhaps as a secondary aspect of that," he adds, "was the Commission's
emphasis on the important role for the Federal Government to play, primarily by enhancing local capacities."

These ideas—more money and Federal standards—were important because the Commission saw that much of the criminal justice system was
subject to political patronage at the State and local levels. "That is why the
Commission was useful," Wechsler says. With strong State and local representation on its membership, it could propose reform of what it found
in criminal justice—an underfunded, politically operated nonsystem.

Maintaining a Balance in Rights

"The Commission gave a great deal of attention to the need to balance
concerns about public safety with the continuing recognition that we are a
democratic society and have to care about values and fairness," says Commission staff member Sheldon Krantz.

The Commission was a product of its times, and the times included the
milestone decisions of the Supreme Court, under Chief Justice Earl Warren,
that extended the application of the Bill of Rights to the States. "What the
Warren Court had done was determine that a lot of the States were dealing
in a very harsh and discriminatory and unfair manner with suspects of
crimes or defendants," says Krantz. "The Court thought that there ought
to be a national standard in many instances, a Constitutional standard that

applies everywhere. We were very much a product of that thinking in the late 1960s." He adds:

We had a number of people on both the Commission and staff who were beginning to recognize what developed very substantially in the 1970s and 1980s, and that is that, although we have to be worried about fairness to defendants, we also have to protect our streets and we have to be concerned about victims. The victims' rights thinking was not very ingrained in the Commission's work. The movement came after us.

. . .

ORIGINS AND APPROACH

. . .

Commission Approach: Get the Facts

President Johnson formally established the President's Commission on July 23, 1965, and directed it to report to him early in 1967 with recommendations for preventing crime and delinquency and improving law enforcement and the administration of criminal justice.

The Commission recruited a staff, which eventually grew to 63, of outstanding lawyers, police officers, correctional personnel, prosecutors, sociologists, psychologists, systems analysts, juvenile delinquency prevention planners, and professional writers and editors. Many were on leave or loan from universities and Federal, State, and local governments. Some 175 consultants and hundreds of advisers also contributed. The President appointed James Vorenberg, on leave from Harvard Law, as executive director. The deputy director was Henry Ruth, who had been a prosecutor in the Department of Justice's Organized Crime and Racketeering Section and later a member of the Office of Criminal Justice.

The Commission established itself as a model of the fact-gathering approach. It undertook several historical surveys—on police-community relations, professional criminals, unreported crime, and correctional personnel and facilities. The surveys of corrections and of victims of crime were the first nationwide studies ever made in those areas. More than 2,200 police departments were asked what field procedures they found especially effective against crime. Science and technology experts, under Alfred Blumstein of the Institute for Defense Analyses, brought special expertise in systems analysis and applications of new technologies to law enforcement.

The Commission also sent staff members and consultants into the streets and neighborhoods to talk with residents, and into police departments, courts, and prisons to talk with law enforcement and criminal justice professionals and with accused individuals and convicted felons. It drew on data from Federal and State agencies, held conferences, and engaged in extensive communication with law enforcement agencies throughout the Nation. The Commission produced a report, *The Challenge of Crime in a Free Society*, and a shelf of task force reports that remain useful today.

WHAT THE NATION LEARNED

The President's Commission believed that more money would improve the criminal justice system, enhance the administration of justice, and—perhaps—help to prevent crime and lower the crime rate. It also believed that law and policy should be informed by research, statistics, and knowledge generally.

Still, Federal leadership and financial support go just so far. "Translating the Commission's research, findings, and recommendations into action proved to be difficult," says Vorenberg. "Not everything the Federal Government identifies as a need can be converted into action. Even the Commission rejected the notion of a large new operating office at the Federal level."

Chairman Katzenbach says the Federal role should be—and is—to suggest ideas and directions, help with resources, and disseminate results on the information network—and then to stand aside while State and local governments do their job.

Bridging the Research and Policy Gap

A core concern of the Commission was how to base policy on empirical fact. A "gap" exists between the insight of the elected official, who knows the voter very well, and the analysis of the researcher, who studies the criminal, victim, police officer, prosecutor, judge, and corrections officer. Putting these two areas of expertise together is the nub of the issue. "Legislators think they know the answers." Chairman Katzenbach says, "Or they get caught up in 'get-tough' rhetoric that always seems to sell with the public. Put the felons in jail and throw the key away—which is an expensive solution."

What is the size of the gap today? Some observers believe that it is fairly wide, noting contentions by some criminal justice researchers that drug interdiction is not cost-effective and that prison-building is no long-range, effective answer to the crime problem. Vorenberg disagrees. "I think the gap is somewhat narrower now than in the past," he says. "There is less hysteria about crime in the streets today than at almost any time in the past 25 to 30 years."

Still, Vorenberg and other Commission alumni cite the drug interdiction policy as perhaps the leading example of the gap. Chairman Katzenbach puts it this way:

We have created a situation where it is difficult to have political or public consideration or debate about how we ought to approach the drug problem. It's not that anything we are doing is necessarily wrong, although some of it I would criticize. But we have created exactly the opposite atmosphere—an unwillingness to look at any aspect of it. Nobody in my position—as a citizen—knows whether and how much interdiction, at what price, is good policy.

"The Commission report really emphasizes the need for us to be driven not by rhetoric but by facts," says former staff member Krantz. "The Commission saw a need to make sure that we do not use the great technology that we have to become a police state, when that is not what the United States wants to be. Those messages still need to be recognized today, because I really do think that we are constantly being driven toward more and more repressive forms of dealing with admittedly difficult problems."

Krantz adds his concern that "research in academic communities in this country is pretty far removed from what is going on in the streets." Even thoughtful academics write books about crime and are basically saying that nothing works. "But out there in the communities, all kinds of exciting things are happening," he adds.

Is this, as Krantz implies, an appropriate time for the research community to take a look at itself? To what extent is it ready to accept the challenge of closing the gap? Everyone agrees that policy should be based on science, but the science needs to be both good and relevant. Maybe some programs out there in communities do work. Are they failures because not all such programs work? What measures of success exist beyond the "merely" quantitative?

WHAT HAS HAPPENED TO THE COMMISSION'S IDEAS?

The Commission's contributions to research begin with its emphasis on the very notion of marrying research with criminal justice planning and policy. "The Commission played a part in the development of governmental practices of using research instruments," says Wechsler. "Private and university research already existed, and [Felix] Frankfurter and the [Sheldon and Eleanor] Gluecks had done good work. But the Commission developed new methods of gathering and using information."

Where did the law enforcement and criminal justice community go from there? Professor Alfred Blumstein of Carnegie Mellon University, chairman of the Commission's Task Force on Science and Technology, has reviewed the current status of several of the Commission's most important proposed innovations. Here is a summary of his findings.

In 1967, automatic fingerprint recognition technology did not exist. With the speed and ability to process digitized fingerprint images now afforded by new computer technologies, latent fingerprints are now used to solve some crimes, and storage and retrieval of fingerprint records have become more efficient.

DNA identification is one of the most important new approaches to forensic identification developed over the past 15 years. But DNA testing is still too expensive for routine use. As costs decrease, a broad-based database of individual DNA will allow comparisons of crime scene evidence with DNA records of known offenders.

Communication networks that link police to each other, to central command and control systems, and ultimately to individual callers who report crimes are the most important police technologies. Most large police departments now have computerized command-and- control systems for communications between and among officers in the field and headquarters personnel.

In the 1960s, many questioned the legality of personal electronic monitors—the bracelets that allow police to put offenders under "house arrest" and track them if they attempt to leave their place of confinement. Today they are considered an appropriate means for dealing with offenders short of incarceration.

In 1967, data reported by the police to the Federal Bureau of Investigation (FBI) and published annually in the *Uniform Crime Reports* were the only source of statistical information available on crime in this country. *The National Crime Survey* and a number of self-report studies now add the perspectives of victims to crime statistics reporting.

Although theories of criminal behavior abounded 30 years ago, those theories were based on intuition rather than empirical evidence. Research is now used to calculate the benefits of a wide variety of criminal justice programs.

Widespread use of computers is the most important development in the criminal justice system of the past 30 years. Although few conceptual innovations have occurred, computer applications and availability have become much more widespread, even in the smallest operating units. For police, innovations in the use of this technology typically involve geographic information systems to replace traditional pin maps, and the use of that information in police patrol allocation programs. The courts also employ computers to organize their calendars, send basic notices to the various participants in legal hearings, and for other purposes.

Issues surrounding computerized individual criminal history records have been debated for many years. The Commission recommended that each State maintain its own records, with a central index indicating merely the identity of individuals with a record in at least one of the States, and with an indication of which State or States held the detailed records. This basic structure has been pursued in the criminal-history network currently being coordinated by the FBI and supported by BJS. . . .

BIOGRAPHIES OF SOURCES

Alfred Blumstein, Director of Science and Technology for the Commission, was a science and technology expert from the Institute for Defense Analyses. He is now the J. Erik Jonsson University Professor at the H. John Heinz III School of Public Policy and Management at Carnegie Mellon University.

Thomas J. Cahill, a Commission member, was Chief of Police of the San Francisco Police Department. He entered the police department as a patrolman in 1942. He now lives in retirement in San Francisco.

Nicholas deB. Katzenbach, Chairman of the Commission, served as Attorney General of the United States under President Lyndon B. Johnson; Deputy Attorney General under President John F. Kennedy; and an Assistant Attorney General, Office of Legal Counsel, also under President Kennedy. He lives in retirement in Princeton, New Jersey.

Sheldon Krantz was a staff member of the President's Commission. He served as a professor at Boston University and as dean of the University of San Diego Law School. He now practices law in the Washington, DC, office of Piper & Marbury.

Elmer K. Nelson, Associate Director of the Commission, is now a professor (emeritus) of public administration at the University of Southern California.

Charles Rogavin was Assistant Director for organized crime for the Commission. He is now a Professor of Law at Temple University.

Henry S. Ruth, Jr., Deputy Director of the Commission, was a prosecutor in the Department of Justice's Organized Crime and Racketeering Section and later a member of the Office of Criminal Justice. He is an Adjunct Professor of Law at the University of Arizona and lives in Tuscon, Arizona.

Donald Santarelli was not a member of the Commission or its staff, but as a counsel to the House Judiciary Committee he was involved in drafting and later, as an administrator, administering the LEAA statute that grew out of the Commission's report. A former Associate Deputy Attorney General, he is now a partner in private practice with the law firm of Bell, Boyd & Lloyd in Washington, DC.

James Vorenberg, Executive Director of the Commission, was a Professor of Law at the Harvard Law School, a post he still holds.

Herbert Wechsler, a Commission member, was the Harlan Fiske Stone Professor of Constitutional Law at Columbia Law School. He had served as an Assistant Attorney General of the United States under President Franklin D. Roosevelt and was the director of the American Law Institute. He lives in retirement in New York City.

FURTHER READING

Conley, John A., ed. (1994). *The 1967 President's Crime Commission Report: Its Impact 25 Years Later*. Cincinnati, OH: Anderson Publishing Co.

Lipsky, M. & D. J. Olson (1977). *Commission Politics: The Processing of Racial Crisis in America*. New Brunswick, NJ: Transaction Books.

National Commission on Law Observance and Enforcement (1931). *Reports*. Washington, DC: U.S. Government Printing Office.

Office of Justice Programs, U.S. Department of Justice. *LEAA/OJP Retrospective: 30 Years of Federal Support to State and Local Criminal Justice* (Summary). Washington, DC: July 11, 1996.

Platt, T. (1971). *The Politics of Riot Commissions, 1917–1970*. New York, NY: Macmillan.

President's Commission on Law Enforcement and Administration of Justice (1967). *The Challenge of Crime in a Free Society*. Washington, DC: U.S. Government Printing Office.

Skolnick, J. H. (1969). *The Politics of Protest*. New York, NY: Simon and Schuster.

Tonry, M. (1991). "The Politics and Processes of Sentencing Commissions," *Crime and Delinquency*, 37:3, 307–329.

U.S. Department of Justice, National Institute of Justice (1994). *25 Years of Criminal Justice Research*. Washington, DC: U.S. Government Printing Office.

Walker, S. (1978). "Reexamining the President's Crime Commission," *Crime and Delinquency*, 24: 1–12.

Zalman, M. (1987). "Sentencing in a Free Society: The Failure of the President's Crime Commission to Influence Sentencing Policy," *Justice Quarterly*, 4:4, 546–569.

OFFICE OF JUSTICE PROGRAMS

ABOUT OJP*

Since 1984 the Office of Justice Programs has provided federal leadership in developing the nation's capacity to prevent and control crime, improve the criminal and juvenile justice systems, increase knowledge about crime and related issues, and assist crime victims. OJP's senior management team—comprised of the Assistant Attorney General (AAG), the Deputy Assistant Attorney General (DAAG), and the five bureau heads—works together with dedicated managers and line staff to carry out this mission.

The *Assistant Attorney General* is responsible for overall management and oversight of OJP. The AAG sets policy, ensures that OJP policies and programs reflect the priorities of the President, the Attorney General, and the Congress.

The AAG promotes coordination among the bureaus and offices within OJP. The bureaus are the *Bureau of Justice Assistance*, the *Bureau of Justice Statistics*, the *National Institute of Justice*, the *Office of Juvenile Justice and Delinquency Prevention*, and the *Office for Victims of Crime*.

OJP also includes the *Violence Against Women Office*, the *Executive Office for Weed and Seed*, the *Corrections Program Office*, the *Drug Courts Program Office*, the *Office for State and Local Domestic Preparedness Support*, the *Office of the Police Corps and Law Enforcement Education*. OJP's *American Indian and Alaska Native (AI/AN) Affairs Office*, coordinates AI/AN-related programmatic activity across the bureaus and program offices and serves as an information resource center for American Indian and Alaskan Native criminal justice interests.

Seven other offices within OJP provide agency-wide support. They are the *Office of Congressional and Public Affairs*, the *Office of Administration*, the *Equal Employment Opportunity Office*, the *Office for Civil Rights*, the *Office of Budget and Management Services*, the *Office of the Comptroller*, and the *Office of General Counsel*. Additionally, the *National Criminal Justice Reference Service* (NCJRS) provides information services in support of the bureaus and program offices.

Through the programs developed and funded by its bureaus and offices, OJP works to form partnerships among federal, state, and local government officials to control drug abuse and trafficking; reduce and prevent crime; rehabilitate neighborhoods; improve the administration of justice in America; meet the needs of crime victims; and address problems such as gang violence, prison crowding, juvenile crime, and white-collar crime. The func-

*Reprinted from the OJP web page.

tions of each bureau or program office are interrelated. For example, the statistics generated by the Bureau of Justice Statistics may drive the research that is conducted through the National Institute of Justice and the Office of Juvenile Justice and Delinquency Prevention. Research results, in turn generate new programs that receive support from the Bureau of Justice Assistance and the Office of Juvenile Justice and Delinquency Prevention. Although some research and technical assistance is provided directly by OJP's bureaus and offices, most of the work is accomplished through federal financial assistance to scholars, practitioners, experts, and state and local governments and agencies.

Many of the program bureaus and offices award formula grants to state agencies, which, in turn, subgrant funds to units of state and local government. Formula grant programs in such areas as drug control and system improvement, juvenile justice, victims compensation, and victims assistance, are administered by state agencies designated by each state's governor. Discretionary grant funds are announced in the Federal Register or through program solicitations that can also be found through bureau and OJP Websites. Grant applications are made directly to the sponsoring OJP bureau or program office.

Last updated 12/14/2000 12:38:26.
Office of Justice Programs, 810 Seventh Street, N.W.
Washington, DC 20531
Telephone: 202/307–0703
About the Office of Justice Programs <http://www.ojp.usdoj.gov/aboutinfo.htm>

OJP'S ORGANIZATION*

OJP is comprised of five bureaus, six program offices, and a number of administrative offices. The five OJP bureaus are:

- *The Bureau of Justice Assistance (BJA)* provides funding, training, and technical assistance to state and local governments to combat violent and drug-related crime and to help improve the criminal justice system. Its programs include the Edward Byrne Memorial State and Local Law Enforcement Assistance formula and discretionary grant programs and the Local Law Enforcement Block Grants (LLEBG) program. BJA also administers the Bulletproof Vest Partnership Program, the State Criminal Alien Assistance Program, and the State Identification Systems Formula Grant Program.

- *The Bureau of Justice Statistics (BJS)* collects and analyzes statistical data on crime, criminal offenders, crime victims, and the operations of justice systems at all levels of government. It also provides financial and technical support to state

*Reprinted from *OJP Fiscal Year 1999 Program Plan*, pp. 1–3.

statistical agencies and administers special programs that aid state and local governments in improving their criminal history records and information systems.

• *The National Institute of Justice (NIJ)* supports research and development programs, conducts demonstrations of innovative approaches to improve criminal
justice, develops new criminal justice technologies, and evaluates the effectiveness
of OJP-supported and other justice programs. NIJ also provides major support
for the National Criminal Justice Reference Service (NCJRS), a clearinghouse of
information on justice issues.

• *The Office of Juvenile Justice and Delinquency Prevention (OJJDP)* provides
grants and contracts to states to help them improve their juvenile justice systems
and sponsors innovative research, demonstration, evaluation, statistics, replica-
tion, technical assistance, and training programs to help improve the nation's
understanding of and response to juvenile violence and delinquency.

• *The Office for Victims of Crime (OVC)* administers victim compensation and
assistance grant programs created by the Victims of Crime Act of 1984 (VOCA).
OVC also provides funding, training, and technical assistance to victim service
organizations, criminal justice agencies, and other professionals to improve the
nation's response to crime victims. OVC's programs are funded through the
Crime Victims Fund, which is derived from fines and penalties collected from
federal criminal offenders, not taxpayers.

OJP's six program offices are:

• *The Violence Against Women Office (VAWO)* coordinates the Department of
Justice's legislative and other initiatives relating to violence against women and
administers grant programs to help prevent, detect, and stop violence against
women, including domestic violence, sexual assault, and stalking.

• *The Corrections Program Office (CPO)* provides financial and technical assistance to state and local governments to implement corrections-related programs,
including correctional facility construction and corrections-based drug treatment
programs.

• *The Drug Courts Program Office (DCPO)* supports the development, implementation, and improvement of drug courts through grants to local or state governments, courts, and tribal governments, as well as through technical assistance and
training.

• *The Executive Office for Weed and Seed (EOWS)* helps communities build
stronger, safer neighborhoods by implementing the Weed and Seed strategy, a
community-based, multi-disciplinary approach to combating crime. Weed and
Seed involves both law enforcement and community-building activities, including
economic development and support services.

• *The Office of State and Local Domestic Preparedness Support (OSLDPS)* is responsible for enhancing the capacity and capability of state and local jurisdictions
to prepare for and respond to incidents of domestic terrorism involving chemical
and biological agents, radiological and explosive devices, and other weapons of

mass destruction (WMD). It awards grants for equipment and provides training and technical assistance for state and local first responders.

- *The Office of the Police Corps and Law Enforcement Education (OPCLEE)*, which in November 1998 transferred to OJP from the Justice Department's Office of Community Oriented Policing Services (COPS), provides college educational assistance to students who commit to public service in law enforcement, and scholarships—with no service commitment—for dependents of law enforcement officers who died in the line of duty.

FORMULA VERSUS DISCRETIONARY GRANT PROGRAMS

OJP awards grants and contracts or enters into cooperative agreements to implement programs, provide technical assistance and training, conduct research and evaluations, and collect and analyze data. Grants are awarded in two forms: formula (or block grants) and discretionary grants. Formula grants are awarded to states or units of local government, which, in turn, decide how funds are distributed to state, local, and nonprofit organizations. Formulas vary among programs and consider such factors as population, juvenile population, crime rate, etc. Discretionary funds are awarded directly by OJP bureaus and offices to state and local agencies and private organizations. . . . The following briefly describes OJP's formula grant programs:

- *BJA's Edward Byrne Memorial State and Local Law Enforcement Assistance* formula grant program provides funds to assist states and units of local government in controlling and preventing drug abuse, crime, and violence, and in improving the functioning of the criminal justice system. Byrne funds are awarded for projects addressing 26 purpose areas, including law enforcement, adjudication, community crime prevention, and development of criminal justice information systems. Each chapter in this *Program Plan* notes the related Byrne purpose areas for which formula funds may be used.
- *The Local Law Enforcement Block Grants (LLEBG)* program, which is also administered by BJA, awards block grants to units of local government to reduce crime and enhance public safety. Grants must be used for one or more of certain purposes, including hiring law enforcement personnel, purchasing law enforcement equipment, enhancing school security, establishing or operating drug courts, adjudicating violent offenders, multijurisdictional task forces, and crime prevention programs.
- *BJA's State Identification Systems (SIS) Grants* program gives states resources to develop or improve their computerized identification systems and integrate those systems with the FBI's national identification databases. SIS grants can be used to: 1) create computerized identification systems that are compatible and integrated with databases of the FBI's National Crime Information Center; 2) improve forensic laboratories' ability to analyze DNA in ways that are compatible and integrated with the FBI's Combined DNA Identification System; or 3) develop

automated fingerprint systems that are compatible and integrated with the FBI's Integrated Automated Fingerprint Identification System.

- *OJJDP's Formula Grants Program, Title V Incentive Grants for Local Delin- quency Prevention Programs and Part E State Challenge Grants* programs sup- port state and local efforts to improve the juvenile justice system and prevent delinquency.
- *Another OJJDP program, the Juvenile Accountability Incentive Block Grant (JAIBG)*, supports state and local efforts to address juvenile crime by encouraging reforms that hold all offenders accountable for their crimes. Funds may be used for any of 11 purposes, including building juvenile detention facilities, hiring juvenile justice personnel, juvenile drug and gun courts, and accountability-based programs for juvenile offenders. Congress has specified minimum amounts for certain purposes.
- *The Residential Substance Abuse Treatment for State Prisoners (RSAT)* program, administered by CPO, funds programs that provide individual and group sub- stance abuse treatment activities for offenders in residential facilities operated by state and local correctional agencies.
- *The Violent Offender Incarceration/Truth in Sentencing* grant programs, also ad- ministered by CPO, help states build or expand correctional facilities for adult or juvenile offenders. The Violent Offender Incarceration grant program is ad- ministered on a three-tiered formula basis, while Truth in Sentencing awards are distributed as an incentive to states to enact sentencing reforms to ensure that violent offenders serve at least 85 percent of their sentences.
- *VAWO's STOP Violence Against Women formula grants program* supports im- provements in the abilities of law enforcement to respond to violence against women, development of more effective strategies and programs to prevent violent crimes against women, and improvements in data collection and tracking systems. By law, at least a quarter of STOP funds must be dedicated each to enhancing direct services for crime victims, for law enforcement, and for prosecution.
- *The VOCA Victim Compensation Formula Grants*, administered by OVC, are awarded to states and territories to alleviate the economic impact of crime on victims. Awards are based on 40 percent of state payouts during the previous federal fiscal year. In general, these grants reimburse victims of violent crimes and their service providers for medical, mental health, funeral, and other crime-related expenses, and provide for loss of support and lost wages.
- *The VOCA Victim Assistance Formula Grants*, also administered by OVC, are awarded to states and territories to support direct services to crime victims. Awards are prorated based on population. The majority of the funds are sub- granted to community-based programs, including rape crisis centers, battered women's shelters, children's advocacy centers, and victim service units within law enforcement agencies. A minimum of 10 percent of funds must be spent on each of four populations: domestic violence, sexual assault, child abuse, and under- served crime victims.

More detailed information about any of these programs, or a referral to the appropriate contact in the administering state office, is available by calling the Department of Justice Response Center at 1–800/421-6770 or by visiting the OJP Website at. *www.ojp.usdoj.gov.*

WHAT'S NEW AT OJP*

OJP's topically organized web site. Links to related publications, programs, trainings and conferences are pulled together to make them more accessible to the user. All the old favorites remain. We welcome your interest and comments. Specific topic comments should be directed to the *Topic Editors* at *ASKOJP@ojp.usdoj.gov.*

State Criminal Alien Assistance Program (SCAAP) Updates.

Promising Strategies to Reduce Substance Abuse (Text or PDF) (2000) is an assessment of effective strategies used in urban, suburban, and rural communities nationwide to reduce illicit drug and alcohol abuse and related crime. The report is intended to serve as a guide to communities by identifying the core elements of promising strategies and illustrating these strategies with examples of programs that are making a difference locally.

The *Global Justice Information Network* is now at OJP. The Global Initiative envisions safe communities through cooperative and collaborative efforts that will ensure that information is readily available to the justice community on a need to know basis.

Office of Justice Programs Fiscal Year 1999 Annual Report to Congress (September 2000).

Information About the Crime Identification Technology Act.

Fiscal Year 2000 Program Plan (April 2000).

Fiscal Year 2000 At-A-Glance (June 2000 edition).

Funding Opportunities lists all current grants or download copies.

Guidelines, Solicitations and Application Kits.

Archived Items.

Last updated 12/15/2000 12:37:10.

---

*Reprinted from the OJP web page.

THE U.S. GENERAL ACCOUNTING OFFICE

WHAT IS GAO?*

The U.S. General Accounting Office (GAO) is an agency that works for Congress and the American people. Congress asks GAO to study the programs and expenditures of the federal government. GAO, commonly called the investigative arm of Congress or the congressional watchdog, is independent and nonpartisan. It studies how the federal government spends taxpayer dollars. GAO advises Congress and the heads of executive agencies (such as Environmental Protection Agency, EPA, Department of Defense, DOD, and Health and Human Services, HHS) about ways to make government more effective and responsive. GAO evaluates federal programs, audits federal expenditures, and issues legal opinions. When GAO reports its findings to Congress, it recommends actions. Its work leads to laws and acts that improve government operations, and save billions of dollars. <http://www.gao.gov>

HOW IS GAO STRUCTURED?

. . . The agency is headed by the Comptroller General, who is appointed to a 15-year term. The long tenure of the Comptroller General gives GAO a continuity of leadership that is rare within government. GAO's independence is further safeguarded by the fact that its workforce is comprised almost exclusively of career employees who have been hired on the basis of skill and experience. Its 3,300 employees include experts in program evaluation, accounting, law, economics, and other fields.
4 06/28/2000

Address: GAO Headquarters
441 G St., NW
Washington, D.C. 20548
Telephone no.: (202) 512–3000 (employee locator)
Agency head: David M. Walker
Comptroller General of the United States
Appointed October 1998; term of office expires in October 2013.

*Reprinted from the U.S. General Accounting Office web page.

DRUG COURTS: OVERVIEW OF GROWTH, CHARACTERISTICS, AND RESULTS
EXECUTIVE SUMMARY

PURPOSE

Since the 1980s, the drug epidemic in the United States and the adoption of tougher drug policies by lawmakers and officials have contributed to an overload of drug cases on judicial dockets. In response to the deluge of drug cases and the cycle of criminal recidivism[7] common among drug offenders, some state and local jurisdictions began in the late 1980s creating drug courts. These are special judicial proceedings generally used for non-violent drug offenders that feature supervised treatment and periodic drug testing.

Title V of the Violent Crime Control and Law Enforcement Act of 1994 (P.L. 103-322) (hereafter referred to as the Violent Crime Act) specifically authorizes the award of federal grants for drug court programs that include court-supervised drug treatment.[8] The act requires that GAO assess the effectiveness and impact of these grants and report to Congress. In response to this requirement and on the basis of discussions with the Senate and House Judiciary Committees, GAO focused its work on determining: (1) the universe of and funding for drug court programs; (2) the approaches, characteristics, and completion and retention rates of existing programs; and (3) the extent to which program and participant data are maintained and used to manage and evaluate drug court programs.

GAO also focused on determining what conclusions can be drawn from existing published and available unpublished evaluations or assessments of drug court programs on the impact of such programs, particularly as they relate to the following specific issues raised in Title V of the 1994 Violent Crime Act and in GAO's discussions with Senate and House Judiciary Committees: (1) criminal profile of program participants compared to similar offenders processed through the traditional adjudication system, (2) completion rates of participants, (3) differences in characteristics between program graduates and dropouts, (4) sanctions imposed on persons who failed to complete drug court programs or comply with program require-

Reprinted from "The Executive Summary," taken from *Drug Courts: Overview of Growth, Characteristics, and Results* (GAO/GGD-97–106 July 1997). The report was prepared in response to the congressional mandate found in Title V of the Violent Crime Control and Law Enforcement Act of 1994. The act required that GAO assess the effectiveness and impact of the federal grants for drug court programs, established in the same act, and report the findings to Congress.

ments, (5) drug use and criminal recidivism rates of program and nonprogram participants, and (6) costs and benefits of drug court programs to the criminal justice system.

In 1995, GAO issued an initial report[9] on drug court programs, which provided preliminary information on programs operating at that time.

BACKGROUND

The main purpose of drug court programs is to use the authority of the court to reduce crime by changing defendants' drug-using behavior. Under this concept, in exchange for the possibility of dismissed charges or reduced sentences, defendants are diverted to drug court programs in various ways and at various stages of the judicial process depending on the circumstances. Judges preside over drug court proceedings; monitor the progress of defendants through frequent status hearings; and prescribe sanctions and rewards as appropriate in collaboration with prosecutors, defense attorneys, treatment providers, and others. Although there are basic elements common to many drug court programs, the programs vary in terms of approaches used, participant eligibility and program requirements, type of treatment provided, sanctions and rewards, and other practices.

With the assistance of the Drug Court Clearinghouse,[10] GAO identified existing drug court programs. GAO, among other things, then surveyed and obtained responses from 134 of the 140 drug court programs that were identified as operating as of December 31, 1996. GAO also did an evaluation synthesis of 20 studies[11] that included some relevant information on the impact of specific drug court programs and identified a variety of other documents that described program objectives and operations; provided judicial commentary on these programs; and, in some cases, provided a summary description of a number of programs.

RESULTS IN BRIEF

There has been a substantial increase in the number of drug court programs started in the United States and the availability of federal funding to support such programs. Between 1989 and 1994, 42 drug court programs were started.[12] Since 1994, the total number of operating drug court programs had grown to 161 as of March 31, 1997. The number of drug court programs in various developmental stages as of the same date indicates that the number of operating programs will likely continue to grow.

Over $125 million has been made available for the planning, implementation, enhancement, and/or evaluation studies of drug court programs from a variety of funding sources since 1989. Federal funding, which has increased substantially since 1993, has provided over $80 million of the total. Over 95 percent of the federal funding has been provided through federal grants administered by the Department of Justice and the Department of Health and Human Services. State and local governments, private donations, and fees collected from program participants have provided about $45 million.

The drug court programs GAO surveyed were very diverse in approach, characteristics, and completion and retention rates.[13] Some programs reported that they deferred prosecuting offenders who entered the program, some allowed offenders to enter the program after their case had been adjudicated, and others allowed offenders to enter their program on a trial basis after entering a plea. Although all of the programs GAO surveyed reported having a treatment component as a part of their overall program, results from a Drug Court Clearinghouse survey indicated that the type and extent of treatment provided to program participants varied among the programs. Populations targeted by these programs also varied among the drug court programs and included adults and juveniles, nonviolent and some violent offenders,[14] offenders with and without a substance addiction,[15] and first-time and repeat offenders. However, drug court programs most frequently reported that participants were typically adult, nonviolent offenders with a substance addiction. The drug court programs GAO surveyed reported that, since 1989, they had admitted over 65,000 offenders. The completion and retention rates for participants in these programs were reported to range, respectively, from about 8 to 95 percent and 31 to 100 percent.

With the exception of follow-up data on program participants after leaving the program, most drug court programs surveyed by GAO reported that they maintained various types of data on program participants as suggested by the Department of Justice in its guidance to jurisdictions applying for federal grants under (1) Title V of the Violent Crime Act; (2) the Health and Human Services' Center for Substance Abuse and Treatment in its drug court treatment guidelines; and (3) the National Association of Drug Court Professionals' Standards Committee, which develops standards and provides guidance to drug court programs, in its recently issued drug court program "Key Components" guide. In addition, collaborative efforts among drug court program stakeholders have been undertaken to study the feasibility of and suggest ways to overcome obstacles, including cost and legal issues, associated with a recognized need in the drug court community to collect and maintain follow-up and other data on drug court program participants, which some drug court programs and stakeholders have demonstrated to be feasible to collect.

GAO, for several reasons, could not draw any firm conclusions on the overall impact of drug court programs or on certain specific issues raised by Congress about the programs or their participants. For example, many of the evaluations available at the time of GAO's review (1) involved programs that were relatively new at the time of the evaluations and were diverse in nature; (2) had differences and limitations in their objectives, scopes, and methodologies, including (in 11 of the 20 studies) no assessment of program participants after they left the programs, and (in 14 of the 20 studies) no comparison of how participants and nonparticipant arrest rates compared after program completion; and (3) showed varied results regarding program impact and the specific issues raised about drug court programs and their participants.

Justice, in conjunction with various stakeholders in the drug court community, has initiated an impact evaluation, to be completed in 1999, of four of the oldest drug court programs. This evaluation is designed to address some of the factors associated with existing studies that prevented GAO from reaching firm conclusions. However, GAO notes that the outcomes of any future evaluations of drug court programs may be hindered by the lack of available follow-up data, which drug court programs are not currently required to collect. If issues raised by Congress and others about the efficacy of drug court programs are to be addressed, following up on participants and nonparticipants (i.e., eligible offenders who chose not to participate) for some period after they leave the program to find out whether they committed new crimes or relapsed into drug use would be important.

PRINCIPAL FINDINGS

The Number of Drug Court Programs and the Availability of Funding Have Increased.

Based on GAO's survey, 42 drug court programs were started between 1989 and 1994. Since then, 4 have closed and 123 more have started, bringing the total number of drug court programs operating to 161 as of March 31, 1997. Moreover, an additional 154 drug court programs were in various developmental stages as of the same date, indicating potential future growth in the number of operating courts. Drug court programs were operating in 38 states, the District of Columbia, and Puerto Rico and were being planned or studied in 8 of the remaining 12 states and Guam. About 40 percent of the drug court programs operating were in California and Florida.

Overall, information obtained directly from federal funding sources and 134 of the 140 drug court programs identified as operating as of December 31, 1996, showed that over $125 million in resources was obtained from federal, state, and local governments; private sources; and participant fees for planning, implementing, enhancing, and/or evaluating drug court programs.[16] Federal funding, which has increased substantially since 1993,[17] has provided over $80 million of the funding. From fiscal years 1990 through 1993, federal multipurpose funding sources provided about $6 million in federal grants to support drug court programs. Since then, about $75 million in additional federal funds have been awarded through March 31, 1997. These funds were obtained from existing multipurpose grants and three additional federal funding sources that made funds specifically available for planning, implementing, enhancing, and/or evaluating drug court programs.

Over 95 percent of the federal funding has been provided through federal grants administered by the Departments of Justice and Health and Human Services. Drug court programs reported that about $45 million was provided by state and local governments, private sources, and/or fees collected from program participants since 1989. However, in commenting on a draft of this report, some drug court program stakeholders expressed the opinion that this amount may understate the actual amount of funding provided by state and local governments and other sources because some of the respondents to GAO's survey may have failed to include the state/local jurisdictions' contributions towards the administrative cost of the program staff (judges, prosecutors, pretrial service staff, court clerks, program coordinators, etc.) and/or cost of program facilities (courthouse and other administrative facilities) that are often contributed by the local jurisdiction.

Approaches, Characteristics, and Completion and Retention Rates of Existing Drug Court Programs Are Diverse.

In response to GAO's survey, about 44 percent of the drug court programs operating as of December 31, 1996, reported deferring prosecution of drug offenders who agreed to enter a drug treatment program, and about 38 percent said that they allowed offenders to enter the program after being adjudicated. About 10 percent reported that they used both approaches, and the remaining 8 percent said they used some other approach.

All of the drug court programs operating as of December 31, 1996, that were surveyed by GAO reported having a treatment component, and 82 percent reported that participants generally started treatment within a week of entering the program. However, the type and extent of treatment provided to program participants varied among the drug court programs. For example, drug court programs responding to a Drug Court Clearinghouse survey reported using an array of treatment services, with the use of these services varying among programs. In addition, some programs reported that a weekly visit to the treatment provider was required; others a minimum of three visits; and in some more extensive programs, four to five visits per week were required.

The drug court programs responding to GAO's survey reported targeting various populations, including adults, women, juveniles, nonviolent and violent offenders, offenders with and without a substance addiction, first-time and repeat offenders, and probation violators. For example:

- About 16 percent reported that juveniles were eligible to participate in their drug court program.
- About 6 percent accepted offenders with a current conviction for a violent offense.
- About 16 percent accepted offenders with a prior conviction for a violent offense.
- About 17 percent accepted offenders without a substance addiction.
- About 78 percent accepted repeat offenders.
- About 63 percent accepted probation violators.

Drug court programs most frequently reported that program participants were adult, nonviolent offenders with a substance addiction.

GAO's analysis of responses to its survey further showed that as of December 31, 1996, 65,921 people had been admitted to drug court programs in the United States since 1989. About 31 percent (20,594) had completed programs, and about 24 percent (16,051) had failed to complete programs because they were terminated or they voluntarily withdrew or died while in the program. About 40 percent, or 26,465 offenders, were reported to be enrolled in drug court programs as of December 31, 1996.[18] The status of the remaining 4 percent, or about 2,800 people, was unknown.[19]

The completion rate for participants in 56 of the 62 drug court programs surveyed that were identified as operating as of December 31, 1996, for more than 18 months ranged from about 8 to 95 percent and averaged about 48 percent.[20] The retention rate for 131 of the 134 programs GAO surveyed ranged from about 31 to 100 percent and averaged about 71 percent.[21]

Except for Follow-Up Data, Most Drug Court Programs Reported Collecting and Using Suggested Management and Evaluation Data.

Guidelines issued by Justice in 1996 require recipients of federal funds from the Violent Crime Act to demonstrate the capability to ensure adequate program management through ongoing monitoring, tracking, and program evaluation. In this regard, the guidelines suggest that, among other things, the following information be collected for drug court participants and, to the extent possible, similarly situated nonparticipants:

- criminal justice history,
- history of substance abuse,
- level of use of controlled or addictive substances at the point of entry into the program,
- data on substance abuse relapse while in the program,
- data on rearrest and/or conviction for a crime while in the program,

- completion/noncompletion of drug court program,
- follow-up data on substance abuse relapse after completing the program, and
- follow-up data on rearrest and/or conviction for a crime after completing the program.

In commenting on a draft of this report, Justice pointed out that it does not have the statutory authority to mandate that states or local jurisdictions collect specific program data for drug court programs funded by its block grants.

In its 1996 and 1997 guidance, the Department of Health and Human Service's Center for Substance Abuse Treatment adopted similar suggestions for collecting and maintaining data on program participants. In its recently issued drug court program guide, the National Association of Drug Court Professionals' Drug Court Standards Committee also adopted similar suggestions, including suggesting that data be collected and maintained on relapse and criminal recidivism of program participants after they leave the program and comparative data on similarly situated nonparticipants. However, recipients of other federal funds administered by the Department of Justice, as well as those receiving funds administered by the State Justice Institute[22] are not subject to similar guidance.

Over 90 percent of the drug court programs operating as of December 31, 1996, reported maintaining most of the suggested data to enable them to manage and evaluate their programs. However, about 67 percent of the drug court programs reported not maintaining follow-up drug relapse data, and about 47 percent reported not maintaining suggested follow-up data on rearrest or conviction for a crime once participants leave the programs. GAO's survey results showed that no significant difference was associated with the source of funding (federal, state/local, private, etc.) received and the extent to which drug court programs collected and maintained suggested follow-up data. GAO notes that since its survey was conducted, additional evidence has become available to indicate that collaborative efforts among stakeholders in the drug court community have been undertaken to study the feasibility of and address obstacles, including cost and legal issues, associated with a recognized need in the drug court community to collect and maintain follow-up and other data on drug court program participants.

A significant number of drug court programs and some drug court community stakeholders have demonstrated that it would be feasible to collect and maintain follow-up data on criminal recidivism of program participants, and others have demonstrated that it would be somewhat feasible to collect and maintain follow-up data on drug use relapse. For example, in March 1997, the Department of Justice through a cooperative agreement with the Justice Management Institute sponsored a meeting involving var-

ious drug court stakeholders that focused on, among other things, the need
for and ways to overcome obstacles associated with obtaining follow-up
data on program participants to adequately monitor and evaluate the impact of drug court programs.

Existing Evaluations Provide Some Limited Information but Do Not Permit Firm Conclusions Regarding Drug Court Impact.

The 20 evaluation studies that GAO reviewed and synthesized did not
permit GAO to reach definitive conclusions concerning the overall impact
of drug courts or the other specific issues mentioned earlier that have been
raised by Congress and in GAO's discussions with the Senate and House
Judiciary Committees about drug court programs and the offenders who
participate in them. For example, many of the available studies involved
program approaches and characteristics that were diverse in nature, including, among other things, differences in eligible participants, differences
in completion requirements, and differences in the type and extent of treatment provided. Also, various differences and limitations were associated
with the objectives, scopes, and methodologies of these studies. Among
other things, most of the studies evaluated drug court programs that were
still in their first or second year of operation, with many of the program
participants being evaluated still active in the programs. Most of the available studies involved very short follow-up periods. Eleven of the 20 studies
did not include an assessment of postprogram criminal recidivism among
program participants, and none of the studies included an assessment of
postprogram drug use relapse. Also, most of the available studies (in 14 of
the 20 studies) involved no comparison between participants and nonparticipant arrest rates after program completion.

Although GAO cannot draw any firm conclusions on the overall impact
of drug court programs or on specific issues that have been raised, GAO
does provide some limited information in chapter 5 on these issues [see
original GAO report] to the extent they are addressed in the 20 available
studies it reviewed and synthesized.

In April 1997, Justice issued a solicitation for an impact evaluation of
four of the oldest drug court programs, which included an assessment of
program participants after they leave the program. Also, during a March
1997 meeting involving Justice and various drug court program stakeholders, attention was given to the need for maintaining follow-up information
on program participants and using it in any future impact evaluations.
Justice expects these efforts to address some of the factors associated with
existing studies that prevented GAO from drawing firm conclusions.

RECOMMENDATIONS

Congress and others have raised reasonable questions about whether drug court programs are effective. However, these questions have not been answered definitively by the programs themselves or studies done to date, in large part because critical data about program participants after they leave the program or similarly situated non-participants have not been available. Accordingly, to help ensure more effective management and evaluation of drug court programs, GAO recommends that the Attorney General and the Secretary of Health and Human Services

- require drug court programs funded by discretionary grants administered by Justice and Health and Human Services to collect and maintain follow-up data on program participants' criminal recidivism and, to the extent feasible, follow-up data on drug use relapse.
- require drug court programs funded by formula or block grants administered by Justice and Health and Human Services, to the extent permitted by law, to collect and maintain follow-up data on program participants' criminal recidivism and, to the extent feasible, follow-up data on drug use relapse. Where no statutory authority exists to impose such requirements, GAO recommends that Justice and Health and Human Services include in their respective grant guidelines language to suggest that drug court programs funded by these sources similarly collect and maintain such data.

To better ensure that conclusions about the impact of drug court programs on participants' criminal recidivism and/or drug use relapse can be drawn, GAO recommends that the Attorney General, the Secretary of Health and Human Services, and the Executive Director of the State Justice Institute require that the scope of future impact evaluations of drug court programs funded by their respective agencies include an assessment of program participants' postprogram criminal recidivism and drug use relapse and, whenever feasible, compare drug court participants with similar non-participants.

AGENCY COMMENTS AND GAO'S EVALUATION

The Departments of Justice and Health and Human Services, the State Justice Institute, the National Association of Drug Court Professionals, and the Drug Court Clearinghouse provided written comments on a draft of this report. These comments are discussed at the end of chapters 1, 2, and 5 [see original GAO report]. These organizations generally agreed with GAO's findings relating to the growth, characteristics, and results of drug court programs and the conclusions and recommendations relating to the collection and maintenance of follow-up data on program participants and impact evaluations of these programs. However, Justice raised a legal concern about its ability to impose mandatory requirements on congressionally authorized entitlement grants—formula or block grant programs. The State Justice Institute raised concern about its ability to impose data collection requirements on programs for which it only provides short-term funding. Also, Justice and the National Association of Drug Court Professionals indicated that one of the difficulties associated with GAO's recommendation that evaluations of drug court programs include follow-up data and comparison groups is the lack of ongoing technical assistance and sufficient resources available to drug court programs to enable them to develop the capacity for data collection and program evaluation. While Justice reiterated that it has taken a number of steps to develop the capacity for data collection and evaluation among its drug court grantees, Justice notes that it will work with Congress to increase its funding for technical assistance.

GAO revised its recommendations to recognize statutory limitations that may be associated with formula and block grant programs administered by Justice and the Department of Health and Human Services. GAO did not, however, systematically review and therefore cannot comment on the sufficiency and adequacy of technical assistance and related resources that are currently being provided to drug court programs.

The National Association of Drug Court Professionals and the Drug Court Clearinghouse commented that while it may be too early to reach firm conclusions on the impact of drug court programs, the retention and completion rates from GAO's survey results and the differences in recidivism rates revealed in the evaluation studies reviewed by GAO permit a more positive conclusion about drug court programs than GAO arrives at in its report. GAO continues to believe it is essential to emphasize that there are shortcomings associated with many of the evaluations of drug court programs that have been done, and thus there are good reasons for withholding final judgment until more and better data are collected and additional studies are completed.

The Department of Health and Human Services expressed concerns with the lack of a thorough assessment of the adequacy of treatment being provided to drug court program participants in the scope of GAO's study. While GAO recognizes the Department's view that it would be helpful to have a detailed assessment of the quality and adequacy of the treatment component of the drug court program, such an effort would have gone well beyond the objectives and scope of this overview assessment of drug court programs.

NOTES

1. BJA's status was placed directly under OJP at the end of the Clinton administration. Plans for reorganization of BJA and OJP await the new presidential administration.

2. Office of Justice Programs, *Fiscal Year 1999 Program Plan* (Washington, DC: U.S. Department of Justice, Office of Justice Programs), p. 3.

3. Larry Sherman et al., *Preventing Crime: What Works, What Doesn't, What's Promising* (Washington, DC: National Institute of Justice, Office of Justice Programs, July 1998).

4. *Drug Courts: Overview of Growth, Characteristics, and Results* (GAO/GGD-97–106) (Washington, DC: U.S. General Accounting Office, 1997).

5. Ibid.

6. See National Commission on Law Observance and Enforcement, *Reports* (Washington, DC: U.S. Government Printing Office, 1931).

7. GAO uses the term recidivism to refer generally to the act of committing new criminal offenses after having been arrested and/or convicted of a crime.

8. Under this act, the attorney general in administering the federal drug court grant program is required to consult with the secretary of Health and Human Services, who is responsible for providing grants to public and private entities that provide substance abuse treatment for individuals under criminal justice supervision.

9. *Drug Courts: Information on a New Approach to Address Drug-Related Crime*, GAO/GGD-95-159BR, May 22, 1995.

10. The Drug Court Clearinghouse and Technical Assistance Project at the American University, which is funded by the Department of Justice's Drug Court Program Office, among other things, compiles, publishes, and disseminates information and materials on drug courts and provides technical assistance to jurisdictions involved with planning and implementing drug court programs.

11. GAO's literary search and data collection efforts identified over eighty documents available as of March 31, 1997, that were either published or unpublished evaluation studies; described program objectives and operations; provided judicial commentary; and, in some cases, provided a summary description of a number of programs. Only twenty of these documents met the criteria for inclusion in GAO's evaluation synthesis, including providing some information on the impact and/or effectiveness of drug court programs.

12. This number, which is based on GAO's independent survey and other sources, differs from the thirty-six drug court programs cited in GAO's prior report (GGD-95-159BR) as started between 1989 and 1994, which was based on information obtained from the Drug Court Clearinghouse at the time.

13. "Completion rates" and "retention rates" are indicators commonly used in the drug court community to measure the impact of drug court programs. Completion rates refer to individuals who completed or were favorably discharged from a drug court program as a percentage of the total number admitted and not still enrolled. This measure is an indicator of the extent to which offenders successfully complete their drug court program requirements. Retention rates refer to individuals who are currently active participants in or have completed or were favorably

discharged from a drug court program as a percentage of the total number admitted. This measure is an indicator of the extent to which a program has been successful at retaining program participants in the program at the time of GAO's survey. Although interrelated, both measures are helpful in assessing program performance. A program that had been operating consistently over a longer period would be expected to have similar completion and retention rates.

14. Survey responses were based on individual jurisdictions' definitions of a "violent offender," which may or may not differ from the federal definition as defined under the Violent Crime Act to mean a person who: (1) is charged with or convicted of an offense, during the course of which offense or conduct (a) the person carried, possessed, or used a firearm or dangerous weapon; (b) there occurred the death of or serious bodily injury to any person; or (c) there occurred the use of force against the person of another, without regard to whether any of the circumstances described in the aforementioned subparagraphs is an element of the offense or conduct of which or for which the person is charged or convicted; or (2) has one or more prior convictions for a felony crime of violence involving the use or attempted use of force against a person with the intent to cause death or serious bodily harm.

15. According to the Department of Health and Human Services officials and other drug court program stakeholders, persons admitted without substance addictions are likely to include persons with substance abuse problems who were not identified as being addicted during their initial screening. In addition, some drug court programs target special populations. For example, the Jackson County, Missouri, drug court program, in addition to targeting others, targets prostitutes because of the likelihood that their drug abuse is the reason for their criminal behavior. Another program in Las Vegas, Nevada, targets parents or guardians of juveniles who have been identified as having a substance addiction.

16. The total amount of funding supporting drug court programs is likely understated because (1) some drug court programs were not able to determine the precise amount of funding they received from federal, state, and local governments; private funding sources; and/or participant fees and (2) certain multipurpose federal funding sources, which did not specifically target drug court programs, had not been tracking the funding of drug court programs. In addition, information on the total amount of various federal block grant funding awarded to jurisdictions and used to support drug court programs, as well as Medicaid funding that may have been used by drug court participants to pay for the cost of treatment, was not available from either the funding sources or recipients.

17. Although GAO did not analyze the extent of increases in state and local funding, it has likely increased during this same time period due to the requirements for matching funds associated with most federal grants.

18. Of the 26,465 enrollees, about 25 percent, or 6,564, did not regularly attend programs or were wanted on bench warrants for failure to appear as of December 31, 1996. However, the median for the 128 drug court programs that were able to account for the status of enrolled program participants was 5 inactive participants, and 1 drug court program accounted for about 1,200 of the 6,564 inactive enrollees.

19. Percentages do not add to 100 percent due to rounding.

20. Completion rates were not applicable for three of the programs because they had retained 100 percent of the program participants admitted at the time of GAO's

survey. For the remaining three programs, GAO was unable to calculate a completion rate because complete information on the status of certain program participants could not be provided by the drug court programs surveyed.

21. GAO was unable to calculate retention rates for three programs, because complete information on the status of certain program participants could not be provided by the drug court programs surveyed.

22. The State Justice Institute is a nonprofit organization created by federal law and funded through congressional appropriations. Among other things, the State Justice Institute has provided grants for evaluation studies of drug court programs.

Chapter 6

The Bureaucracy: Implementation and Street-Level Criminal Justice Policy Making

INTRODUCTION

Policy, in general, and criminal justice policy, in particular, is implemented through bureaucracy. Policies established by federal, state, and local governments are carried out within communities. Each level of government or agencies, through which the policy or program passes to the client or recipient of services, affects, through its interpretation, for example, regulations, guidance, or guidelines, the clients' and the communities' perceptions of that policy or program. Ultimately, the policy or program is carried out at the community level and is affected by the political environment—political cultures and structures—within those communities. Finally, the decisions made by the individuals at the lowest levels of those bureaucracies—the bureaucrats who come in direct contact with those for whom or against whom the policies are implemented—affect what, in fact, policy is. These lowest level policymakers are referred to in the public administration literature as "street-level bureaucrats."

Criminal justice policy is implemented through a number of bureaucracies—police, judicial, probation, parole, and correctional agencies. The criminal justice "street-level bureaucrat," as he or she implements criminal justice policy, affects what the public perceives to be criminal justice policy. For example, public perceptions of traffic law enforcement are affected by how police enforce these laws.

To analyze how criminal justice street-level bureaucrats can influence criminal justice policy, it is necessary to understand the context in which

these bureaucrats carry out policy. The policies and programs that the police or corrections bureaucrat implements usually has been interpreted by
the various levels of government, for example, federal bureaucracies from
Washington, D.C., through the state and municipality structures, before
the street-level bureaucrat receives his/her charge. The implementation process is further influenced by the political culture and political structures of
the community and criminal justice bureaucracies in which these bureaucrats carry out their jobs. Seemingly, however, one of the most important
factors affecting policy implementation and how the public perceives that
policy or program are certain job conditions common to street-level bureaucrats that affect how the bureaucrat carries out his/her job.[1] Such conditions include inadequate resources, the threat and challenge to authority,
and contradictory or ambiguous job expectations. These factors also affect
the bureaucrat's vulnerability to corruption.

Using police as the example of the criminal justice street-level bureaucrat,
this chapter discusses the criminal justice policy implementation process.
Specifically, the articles included examine how community values through
political culture set parameters for street-level policy making, how street-
level bureaucrats affect policy, and how these factors may influence corruption as well as effective responses to corruption.

POLICY IMPLEMENTATION AND POLITICAL CULTURE

The street-level bureaucrat does not function in a vacuum. He or she is
part of a community and carries out his/her job within the context of the
values of that community. To what extent the community determines, for
example, police policy, and to what extent the police, themselves, determine
policy is a subject for analysis.

In *Varieties of Police Behavior*, James Q. Wilson examines how the political culture of four cities affected police style.[2] He identifies three police
styles—watchman, service, and legalistic. Three different types of political
systems—caretaker, service, and legalistic coincide, respectively, with each
police style. Each political style has a different structure, as well as emphasizing different values, which affect what and how police enforce the law.
For example, a caretaker political system, which is characterized by party
loyalty, ethnic identification, personal ties, low tax rates, and partisanship,
can be expected to be tolerant of gambling and vice, and supports a watchman (more personalized) style of policing. He furthers states, however, that
while community decisions do not explicitly determine the prevailing police
style, police in all cases are keenly sensitive (they are alert to and concerned
about) their political environment without in all cases being governed by
it. The community can determine police policy within broad limits when
they observe some condition, for example, widespread gambling, for which
the police can be held responsible. That is, political authorities can decide

how vigorously to crack down on these activities. As individual members of a bureaucracy, police are alert to particular concerns, including, what is said about them publicly; who is in authority over them; how their material and career interests are satisfied; and how complaints about them are handled. With regard to handling petty offenses, treating juveniles, and traffic violations, Wilson asserts that these are, with very few exceptions determined by the police themselves.

With respect to police work, especially patrol work, Wilson asserts that political culture creates a "zone of indifference," an area of community tolerance for discretion, within which police are free to act as they see fit. The narrowness of this area varies from community to community, but is greatest when people are deeply divided over law enforcement issues. Although the most important way in which political culture affects police behavior is through the choice of the police chief, the zone of indifference filters demands to which the chief has to respond and can pass on.

POLICY IMPLEMENTATION AND STREET-LEVEL BUREAUCRATS AS CRIMINAL JUSTICE POLICYMAKERS

Street-level bureaucrats, whether social workers delivering welfare benefits or the police officers implementing criminal laws, affect service delivery and as such the public's view of policy due to the discretion they can exercise in carrying out their jobs. Michael Lipsky has discussed the influence of street bureaucrats in a number of publications.[3] He asserts that the clients of the street-level bureaucrat are nonvoluntary and, generally, not the primary reference group of the bureaucrat.[4] For example, while offenders and suspects are the nonvoluntary clients of the police officer, other officers, police administrators, and law-abiding citizens if not the primary are critical reference groups for the officer.

The typical working environment of street-level bureaucrats is characterized by (1) limited resources that necessitate quick decisions based on inadequate information, (2) a lack of control over physical and psychological threats, and (3) contradictory or ambiguous job expectations.[5] Confronted by these conditions, Lipsky asserts that street-level bureaucrats, generally, address these job problems using several techniques. For example, they develop "simplifications" to facilitate making quick decisions. To reduce stress, they develop defense mechanisms, for example, segmenting themselves from the population they associate with their clientele.[6]

The concept of the "street-level bureaucrat" helps to explain the means by which criminal justice bureaucrats, who come in direct contact with citizens, affect policy. The behaviors of street-level bureaucrats may be better understood when interpreted in the context of job pressures. For example, stereotyping is one means of simplifying decisions. At the same time, understanding the impetus for behavior does not eliminate the responsibility of scrutinizing or even criticizing that behavior. Establishing and implementing profiles of potential lawbreakers, while simplifying law enforcement, is generally viewed as unacceptable. Rather than simply criticizing law enforcement for such behavior, the astute criminal justice policy analyst may instead suggest appropriate responses to the underlying problem that led to the use of profiling—a level of law enforcement resources that is not commensurate with the need for services.

POTENTIAL EFFECTS OF STREET-LEVEL CRIMINAL JUSTICE POLICY MAKING: CORRUPTION AND REFORM

Recent commissions on police corruption have addressed the problem in Chicago and New York City. In New York, the Commission to Investigate Allegations of Police Corruption and the Anti-Corruption Procedures of the Police Department (known as and referred to as the Mollen Commission) identifies police culture, that is, the attitudes and values that shape officers' behavior, as a critical component of police corruption today.[7] It highlights the devastating effects that the code of silence has on honest police officers. It asserts that although the principal victims of police corruption are honest officers, reporting corruption is still viewed by officers as an offense more heinous and dangerous than corruption itself. The Mollen Commission provides insight into the stresses and strains experienced by police as street-level bureaucrats and the coping mechanism they have developed to address these strains, some of which foster corruption. Noting that police corruption has been a consistent and pervasive problem in law enforcement, the Chicago Commission on Police Integrity observed that the nature of corrupt activity has changed dramatically over the years. . . . "Today's police corruption is most likely to involve drugs, organized crime, and relatively sophisticated but small groups of officers engaged in felonious criminal activities."[8]

Corruption most dramatically demonstrates the effect of the street-level bureaucrat's job environment on the interpretation of policies. Both commissions note that most police officers are honest, but, as the Mollen Commission notes, corruption threatens the honest officer. These observations further illustrate how inattention to the policy-making role of street-level bureaucrats can have a negative impact on the public's perception of policy, if that inattention fosters attitudes and values that support corruption. Moreover, these observations underscore the need to study the policy-making role of all criminal justice system street-level bureaucrats in order to understand the public perceptions of criminal justice policies.

Both the Mollen and Chicago Commissions offered recommendations to address corruption. The Mollen Commission's report asserts that the New York City Police Department "must create a culture that demands integrity and works to insure it, establishing an atmosphere in which dishonest cops fear the honest ones, and not the other way around" . . . The Chicago

Commission's report offers a range of recommendations, including changes in hiring standards, additional education, and management improvements.

INCLUDED SELECTIONS

The first selection in this chapter is taken from Wilson's *Varieties of Police Behavior*.[9] It discusses variations in police styles and political culture as influences on police policy making. The second selection by Michael Lipsky describes the street-level bureaucrat as policy maker.[10] Written in the late 1960s and early 1970s, respectively, these articles introduce the reader to concepts—"political culture" and "street-level bureaucrat"—that are essential to the understanding of criminal justice policy making and criminal justice policy. The final two selections from the Mollen and Chicago Commission reports examine the problem of police corruption and the steps that may be taken to address the problem.[11]

FOR DISCUSSION

In this chapter, the reader should consider:

1. The relationship between the political environment of a community and its police style.
2. The job conditions that affect how street-level bureaucrats, for example, police, carry out their jobs.
3. The steps that street-level bureaucrats take to address unfavorable job conditions and how these steps affect the implementation of policy.
4. The relationship between street-level bureaucrats making policy and the occurrence of corruption.
5. Given the role of street-level bureaucrats in policy making, the steps, such as those recommended by the various commissions, that might be taken to reduce opportunities for corruption.

RECOMMENDED READINGS AND OTHER SOURCES

Specific References

City of New York, The Commission to Investigate Allegations of Police Corruption and the Anti-Corruption Procedures of the Police Department, *The Report*. New York, July 7, 1994.

Lipsky, Michael. *Street-Level Bureaucracy: Dilemmas of the Individual in Public Services*. New York: Russell Sage Foundation, 1980.

The Report of the Commission on Police Integrity. Chicago, Illinois, November 1997.

Wilson, James Q. *Varieties of Police Behavior*. Cambridge, MA: Harvard University Press, 1968.

VARIETIES OF POLICE BEHAVIOR
(EXCERPT)

James Q. Wilson

To change a police style one must first understand the extent to which that style is subject to the decision-making processes of the community. Differences among police departments that are the result of explicit community choices can presumably be altered by making different choices. Because police practices have a considerable effect on the lives of many citizens and because, in addition, crime—especially "crime in the streets"—is an issue of great importance in many cities, one might suppose that politics (taken broadly as the conflict over the goals and personnel of government) would determine the prevailing police style much as it determines whether an urban renewal project will be undertaken, the water supply fluoridated, or taxes increased.

In fact, deliberate community choices rarely have more than a limited effect on police behavior, though they may often have a great effect on police personnel, budgets, pay levels, and organization. How the police, especially the patrolmen, handle the routine situations that bring them most frequently into contact with the public can be determined by explicit political decisions only to the extent that such behavior can be determined by the explicit decisions of the police administrator, and the administrator's ability to control the discretion of his subordinates is in many cases quite limited by the nature of the situation and the legal constraints that govern police behavior. The maintenance of order, unless it involves the control of large disorders (a riot, for example), is very hard to bring under administrative control and thus very hard to bring under political control—at least insofar as politics operates through the making of conscious decisions by formal institutions (mayors, city councils, and the like). And some law enforcement situations, especially those in which the police response is citizen-invoked, offer few opportunities to the administrator—and thus to his political superiors—for changing the nature or the outcome of police action.

Even in areas of police-initiated law enforcement, where the administrator does have the ability to make policy, that policy is often his and not the community's. He can determine how many traffic tickets will be issued and he can strongly influence, if he chooses, how many drunk arrests will be made, but in no city studied for this book were those decisions by the chief made at the direction of the governing bodies of the community. The reason for a city's failure to exercise influence potentially at its disposal is that in most cases, and certainly in all cases reported in this study, such matters are not of general interest to the citizenry or to public officials. In these matters, citizen interest, and thus political interest, tends to be highly particularistic—it produces specific complaints regarding whether *my* ticket was fairly issued, whether there is a teenager racing his car in front of *my* house, whether *I* have been annoyed by a drunk on the sidewalk. The political institutions of the city may or may not amplify or pass on such complaints, but if they do it is in the form of issuing specific directives or asking specific questions of the chief; to such inquiries or orders, specific responses will be made, but such responses only rarely take the form of a change in over-all police strategy.

The community can determine police policy, within broad limits when the public can observe some general condition for which the police can be held responsible (whether fairly or unfairly is another matter). The existence of widespread gambling or organized prostitution is visible and the political authorities can decide how vigorously the police should crack down on these activities. Just such a decision was made in Oakland by the city manager when he ordered his new police chief to put an end to illegal businesses and, insofar as it was in his power, that is exactly what he did. The mayor of Syracuse expected similar action from his new police chief, and he got it. The officials in Albany and Newburgh, on the other hand, have been less interested in these problems, and the police have acted accordingly.

Other than vice, only two issues of general significance typically become matters of community discussion, but in neither is the discussion conclusive or the police response proportional to the intensity of the emotions aroused. The first is the issue of "crime in the streets"; the second, police handling of citizen complaints.

It is one thing to decide that something should be done about crime in the streets and quite another thing to decide exactly what it is that should be done. The politicians may ask the chief, or he may propose to them, that the police intensify their surveillance over public places in order to deter, or apprehend, persons who are about to commit, or have committed, street assaults, muggings, purse snatches, and the like. But most cities where such problems exist are also cities that are more and more deeply divided on the proper police response to these problems. What in Oakland is a sound police strategy to many whites and most police officers is "harassment" to a substantial part of the Negro community. Furthermore, because the law enforcement benefits of aggressive preventive patrol are rarely, measured with any care and because there is almost no way even in principle to measure the costs in terms of good community relations, this police policy—and the political mandate that may underlie it—tends to become as much an ideological as a practical issue. The police quickly sense that their behavior in this area is being judged by conflicting standards and expectations and that one set of expectations (those opposed to "harass-ment") is being urged by persons who seek to "meddle" in the department or to "play politics"; thus the police often are led to insist that such deci-sions be made by the police themselves and not by the community.

Unlike a discussion of crime in the streets, controversy over police han-dling of grievances is at least over concrete alternatives, such as whether to create a civilian review board or an "ombudsman." In varying ways such an issue has arisen in Albany, Nassau [County], Newburgh, Oakland, and Syracuse; in Oakland it has been a major community controversy. But though the issue is passionately debated, it is not clear that, however it is resolved, it will have much effect on the *substantive* police policies that are in effect—partly because some are not "policies" at all but styles created by general organizational arrangements and departmental attitudes and partly because grievance procedures deal with specific complaints about unique circumstances, not with general practices of the officers.

If an issue of substantive significance *is* raised, it is often raised by a member of the law enforcement system—a judge, prosecutor, probation officer, or a group of police officers. The controversy in Nassau County over how the vice squad should be organized and led was an issue between the (Republican) district attorney on the one hand and the (Democratic) county executive and his subordinate, the police commissioner, on the other. The controversy in Brighton and Highland Park over how many traffic tickets should be issued was in each case precipitated, not by the public, but by the patrolmen some of whom, of course, tried to involve politicians on their side. Complaints about whether judges are "too soft" on suspects or police "too zealous" in making arrests, though they rarely become full-scale public issues, are usually exchanged among members of the criminal justice system. And because the system lacks any central au-thority or decision-making process that supervises its component parts or that can set general policy for it, such complaints usually sputter out with no effect to confirm in the eyes of all parties that the other fellow doesn't know what he is talking about.

In sum, the prevailing police style is not explicitly determined by com-munity decisions, though a few of its elements may be shaped by these decisions. Put another way, the police are in all cases keenly sensitive to their political environment without in all cases being governed by it. By *sensitive* is meant that they are alert to, and concerned about, what is said about them publicly, who is in authority over them, how their material and career interests are satisfied, and how complaints about them are handled. In short, they are alert to their particular concerns as individual members of a bureaucracy. To be *governed* means that the policies, operating procedures, and objectives of the organization are determined deliberately and systematically by someone with authority to make these decisions. The policies described in this study—handling petty offenses and traffic violations, treating juveniles—are, with very few exceptions, determined by the police themselves without any deliberate or systematic intervention by political authorities. (These policies may be affected in *unintended* ways by various political actions, but that is another matter.)

Such intervention as occurs usually concerns the selection of a new chief or the career interests of the individual officers (wages, working conditions, promotions, charges of misconduct, and the like). Even the conflict over the racial issues—obviously a matter of growing importance—is typically conflict over police behavior in the *particular* case and is framed in terms of whether an *individual* officer has or has not exceeded his authority and, if so, what procedures should be followed to punish him. The more general question—how the police allocate their resources, which laws they choose to enforce vigorously and which they choose to slight, whether they employ warnings or arrest in cases where they have discretion—are rarely raised, even in racial issues. Thus, the police officer sees the struggle over police-minority relations primarily as political efforts to challenge the authority of individual police officers and constrain them by threatening their career interests—their salaries, promotion prospects, self-respect, and morale. He sees challenges by Negroes as no different from the challenges of politicians or any other outside group, all of which are equally resented even when they cannot be resisted.

In other words, the police view most issues—whether they arise from a city manager's efforts to "reform" a department, an alderman's efforts to name a new deputy chief, or a Negro organization's efforts to establish a civilian review board—as a struggle for control of the department by "outside" forces. Of course, the issues are in principle quite different in each case, but because they affect the individual officer in essentially the same way, by making him less certain of his position and prospects, these differences are not taken seriously. This is not to say that if public authorities made systematic and deliberate efforts to set law enforcement policies the way the Joint Chiefs of Staff and the Secretary of Defense presumably set military policy, the rank-and-file police officer would be content and compliant. Far from it; any organization resists change, and the police role, with its vulnerability to legal sanctions, its (perceived) low social esteem, and its absence of professional reference groups, produces a sufficient sense of insecurity to be especially resistant to change. But when public control over the police is exercised *primarily* in terms of complaints, grievances, struggles over salary and retirement benefits, and legal sanctions, then the normal resistance to change is greatly increased.

In general, then, understanding the political life of a community will not provide a sufficient explanation of the police policies in effect. They are

left, in many areas, to the police themselves. There was no political involvement in the Syracuse police decision to intensify traffic and parking arrests
or in the Oakland decision to arrest drunks in large numbers. There was
public pressure to "do something" about juveniles in Nassau, but the means
were left to the police, and . . . the Nassau police response was the opposite
of that in neighboring Suffolk (the former created a bureau to emphasize
prevention and counselling, the latter created one to increase arrests). The
Highland Park chief in the mid-1950's introduced the legalistic police style
without any particular directives from the city manager and when a new
city manager privately decided that the chief should ease up a bit, he took
no special steps to obtain a change in policy: Certain party leaders in Brighton tried to get the chief to abandon his traffic ticket "norm" (not so much
because of public concern as police concern), but although the ticketing
rate dropped for a while, it soon returned to its former level.

Organizational changes in all these departments (for example, hiring
more men, buying major new pieces of equipment, and reorganizing important units) involve consultation with mayors and city managers; such
changes have important legal and budgetary implications, and public approval is often mandatory and always prudent. And in almost all cases,
public officials transmit to the police specific complaints and demands.

But if the police are not, in the routine case, governed by the community,
neither are they immune to community interests and expectations. As a
source of pay and promotions, the city government naturally interests all
police officers a great deal and in most cities they are well organized to
express those interests. But in addition the community is a source of cues
and signals—some tacit, some explicit—about how various police situations should be handled, what level of public order is deemed appropriate,
and what distinctions among persons ought to be made. Finally, the police
are keenly aware of the extent to which the city government does or does
not intervene in the department on behalf of particular interests.

Thus, police work is carried out under the influence of a *political culture*
though not necessarily under day-to-day political direction. By political culture is meant those widely shared expectations as to how issues will be
raised, governmental objectives determined, and power for their attainment
assembled; it is an understanding of what makes a government legitimate.
Since community attitudes were not surveyed for this study, the political
culture can only be inferred from the general behavior of political institutions. Nor does the word "culture" imply that everyone in the community
supports and approves of the way things get done; it only suggests that
most people would expect, for better or worse, things to be done that way.
With respect to police work—or at least its patrol functions—the prevailing
political culture creates a "zone of indifference"[12] within which the police
are free to act, as they see fit.[13]

The most important way in which political culture affects police behavior is through the choice of police administrator and the molding of the expectations that govern his role. Just as the most important decision a school board makes is its choice of superintendent, so the most important police decision a city council makes (or approves) is the selection of chief. In some communities, it is expected that he will be the "best man available"; in others it is that he will be the "deserving local fellow" or the man "closest to the party." And once in office, the chief will confront a zone of community indifference to his policies of varying dimensions. In Albany, where political power is concentrated at the top in party hands, that zone may be very narrow for any matter that affects the party or its favored supporters but quite broad otherwise. Where the political system tends toward the nonpartisan, professionally administered, good-government ideal, the zone may be narrow only with respect to actions that could be construed as corrupt or self-serving but quite broad with respect to everything else (except, perhaps, for certain critical events). And the political culture acts as a filter, different for each community, that screens out certain complaints and demands, leaving the chief free to ignore them, and passes through (or even amplifies) others.

The character of the chief can have a great effect within the limits set by his ability to control his subordinates . . . and the zone of indifference of the community. The outsiders who came to Syracuse and Highland Park are the most striking examples, though there are others as well. The men who became chief in Oakland in the 1950's and chief in Nassau in the 1940's were both insiders, but both made sweeping departmental changes. In Highland Park and Oakland, police changes accompanied broader political changes (the arrival of a professional city manager)—that is to say, the zone of indifference changed. In Syracuse and Nassau, the police changed though the political system did not—the police moved within the existing zone of indifference.

Except in Albany, where the chief is part of the party organization, and in one or two other communities where political constraints on the police are numerous, the attitude of most city officials interviewed for this study suggested that their job was to select, within the latitude open to them, the "best man" for the chief's job and then let him run the department the way he wanted. Everyone conceded that who the chief was made a difference, and all mayors and managers spent a good deal of time on this decision. But rarely, with the exceptions noted, was there any strong desire to "get involved" in police matters. The police department is regarded as a city agency that provides a service, and the man in charge can be evaluated, so the theory goes, in terms of how well or how "efficiently" he provides it. As this study should have made clear, this view is not quite correct. The police are not a municipal service like trash collection, street sweeping, or road maintenance, and to govern them as if they were leads to difficulties. Trash collection or street sweeping is a *routine* service provided to the population *generally*. Everybody gets it (though perhaps some a bit more than others) and everybody can evaluate what he gets by reasonably evident standards. When citizens get too little, they complain, and the service level, if the city is alert to these matters, is adjusted accordingly or an explanation of why it cannot be adjusted is offered. Police protection is an *exceptional* service, which exists to prevent things from happening. It is largely invisible, and the average citizen comes into contact with it only in the exceptional case. He has no way of telling whether he is getting good service or not, except in the (rare) case when he experiences it—and perhaps not even then. He has no way of knowing if he is being treated, either as victim or suspect, differently from others. If his call for help is ignored or the response delayed, is it because the police are lazy or because all their cars are tied up on something more important? If the police fail to catch the burglar, is it because they are incompetent or because the burglar has left no clue? And if a mayor receives a complaint about the police, it is as likely to be a measure of how well they are doing their job as how poorly— what is "harassment" to one person is "good police protection" to his neighbor.

In short, if public authorities evaluate routine municipal services they cannot, except by happy accident, produce the kind of suboptimization that the "service-adjusted-to-complaints" system of managing street sweeping produces. Just as the absence of reliable performance criteria makes the police administrators task so difficult and gives rise to many of the tensions within the police department, so the mayor's, or manager's, lack of reliable performance criteria gives rise to the same kinds of tensions between the mayor and the police chief. The difference, of course, is that the mayor can, more easily than the chief, wash his hands of the whole affair or confine his concern with the police to particularistic matters—promotions, budgets, assignments, favors, citizen complaints—rather than law enforcement, which is just what he is likely to do. . . .

STREET-LEVEL BUREAUCRACY AND THE ANALYSIS OF URBAN REFORM

Michael Lipsky[14]

In American cities today, policemen, teachers, and welfare workers are under siege. Their critics variously charge them with being insensitive, unprepared to work with ghetto residents, incompetent, resistant to change, and racist. These accusations, directed toward individuals, are transferred to the bureaucracies in which they work.[15]

STREET-LEVEL BUREAUCRACY

Men and women in these bureaucratic roles deny the validity of these criticisms. They insist that they are free of racism, and that they perform with professional competence under very difficult conditions. They argue that current procedures are well designed and that it is only the lack of resources and of public support and understanding which prevents successful performance of their jobs. Hence bureaucrats stress the need for higher budgets, better equipment, and higher salaries to help them do even better what they are now doing well, under the circumstances.

How are these diametrically opposed views to be reconciled? Do both sides project positions for advantage alone, or is it possible that both views may be valid from the perspective of the policy contestants? Paradoxically, is it possible that critics of urban bureaucracy may correctly allege bias and ineffectiveness of service, at the same time that urban bureaucrats may correctly defend themselves as unbiased in motivation and objectively responsible to bureaucratic necessities?

What is particularly ominous about this confrontation is that these "street-level bureaucrats," as I call them, "represent" American government to its citizens. They are the people citizens encounter when they seek help from, or are controlled by, the American political system. While, in a sense, the Federal Reserve Board has a greater impact on the lives of the poor than, say, individual welfare workers (because of the Board's influence on inflation and employment trends), it nonetheless remains that citizens *perceive* these public employees as most influential in shaping their lives. As ambassadors of government to the American people, and as ambassadors with particularly significant impacts upon the lives of the poor and of rel-

Reprinted from Michael Lipsky, "Street-Level Bureaucracy and the Analysis of Urban Reform," *Urban Affairs Quarterly* (June 1971), pp. 391–409, Copyright © 1971 by Sage Publications. Reprinted by permission of Sage Publications.

atively powerless minorities, how capable are these urban bureaucrats in providing high levels of service and responding objectively to individual grievances and needs?

It is one conclusion of this paper that both perspectives have some validity. Their simultaneous validity, reflecting differences in perspective and resulting from the responses of street-level bureaucrats to problems encountered in their jobs, focuses attention on one aspect of the institutional racism with which the Kerner Commission charged American society.

In analyzing the contemporary crisis in bureaucracy, and the conflicting claims of urban bureaucrats and their nonvoluntary clients, I will focus on those urban bureaucrats whose impact on citizens' lives is both frequent and significant. Hence the concentration on street-level bureaucrats—those government workers who directly interact with citizens in the regular course of their jobs; whose work within the bureaucratic structure permits them wide latitude in job performance; and whose impact on the lives of citizens is extensive. Thus, the analysis would include the patrolman on the beat, the classroom teacher, and the welfare investigator. It would be less relevant to the school principal, who deals primarily with subordinates rather than with pupils, or to the traffic cop, whose latitude in job performance is relatively restricted.

Further, I want to concentrate on ways in which street-level bureaucrats respond to conditions of stress imposed by their work environment, where such stress is relatively severe. Analytically, three kinds of stress may be readily observed in urban bureaucracies today.

(1) Inadequate resources. Street-level bureaucracies are widely thought to lack sufficient organizational resources to accomplish their jobs. Classrooms are overcrowded. Large welfare caseloads prevent investigators from providing all but cursory service. The lower courts are so overburdened that judges may spend their days adjourning but never trying cases. Police forces are perpetually understaffed, particularly as perceptions of crime and demands for civic order increase.[16]

Insufficiency of organizational resources increases the pressures on street-level bureaucrats to make quick decisions about clients and process cases with inadequate information and too little time to dispose of problems on their merits. While this may be said about bureaucratic decision-making in general, it is particularly salient to problems of street-level bureaucracy because of the importance of individual bureaucratic outcomes to citizens subject to the influence of urban institutions. The stakes are often high— both to citizen and to bureaucrat.

(2) Threat and challenge to authority. The conditions under which street-level bureaucrats work often include distinct physical and psychological threats. Policemen are constantly alert to danger, as are other street-level bureaucrats who function in neighborhoods which are alien to them, are generally considered dangerous, or are characterized by high crime rates.

Curiously, it may make little difference whether or not the probabilities of encountering harm are actually high, so long as people think that their jobs are risky. Even if actual physical harm is somewhat remote, street-level bureaucrats experience threat by their inability to control the work-related encounter. Teachers especially fear the results of loss of classroom discipline or their ability to manage a classroom. Policemen have been widely observed to ensure the deference of a suspect by anticipatory invocation of authority.

(3) Contradictory or ambiguous job expectations. Confronted with resource inadequacies and threats which increase the salience of work-related results, street-level bureaucrats often find their difficulties exacerbated by uncertainties concerning expectations of performance. Briefly, role expectations may be framed by peers, by bureaucratic reference groups, or by public expectations in general.[17] Consider the rookie patrolman who, in addition to responding to his own conceptions of the police role, must accommodate the demands placed upon him by

(1) fellow officers in the station house, who teach him how to get along and try to "correct" the teachings of his police academy instructors;

(2) his immediate superiors, who may strive for efficiency at the expense of current practices;

(3) police executives, who communicate expectations contradictory to station-house mores; and

(4) the general public, which in American cities today is likely to be divided along both class and racial lines in its expectations of police practices and behavior.

One way street-level bureaucrats may resolve job-related problems without internal conflict is to drift to a position consistent with dominant role expectations. This resolution is denied bureaucrats working under conflicting role expectations.

Controversy over schools, police behavior, or welfare practices exacerbate these stress conditions, since they place in the spotlight of public scrutiny behavior which might otherwise remain in the shadows. These stresses result in the development of psychological and behavioral reactions which seem to widen the already existing differences between street-level bureaucrats and spokesmen for the nonvoluntary clienteles. Three such developments may be mentioned here.

First, it is a common feature of organizational behavior that individuals in organizations need to develop simplifications, or some kind of "shorthand," by which they can make decisions quickly and expeditiously. A policeman develops simplifications which suggest to him that crimes are in the process of being committed. Teachers develop simplifications to allow them to determine which pupils are "good" students and which are "troublemakers."

This is a cliche of organizational behavior.[18] But it is portentous, and not trivial, when we recognize the conditions under which these simplifications tend to be developed in stereotypic ways with racist orientations. When a black man driving through a white neighborhood is stopped by a policeman merely because he is black and therefore (according to the policeman's mode of simplification) suspiciously out of place, he has been stopped for good reason by the policeman, but for racist reasons, according to this aggrieved citizen. Teachers may select students for special attention or criticism because of their manners of speech, modes of dress, behavior in class, parental backgrounds, or other characteristics unrelated to their ability. Policemen, judges, and welfare investigators may be significantly influenced by symbols of deference or defiance to themselves or their authority. These signs may be related to general and generational responses to the enforced passivity of the past, and unrelated to the bureaucracies or bureaucrats themselves.

Race-oriented simplifications are particularly explosive even if only a few street-level bureaucrats engage in racist name calling. The objects of bureaucratic abuse understandably engage in the same kind of simplifying of the world that bureaucrats do. Thus, it takes only a few racist incidents to develop and sustain the impression that overall police behavior toward blacks is discriminatory. We are truly in a crisis because greater black community solidarity and greater willingness to object to police behavior create the very conditions under which race-oriented simplifications are increasingly invoked leading to an escalation of tension and hostility. The greater the tensions and the images of conflict in the minds of street-level bureaucrats, the more likely they will be to invoke the simplifications they think provide them with a measure of protection in their work. This increase in discrimination under tension occurs above and beyond the more overtly discriminatory attitudes that are sanctioned by the larger community and society.

The second development heightening the existing bureaucratic crises is the tendency on the part of street-level bureaucrats to develop defense mechanisms, in order to reach accommodation and resolution of stress tendencies, that result in a distortion of the perceived reality.[19]

One such reaction is the tendency to segment psychologically, or fragment conceptually, the population which the bureaucrat considers his clientele. Some police bureaucracies have regularly dealt with Negro crime through this technique.[20] If one can think of black people as "outside" the community, then one can perform according to "community standards" without experiencing the stresses exerted by diverse community elements. The police riots during the 1968 Chicago Democratic Convention, and more recently in various university communities, can only be understood by assuming that long-haired, white college students, some of whom are verbally abusive, are thought by the police to be "outside" the community which can expect to be protected by norms of due process.[21]

Similarly, teachers reduce their own sense of stress by defining some students as uneducable or marginally educable. Early selection of some students for higher education, based on such characteristics as the ability to speak English and class background, permits the educators to perform in their expected roles according to a more limited definition of the population to be served. As Nathan Glazer[22] has suggested, tensions in city schools and over police practices in ghetto neighborhoods are not only a function of the apparent "foreignness" of teachers and policemen to blacks. The process determining "foreignness" did not begin yesterday with black people. If nothing else, black labeling of whites as "foreigners" has been reinforced, if not inspired, by bureaucratic processes of categorizing nonvoluntary clients.

The development of tracking systems in public schools illustrates the development of *institutional* mechanisms for segmenting the population to be served so as to better ensure teacher success through population redefinition.[23] This is the intent function of tracking systems. It should be noted that population redefinition, as I have described it, must find support in general community attitudes, or else cross-pressures would emerge to inhibit this development. The growing cleavage in American cities between whites and blacks may never result in actual apartheid, as threatened by the Kerner Commission. But the subtle psychological apartheid resulting from redefinitions of the populations served by public programs and institutions is equally ominous and may be already accomplished.

A third development in the bureaucratic crisis is the way in which the kind of behavior described here may work to create the very reality which people either fear or want to overcome. For example, in categorizing students as low or high achievers—in a sense predicting their capacities to achieve—teachers may create validity for the very simplifications concerning student potential in which they engage. Recently, evidence has been presented to demonstrate that on the whole, students will perform better in school if teachers think they are bright, regardless of whether or not they are.[24] Similarly, the propensity to arrest black youngsters for petty crimes, the increasing professionalization of police forces (resulting in the recording of more minor offenses), and society's concern for clean arrest records as criteria for employment may create a population inclined toward further illegal activity per force if not by choice. The society's penal institutions have been characterized as schools for criminal behavior rather than for rehabilitation. Thus we create a class of criminal types by providing them with informal vocational training.

Not only individual teachers, but schools themselves communicate expectations to students. Increasingly, educators of disadvantaged minorities are convinced that student high school achievement is directly related to the extent to which schools communicate expectations of high potential to their student. Various street academies which have grown up in New York, Newark, and other cities, the Upward Bound program, and other experimental programs for poor and ghettoized youth, are premised on the assumption that if educators behave as if they think college—and hence upward mobility—is a realistic possibility for their students, high school dropouts and potential dropouts will respond by developing motivation currently unsuspected by high school personnel.

In their need to routinize and simplify in order to process work assignments, teachers, policemen, and welfare workers may be viewed as bureaucrats. Significantly, however, the workload of street-level bureaucrats consists of *people*, who in turn are reactive to the bureaucratic process. Street-level bureaucrats, confronted with inadequate resources, threat and challenge to authority, and contradictory or ambiguous role expectations, must develop mechanisms for reducing job-related stresses. It is suggested here that these mechanisms, with their considerable impact on clients' futures, deserve increasing attention from students of urban affairs.

PUBLIC POLICY REFORM IN STREET-LEVEL BUREAUCRACIES

Although much more could be said about the stresses placed on street-level bureaucrats, the remainder of this paper will focus on the implications for public policy and for public perceptions of urban bureaucracy, of an analysis of the ways street-level bureaucrats react to problems related to specified work conditions. Where does this kind of analysis lead?

First, it may help bridge that gap between, on the one hand, allegations that street-level-bureaucrats are racist and, on the other hand, insistence by individuals working in these bureaucracies that they are free from racism. Development of perceptual simplifications and subtle redefinitions of the population to be served—both group psychological phenomena—may be undetected by bureaucracies and clientele groups. These phenomena will significantly affect both the perception of the bureaucrats and the reactions of clienteles to the bureaucracies. Perceptual modes which assist bureaucrats in processing work and which, though not developed to achieve discriminatory goals, result in discriminatory bias may be considered a manifestation of institutional as opposed to individual racism. So there must be a distinction between institutional routinized procedures which result in bias and personal prejudice.

Second, we may see the development of human relations councils, citizen review boards, special equal opportunity units, and other "community relations" bureaus for what they are. They may provide citizens with increased marginal access to the system, but, equally important, they inhibit institutional change by permitting street-level bureaucrats to persist in behavior patterns because special units to handle "human related problems" have been created. These institutional developments do not fundamentally affect general bureaucratic performance. Instead, they insulate bureaucracies from having to confront behavioral factors affecting what appears to be racist work performance. These observations particularly obtain when, as is often the case, these units lack the power to impose on the bureaucracy decisions favorable to aggrieved citizens.

Third, tracking systems, vocational schools with basically custodial functions, and other institutionalized mechanisms for predicting capacities should be recognized as also serving to ease the bureaucratic burden at the expense of equal treatment and opportunity.

Fourth, the inherent limitation of "human relations" (sensitivity training, T-group training) training for street-level bureaucrats should be recognized as inadequate to the fundamental behavioral needs of street-level bureaucrats. Basic bureaucratic attitudes toward clients appear to be a function of workers' background and of socialization on the job. Training designed to improve relationships with black communities must be directed toward helping bureaucrats improve performance, not toward classroom lessons on equality which are soon forgotten.[25] The psychological forces which lead to the kinds of biased simplifications and discriminatory behavior mentioned earlier, appear sufficiently powerful to suggest skepticism over the potential for changing behavior patterns through human relations training efforts.

Fifth, just as training should be encouraged which relates to job performance needs, incentives should be developed which reward successful performance-utilizing indicators of clientele assistance. While performance standards can be trivialized, avoided, or distorted through selective use of statistics, their potential utility has hardly been explored. For example, it could be entirely appropriate to develop indices for teacher success and to develop appropriate merit rewards, based upon assessed performance indicators. For teachers, pay raises and promotions might be based upon average reading score improvements in relation to the school or citywide average for that grade level. In some ghetto schools, this index might initially reward those teachers who minimize the extent to which their students fall behind citywide averages. Public employee unions, of course, would oppose such proposals vigorously. There is every reason to think such proposals would be strongly endorsed in experimental educational units.

To improve public bureaucracies, the American political system has moved from public service as patronage to public service recruitment through merit examination. But in American cities today, administrators are frustrated because of the great difficulty in bringing talented individuals into government at high levels and introducing innovation at lower levels.

Mobility in the civil service is based too little on merit. "Dead wood" is built into the systems, where the least talented public employees remain in public service.

These conditions have prevailed for some time. What is new to the discussion is that black educators and critics of police forces now argue that (a) merit examinations do not test abilities for certain kinds of tasks that must be performed in ghetto teaching and ghetto police surveillance; and (b) on the basis of the records of ghetto schools and ghetto law enforcement practices, in many cases, civil service protection cannot be justified. The society cannot afford to continue to protect civil servants, or the natural allies of the bureaucracies, at the expense of their clienteles.[26] The criticism and reevaluation of bureaucratic standards that have accompanied demands for community control are supportive of these proposals.

Sixth, this analysis is more generally supportive of proposals for radical decentralization and neighborhood control. Advocacy of neighborhood control has recently revolved around five kinds of possible rewards resulting from a change in present organizational arrangements. It has been variously held that neighborhood control would

(1) increase loyalty to the political system by providing relatively powerless groups with access to governmental influence;

(2) increase citizens' sense of well-being as a result of participation;

(3) provide greater administrative efficiency for overly extended administrative systems;

(4) increase the political responsibility and accountability of bureaucracies currently remote from popular influence; and

(5) improve bureaucratic performance by altering the assumptions under which services are dispensed.[27]

The analysis of street-level bureaucracy presented here has been supportive of that strand of neighborhood control advocacy which focuses on the creation of standards by which to judge improved bureaucratic performance. Specifically, it has been proposed, among other things, that the performance of policemen, teachers, and other street-level bureaucrats is significantly affected by the availability of personal resources in the job situation, the sense of threat which is experienced, the ambiguity of role expectations, and the diversity of potential clientele groups. Most community control proposals are addressed to these considerations.

Recommendations for decentralization of police forces provide an opportunity to demonstrate the applicability of these ideas. For example, it has been proposed that the police function be divided into order maintenance (such as traffic control, breaking up domestic quarrels, parade duty, and so on), and crime fighting. The first is said to be a function that could easily be performed at the neighborhood level, whereas the crime fighting function, requiring both weaponry and greater technical training, might continue to be a citywide function. This kind of task redefinition would restore the cop to the beat, would replace city policemen with neighborhood residents more sensitive to community mores, and would relieve the city police of some of the duties they regard as least rewarding and most aggravating.[28] Such reorganization might reduce the stresses resulting from the variety of duties policemen are currently asked to perform, as well as increase the resources available to individuals in police duties.

Radical decentralization is also commended by this analysis because the increased homogeneity of district populations would permit greater uniformity and responsiveness in designing policies directed toward neighborhood clienteles. The range represented by the new clientele would be narrower and could be planned for with greater confidence. The system would not be so constrained by competing definitions of appropriate bureaucratic methods or by competing demands on the conceptualization of service. Citywide performance standards and appropriate regulations concerning nondiscriminatory behavior could be maintained with the expectation that they would be no *less* honored than currently.

This analysis is further supportive of proposals for radical decentralization to the extent that minority group employment under community control would be increased through changes in recruitment methods and greater attraction (for some) of civic employment. Increasing minority group employment in these street-level bureaucratic roles is not suggested here for the symbolism of minority group inclusion or for the sake of increasing minority groups opportunities (although these reasons are entirely justified). Rather, this analysis suggests that such people will be less likely to structure task performance simplifications in stereotypic ways.

Potential clients might also have greater confidence and trust in individuals with whom they can relate, and who they can assume have greater understanding of their needs. However, it is not clear to what extent such predictions are reliable. Black recruits to police bureaucracies as currently designed would undoubtedly continue to be governed by the incentive systems and job perceptions of the current force. Black patrolmen today may even be the objects of increased community hostility. But in systems encouraging increased community sensitivity, black patrolmen might thrive. The benefits of community control, perhaps like most political arrangements, may ultimately depend upon the development of political consciousness and arousal. Voter turnout is low when community participation is introduced through elections in which people have previously developed little stake or involvement (such as elections for Community Action Agency boards and the recent school elections in New York City).[29] Similarly, the potential for greater rapport between street-level bureaucrats and clients may ultimately depend upon the extent to which community involvement in the issues of community control precedes transfer of power. Without such prior arousal, community control may only provide unrealized structural *opportunities* for increased community participation and greater bureaucracy-client rapport should community groups seek to influence public policy in the future.

These comments are made in full recognition that they are supportive of structural and institutional changes of considerable magnitude. If the analysis developed here is at all persuasive, then it may be said that the bureaucratic crises I have described are built into the very structure of organizational bureaucratic life. Only structural alterations, made in response to a comprehensive analysis of the bureaucratic crisis, may be expected to be effective.

CONCLUSION

Let me conclude and summarize by indicating why the current situation, and this analysis, point to a continuing crisis in city politics. It is not only that bureaucracy-client antagonisms will continue to deepen or that black separatism will continue to place stress on street-level bureaucracies which they are poorly equipped to accommodate. In addition to these factors, we face a continuing crisis because certain modes of bureaucratic behavior effectively act to shield the bureaucracies from the nature of their own shortcomings.

Street-level bureaucrats, perceiving their clients as fully responsible for their actions—as do some policemen, mental hospital workers, and welfare workers—may thereby absolve themselves from contributing to the perpetuation of problems. Police attribution of riots to the riff-raff of the ghetto provides just one illustration of this tendency.[30]

On the other hand, attributing clients' performance to cultural or societal factors beyond the scope of human intervention also works to absolve bureaucrats from responsibility for clients' futures.[31] While there may be some validity to both modes of perception, the truth (as it often does) lies somewhere in between. Meanwhile both modes of perception function to trivialize the bureaucrat-client interaction, at the expense of responsibility.

Changing role expectations provides another mechanism which may shield street-level bureaucrats from recognizing the impact of their actions. This may take at least two forms. Bureaucrats may try to influence public expectations of their jobs, so as to convince the public of their good intentions under difficult conditions. Or they may seek role redefinition in such a way as to permit job performance according to role expectations *in some limited way*. The teacher who explains that "I can't teach them all, so I will try to teach the bright ones," is attempting to foster an image of fulfilling role expectations in a limited way. While this may be one way to utilize scarce resources and deserves some sympathy, it should be recognized that such tendencies deflect pressures *away* from providing for more adequate *routine* treatment of clients.

But perhaps most significantly, it is difficult for street-level bureaucrats to acknowledge the impact of their behavior toward clients because their very ability to function in bureaucratic roles depends upon routines, simplifications, and other psychological mechanisms to reduce stress. Under such circumstances attacks upon the substance or content of these reactions to job stress may be interpreted as criticisms of the basic requirements of job performance. As such, the criticisms are interpreted as ignorant or inaccurate.

Even if street-level bureaucrats are prepared to accept the substance of criticisms, they are likely to view them as utopian in view of the difficulties of the job. They may respond by affirming the justice of criticism in theory, but reject the criticism as inapplicable in the real world. Because they (and we) cannot imagine a world in which bureaucratic simplifications do not take place, they reject the criticism entirely.

This inability to recognize or deal with substantive criticism is reinforced by the fact that street-level bureaucrats find the validity of their simplifications and routines confirmed by selective perception of the evidence. Not only do the self-fulfilling prophecies mentioned earlier confirm these operations, but street-level bureaucrats also affirm their judgments because they depend upon the routines that offer a measure of security and because they are unfamiliar with alternative procedures which might free them to act differently. That street-level bureaucrats are in some sense shielded from awareness of the impact to their job-related behavior ensures that the crisis between street-level bureaucrats and their clients will continue; even while administrators in these bureaucracies loudly proclaim the initiation of various programs to improve community relations, reduce tensions among clientele groups, and provide token measures of representation for clientele groups on lower-level policy-making boards. The shelter from criticism may contribute to conservative tendencies in street-level bureaucracies, widely commented upon in studies of bureaucracy generally. For our purposes they may help to explain the recourse of community groups to proposals for radical change, and the recognition that only radical alternatives are likely to break the circle of on-the-job socialization, job stress, and reaction formation.

An illustration of relatively drastic changes may be available in the recent recruitment of idealistic college students into the police and teaching professions.[32] These individuals are not only better educated, but are presumed to approach their new jobs with attitudes toward ghetto clients quite different from those of other recruits. What higher salaries, better working conditions, and professionalization were unable to accomplish is being achieved on a modest level by the selective service system, the war in Vietnam, and the unavailability of alternative outlets for constructive participation in reforming American society. Higher salaries (which go mostly to the kinds of people who would have become policemen and teachers anyway) have not previously resulted in recruitment of significantly more sensitive or skillful people in these bureaucracies, although this has been the (somewhat self-serving) recommendation for bureaucratic improvement for many years. On the contrary, the recruitment of college students whose career expectations in the past did not include this kind of public service orientation may accomplish the task of introducing people with the desired backgrounds to street-level bureaucratic work independent (or even in spite) of increased salaries, professionalization, seniority benefits, and the like.

It is obviously too early to evaluate these developments. The new breed of street-level bureaucrat has yet to be tested in on-the-job effectiveness, ability to withstand peer group pressures and resentments, or staying power. But their example does illustrate the importance of changing basic aspects of the bureaucratic systems fundamentally, instead of at the margin. If the arguments made here are at all persuasive, then those who would analyze the service performance of street-level bureaucracies should concentrate attention on components of the work profile. Those components discussed here—resource inadequacy, physical and psychological threat, ambiguity of role expectations, and the ways in which policemen, teachers, and other street-level bureaucrats react to problems stemming from these job-related difficulties—appear to deserve particular attention.

REFERENCES

Altshuler, A. *Community Control: The Black Demand for Participation in American Cities.* New York: Western, 1970.

Becker, H. "Social class and teacher-pupil relationships," in B. Mercer and E. Carr (eds.), *Education and the Social Order.* New York: Holt, Rinehart, 1957.

Bordua, D. (ed.). *The Police: Six Sociological Essays.* New York: John Wiley, 1967.

Clark, K. *Dark Ghetto.* New York: Harper & Row, 1965.

Downs, A. *Inside Bureaucracy.* Boston: Little, Brown, 1967.

Gittell, M. and Hevfsi, A. G. (eds.). *The Politics of Urban Education.* New York: Praeger, 1969.

Glazer, N. "For white and black community control is the issue." *New York Times Magazine,* April 27, 1969.

Goffman, E. *Asylums.* Chicago: Aldine, 1969.

Kotler, M. *Neighborhood Government.* Indianapolis: Bobbs-Merrill, 1969.

Lazarus, R. *Psychological Stress and the Coping Process.* New York: McGraw-Hill, 1966.

Lipsky, M. "Is a Hard Rain Gonna Fall: Issues of Planning and Administration in the Urban World of the 1970's." Prepared for delivery at the Annual Meetings of the American Society of Public Administration, Miami Beach, May 21, 1969.

Lipsky, M. "Toward a theory of street-bureaucracy." Prepared for delivery at the Annual Meetings of the American Political Science Association, New York, September 20, 1969.

McNamara, J. "Uncertainties in police work: the relevance of police recruits' background and training," in D. Bordua (ed.), *The Police.*

Niederhoffer, A. *Behind the Blue Shield.* New York: Doubleday, 1967.

Rogers, D. *110 Livingston Street.* New York: Random House, 1968.

Rosenthal, R. and Jacobson, L. *Pygmalion in the Classroom.* New York: Holt, Rinehart & Winston, 1968.

Rossi, P., et al. "Between White and Black, the Faces of American Institutions in the Ghetto." *Supplemental Studies for the National Advisory Commission on Civil Disorders.* Washington, D.C., 1968.

Sarbin, T. and Allen, V. "Role Theory," in G. Lindzey and E. Aronson (eds.), *The Handbook of Social Psychology.* Reading, MA: Addison-Wesley, 1968.

Silver, A. "The demand for order in civil society," in D. Bordua (ed.), *The Police.*

Skolnick, J. *Justice without Trial.* New York: John Wiley, 1967.

Walker, D. *Rights in Conflict.* New York: Bantam, 1968.

Waskow, A. "Community control of the police," *Transaction.* December 1969.

Wilson, J. Q. *Varieties of Police Behavior.* Cambridge, MA: Harvard University Press, 1968.

POLICE CULTURE AND CORRUPTION

"We must create an atmosphere in which the dishonest officer fears the honest one, and not the other way around."

Detective Frank Serpico, Testimony before
the Knapp Commission, December 2, 1971

More than twenty years after Frank Serpico's testimony, this Commission found that the dishonest officers in the New York City Police Department still do not fear their honest colleagues. And for good reason. The vast majority of honest officers still protect the minority of corrupt officers through a code of silence few dare to break. The Knapp Commission predicted that the impact of their revelations would significantly weaken the characteristics of police culture that foster corruption. In particular, they hoped that their success in persuading a number of corrupt police officers to testify publicly about corruption would forever undermine the code of silence, the unwritten rule that an officer never incriminates a fellow officer. Unfortunately, their hope never became reality.

Police culture—the attitudes and values that shape officers behavior—is a critical component of the problem of police corruption today. This Commission, therefore, was not satisfied simply to examine the types of police corruption we found to exist. The more difficult question we asked is why such corruption exists, what are the root causes and prevailing conditions that nurture and protect it, and how they can be effectively addressed. Only by examining the variety of influences and attitudes that contribute to corruption, can we assess and formulate strategies to stop it.

The code of silence and other attitudes of police officers that existed at the time of the Knapp Commission continue to nurture police corruption and impede efforts at corruption control. Scores of officers of every rank told the Commission that the code of silence pervades the Department and influences the vast majority of honest and corrupt officers alike. Although police officers who look the other way while colleagues steal property, sell drugs, or abuse citizens' civil rights may not be directly involved in corruption, they nonetheless support and perpetuate it by abandoning their professional obligations.

These aspects of police culture facilitate corruption primarily in two ways. First, they encourage corruption by setting a standard that nothing

Reprinted from *The Report*, by the Commission to Investigate Allegations of Police Corruption and the Anti-Corruption Procedures of the Police Department. New York City: July 7, 1994, excerpts from pp. 51–69, with permission from the Honorable Milton Mollen.

is more important than the unswerving loyalty of officers to one another—
not even stopping the most serious forms of corruption. This emboldens
corrupt cops and those susceptible to corruption. Second, these attitudes
thwart efforts to control corruption. They lead officers to protect or cover
up for others' crimes—even crimes of which they heartily disapprove. They
lead to officers flooding Department radio channels with warnings when
Internal Affairs investigators appear at precincts, and refusing to provide
information about serious corruption in their commands. Changing these
aspects of police culture must be a central task if corruption controls are
ever to succeed.

The realities of police work bolster these corruptive features of police
culture. As a society, we expect more of police officers than other public
servants. We call upon them to daily to accomplish a variety of competing
responsibilities. We expect them to be daring crime fighters as well as pa-
tient mediators. We call on them to stop crime in our neighborhoods, to
resolve our domestic disputes, and to act as obedient members of a para-
military organization. Most of all, we expect them to confront physical
danger and risk their lives to protect our lives and property. After a time,
particularly in high-crime areas, they begin to identify the criminals they
must confront every day with the community they must serve. They begin
to close ranks against what they perceive as a hostile environment. Consequently, many officers lost sight of the majority of law-abiding citizens
who live in their precincts. When this happens corruption becomes easier
to commit and to tolerate.

Citizens often return this hostility. With crime, drugs, and guns rampant
in parts of our City, the public incorrectly faults the police. When incidents
of police corruption are disclosed, the community incorrectly assumes that
this is the norm. When police officers interfere with citizens' activities, the
public often resents it. Police officers feel this resentment. What the Knapp
commission observed in its time is just as applicable today:

Nobody, whether a burglar or a Sunday motorist likes to have his activities inter-
fered with. As a result most citizens at one time or another, regard the police with
varying degrees of hostility. The policeman feels, and naturally often returns, the
hostility.[33]

Faced with this resentment, the dangers of their work, and their depen-
dence on other officers for their mutual safety, police officers naturally band
together. Often to such degree that officers become isolated from the outside world. They socialize with and depend upon fellow officers not only
on the job, but off. An intense group loyalty, fostered by shared experiences
and the need to rely on each other in times of crisis, emerges as a predominant ethic of police culture.

This loyalty itself is not corruptive. Loyalty and trust are vital attributes that promote effective and safe policing. We cannot ask police officers to abandon their loyalty to each other while simultaneously demanding that they confront danger for us.

But group loyalty often flourishes at the expense of an officer's sworn duty. It makes allegiance to fellow officers—even corrupt ones—more important than allegiance to the Department and the community. When this happens, loyalty itself becomes corrupt and erects the strongest barriers to corruption control: the code of silence and the "Us vs. Them" mentality.

THE CODE OF SILENCE

The pervasiveness of the code of silence is itself alarming. But what we found particularly troubling is that it often appears to be strongest where corruption is most frequent. This is because the loyalty ethic is particularly powerful in crime-ridden precincts where officers most depend on each other for their safety each day—where fear and alienation from the community are most rampant. Thus, the code of silence influences honest officers in the very precincts where their assistance is needed most.

The pervasiveness of the code of silence is bolstered by the grave consequences for violating it: Officers who report misconduct are ostracized and harassed; become targets of complaints and even physical threats; and are made to fear that they will be left alone on the streets in a time of crisis. This draconian enforcement of the code of silence fuels corruption because it makes corrupt cops feel protected and invulnerable. . . .

The inculcation of police culture begins early in police officers' careers, as early as the Police Academy . . .

The fear of violating the code of silence can even lead an officer to accept the blame and punishment for the acts of a fellow officer . . .

There is a tragic irony to the code of silence which provides both the greatest challenge—and hope—in combatting corruption. Although most honest cops will not report serious corruption, they despise corrupt cops and silently hope that they will be removed from the ranks . . .

Thus the most devastating consequence of the code of silence is that it prevents the vast majority of honest officers from doing what they inwardly want to do: help keep their Department corruption free. It is not surprising that the honest cop wants corrupt cops off the job. The consequences of corruption for honest cops are grave: it taints their reputations, destroys their morale, and, most important, jeopardizes their very safety. . . .

What is surprising is that despite these devastating consequences, honest cops refuse to help eliminate corrupt cops from their Department, even though they are the principal victims of police corruption. . . .

Despite corruption's threat to their safety and their genuine desire to work in a corruption-free Department, officers view reporting corruption as an offense more heinous and dangerous than the corruption itself . . .

Honest officers who know about or suspect corruption among their colleagues, therefore, face an exasperating dilemma. They perceive that they must either turn a blind eye to the corruption they deplore, or risk the dreadful consequences of reporting it. The Commission's inquiries reveal that the overwhelming majority of officers choose to live with the corruption . . .

If the Department ever hopes to make lasting improvements in corruption control, it must do something it has failed to do in recent history: acknowledge that the code of silence exists and take steps to overcome it. It must rescue its members from the grip of their self-created predicament. From first-line supervisors to Internal Affairs it must provide constant support and recognition to officers who, by reporting corruption, choose to do what is right rather than what their culture expects of them. The Police Commissioner must make it clear that those who expose corruption will be rewarded, and those who help conceal it punished.

Finally, the Department must provide the same confidentiality protections to officers who report other officers, as it does to civilians who provide information about criminals. There is a widespread perception among officers that this is not the case. Many officers told us that they would not report corruption because the Department does not provide the same basic protections to officers as it does to civilians assisting the Department. This communicates a powerful message: that the Department is not really interested in enlisting the police in the fight against corruption. Until this changes, no reforms will ever change the attitudes that underlie the code of silence.

"US VS. THEM"

The code of the "blue fraternity" extends beyond the "blue" and into the communities they police. The loyalty ethic and insularity that breed the code of silence that protects officers from other officers also erects protective barriers between the police and the public. Far too many officers see the public as a source of trouble rather than as the people they are sworn to serve. Particularly in precincts overtaken with crime, officers sometimes view the public as the "enemy" . . .

CONCLUSION

The code of silence and the "Us vs. Them" mentality were present wherever we found corruption. These characteristics of police culture help explain how bands of corrupt officers can openly engage in corruption over long periods of time with impunity. To achieve lasting success against police corruption, the Department must insure that its systems of corruption control strike at the root causes and conditions of corruption and not just its symptoms. To do that the Department must transform police culture and redirect its power against concealing and perpetuating corruption. It must create a culture that demands integrity and works to insure it; an atmosphere in which dishonest cops fear the honest ones, and not the other way around—as Detective Frank Serpico warned twenty years ago. Without it, no system of corruption control is likely to succeed. The Commission believes that such change is possible. It believes such possibility is enhanced by an independent commission trusted by all concerned.

EXECUTIVE SUMMARY: REPORT OF THE COMMISSION ON POLICE INTEGRITY, PRESENTED TO THE CITY OF CHICAGO, RICHARD M. DALEY, MAYOR, NOVEMBER 1997

The Commission's charge was to examine the root causes of police corruption, to review how other urban police departments approach the issue, and to propose possible changes to department policies and procedures . . .

Recommendations summarized here reflect the reality that there is no simple strategy for preventing potential police corruption:

HIRING STANDARDS

The Commission recommends increasing the minimum requirements to a bachelors degree and a minimum of one year of work history before a candidate is accepted for employment as a Chicago police officer A pool of more mature and educated officers with verifiable work histories will improve the quality of the police force, making them better equipped to handle today's problems and perhaps less likely to engage in misconduct.

NEW POLICE OFFICERS

The Commission recommends completely overhauling the field training officer program to improve training during the new officer's critical first months. It also recommends extending the probationary period for new officers from 12 months to a full 18 months.

MONITORING POTENTIAL PROBLEMS

The Commission recommends establishing an "early warning" system to alert command personnel when an officer may be involved in a pattern of misconduct. The goal would be to stop small problems from becoming larger ones and to help officers who might be experiencing personal problems.

MANAGEMENT ISSUES

The Commission recommends a range of management improvements, including revising the system the Department uses for performance evalu-

Reprinted from Report of the Commission on Police Integrity, Presented to the City of Chicago, Richard M. Daley, Mayor, November 1997.

ations; establishing department-wide standards for selection of tactical officers; emphasizing supervisor accountability; and expanding training for new sergeants.

MANDATORY CONTINUING EDUCATION

The Commission recommends mandatory continuing education or in-service training for officers of all ranks, to reflect the view that policing is a profession.

The Commission is encouraged by the fact that the City and the Police Department are willing to take a hard look at what works and what does not. The policing profession is a rapidly changing one, and enlightened leadership will always be looking for new ideals. Chicago is recognized throughout the country as an innovative leader in the field of community policing. Now it must be a national leader in maintaining the highest possible level of integrity among its police force . . .

NOTES

1. Michael Lipsky, "Street-Level Bureaucracy and the Analysis of Urban Reform," *Urban Affairs Quarterly* (June 1971): 391–409; idem, "Toward a Theory of Street-Level Bureaucracy," in Willis D. Hawley et al., eds., *Theoretical Perspectives on Urban Politics* (Englewood Cliffs, NJ: Prentice-Hall, Inc., 1977), pp. 196–213; *Street-Level Bureaucracy: Dilemmas of the Individual in Public Services* (New York: Russell Sage Foundation, 1980).

2. James Q. Wilson, *Varieties of Police Behavior* (Cambridge: Harvard University Press, 1968).

3. Lipsky, "Street-Level Bureaucracy," "Toward a Theory of Street-Level Bureaucracy," and *Street-Level Bureaucracy: Dilemmas*.

4. Lipsky, "Toward a Theory of Street-Level Bureaucracy," p. 197.

5. Lipsky, "Street-Level Bureaucracy," pp. 393–95.

6. Ibid., p. 395.

7. City of New York, The Commission to Investigate Allegations of Police Corruption and the Anti-Corruption Procedures of the Police Department, *The Report* (New York, July 7, 1994), p. 1.

8. *The Report of the Commission on Police Integrity* (Chicago, Illinois, November 1997).

9. Wilson, *Varieties*, pp. 227–36.

10. Lipsky, "Street-Level Bureaucracy."

11. City of New York, pp. 51–69 in part and the Chicago Commission, pp. 2–3.

12. The term is taken from Chester A. Barnard, who applies it to the authority of an executive in an organization. See his *The Functions of the Executive* (Cambridge, MA: Harvard University Press, 1938), pp. 168–69. Another study that has applied it to community tolerance of administrative discretion (this time in the case of public welfare agencies) is Alan Keith-Lucas, *Decisions About People in Need* (Chapel Hill: University of North Carolina Press, 1957), pp. 246–47.

13. The zone is probably greatest when people are deeply divided over law enforcement issues, as they [were] in nineteenth-century Boston over the question of liquor licensing. See Robert Lane, *Policing the City: Boston, 1822–1885* (Cambridge, MA: Harvard University Press, 1967), p. 137.

14. Author's Note: This essay was prepared for a Conference on New Public Administration and Neighborhood Control held in Boulder, Colorado, in May 1970, and sponsored by the Center for Governmental Studies in Washington, D.C. The essay [appeared] in H. George Frederickson, ed., *Politics, Public Administration, and Neighborhood Control* (San Francisco: Chandler, [1972]).

15. This paper draws heavily upon and extends two recent papers (M. Lipsky, "Is a Hard Rain Gonna Fall: Issues of Planning and Administration in the Urban World of the 1970's." Prepared for delivery at the Annual Meetings of the American Society of Public Administration, Miami Beach, May 21, 1969 and M. Lipsky, "Toward a Theory of Street-level Bureaucracy," Prepared for delivery at the Annual Meetings of the American Political Science Association, New York, September 20, 1969. For a more detailed analysis of street-level bureaucrats and the fact, affecting their performance, see the latter. The reader will recognize the tentative nature of some of the conclusions and analyses which follow. The analysis of street-level bureaucracy thus far has consisted of trying to discover characteristics common to a certain set of urban bureaucrats which obtain beyond the narrow contexts of individual bureaucracies such as the police or teachers. The latter half of this paper is similarly a tentative attempt to relate the analysis to issues of current public policy.

16. A. Silver, "The Demand for Order in Civil Society," in D. Bordua, ed., *The Police: Six Sociological Essays* (New York: John Wiley, 1967).

17. T. Sarbin and V. Allen, "Role Theory," in G. Lindzey and E. Aronson, eds., *The Handbook of Social Psychology* (Reading, MA: Addison-Wesley, 1968).

18. See, for example, A. Downs, *Inside Bureaucracy* (Boston: Little, Brown, 1967), pp. 2–3, 75–78.

19. For a general discussion of psychological reaction to stress, see R. Lazarus, *Psychological Stress and the Coping Process* (New York: McGraw-Hill, 1966), esp. ch. 1, pp. 266–318. This work is particularly useful in providing conceptual distinctions for various phenomena related to the coping process.

20. Wilson, *Varieties*, p. 157.

21. D. Walker, *Rights in Conflict* (New York: Bantam, 1968).

22. Nathan Glazer, "For White and Black Community Control Is the Issue," *New York Times Magazine* (April 27, 1969), p. 46.

23. See the decision of Judge Skelly Wright in *Hobson v. Hanson*, June 19, 1967, 269F Supp. 401 (1967); also see K. Clark, *Dark Ghetto* (New York: Harper & Row, 1965), p. 128 and also see R. Rosenthal and L. Jacobson, *Pygmalion in the Classroom* (New York: Holt, Rinehart & Winston, 1968), pp. 116–18.

24. Rosenthal and Jacobson, *Pygmalion*.

25. J. McNamara, "Uncertainties in Police Work: The Relevance of Police Recruits' Background and Training," in Bordua, ed., *The Police*.

26. For example, the requirements for becoming a building department inspector in New York City have virtually assured the budding trade unions of public employment for their members.

27. A. Altshuler, *Community Control: The Black Demand for Participation in*

American Cities (New York: Western, 1970) and M. Kotler, *Neighborhood Government* (Indianapolis: Bobbs-Merrill, 1969).

28. See, e.g., A. Waskow, "Community Control of the Police," *Transaction* (December 1969) and Wilson, *Varieties*.

29. A number of writers have commented on the low turnout for elections to CAP and Model Cities boards. See, e.g., Altshuler, *Community Control*, pp. 138–39. On decentralized school board elections, see the *New York Times* dated from February 19 to March 22, 1970.

30. See P. Rossi et al., "Between White and Black, the Faces of American Institutions in the Ghetto," *Supplemental Studies for the National Advisory Commission on Civil Disorders* (Washington, D.C., 1968), pp. 110–13.

31. Ibid., p. 136.

32. See, for example, *New York Times*, February 13, 1970.

33. City of New York, *The Report*, p. 6.

Chapter 7

The Supreme Court as Criminal Justice Policymaker

INTRODUCTION

The Supreme Court, by using its power to interpret the law, has engaged in criminal justice policy making. Through its decisions, the Court has affected the rights of adult criminal and juvenile defendants, as well as setting expectations for law enforcement and corrections practice. In doing so, the Court has had an impact on the operation of the criminal justice system, as we know it. The role of the Supreme Court as policymaker is extremely complex due to the intricacies of the Court's decision-making processes and the difficulties involved in implementing its decisions. In addition, judicial decision making reflects the Court's willingness to act, as well as the overriding ideology of the Court at any point in time. Some understanding of these complexities is necessary to comprehend policy outcomes as they emerge from the Court and then as they impact the day-to-day operations of the criminal justice system.

This chapter examines the complexities of the Supreme Court as policymaker, focusing specifically on how the Court has impacted the operation of the juvenile court system. Between the late 1960s and early 1970s, the Supreme Court promulgated in three cases—*Gault, Winship*, and *McKeiver*—decisions that, albeit intentionally or not, changed the juvenile court to an institution different from that envisioned by its creators.[1] Established at the turn of the century, the juvenile court was to serve the needs of the child, to rehabilitate. Today, due to the procedural revolution of the court, it more closely approximates the adult criminal court.

THE SOURCE OF THE SUPREME COURT'S
DECISION-MAKING AUTHORITY

Article III of the Constitution vests the judicial power of the United States in one Supreme Court and in such inferior courts as the Congress may establish from time to time. This power extends to all cases in law and equity, arising under the Constitution, the laws of the United States, and treaties made; all cases affecting ambassadors, other public ministers, and consuls; all cases of admiralty and maritime jurisdictions; controversies between states, between citizens of one state and another state, and between a state or citizens of a state and a foreign state or its citizens. In practice, the federal court system is organized on three levels—the district courts, which are similar to a trial court at the state level; the appellate courts, which focus on issues about how a trial is conducted; and the Supreme Court, which is the court of ultimate review, but which also has initial jurisdiction in rare cases, such as problems between states. The primary focus of the judicial discussion in this text is the Supreme Court and how its interpretation of the law has affected the criminal justice system at all levels of government.

The source of the power of the Supreme Court is the power of judicial review. Although it has been argued that the framers of the Constitution anticipated some sort of judicial review, it was Chief Justice John Marshall who articulated the concept in *Marbury v. Madison*, in 1803. Marshall argued that "it is emphatically the province and duty of the judicial department to say what the law is." If the law is in conflict with the Constitution, then the court has the duty of the judiciary to declare the law void.[2] According to Howard Ball, employing the power of judicial review, the U.S. federal courts (the Supreme Court and others) have performed two functions throughout U.S. history: (1) norm enforcement—validating legislation passed by Congress (and the states) and (2) policy making through examination and interpretation of a statute or the Constitution in cases properly brought to the Court.[3]

It is through its power of judicial review that the Supreme Court has functioned as a criminal justice policymaker. It can create positive policy or negate existing policy through its interpretation of state and federal laws.

LIMITATIONS OF JUDICIAL DECISION-MAKING
AUTHORITY

The role of the Supreme Court as a criminal justice policymaker is not without its limitations. Some of those limitations are functions of judicial decision making. In addition, there are practical impediments to implementing judicial decisions at the federal, state, and local levels that affect the impact of the Court's decision-making authority.

First, the Court must choose the cases it reviews from cases brought to it. The Court may have interest in addressing an issue, but if a case is not sent forward, the court cannot go out and "shop" for a case so that it can address that issue. At the same time, it cannot hear all the cases appealed to it. Once the Court decides to hear a case, it may affirm, modify, or reverse the lower court's decision.[4]

Second, the Supreme Court relies on precedent. A basic doctrine of the Court is stare decisis—let the decision stand.[5] That is, the Court tends to adhere to its previous interpretation of the law.

Third, the Court tends to scope its decisions narrowly. For example, during the 1970s, the Court did not rule on whether or not the death penalty was constitutional, but focused on the constitutionality of the procedures for imposing the death penalty. In some situations, the Court will need additional cases to flesh out its decision—to clarify or extend its decision, but it has no control over whether or not such a case will be brought to it; therefore, judicial policy making may be spotty. For example, the Court's decision making with respect to the right of a defendant to counsel evolved over time. Or, subsequent Courts may interpret cases brought to it in such a way as to weaken or strengthen an earlier Court's ruling, although the decision remains standing. The Court's interpretation of the so-called "exclusionary rule" (regarding the use in court against a defendant of evidence illegally seized by police) shifted, while the basic rule remained standing.[6]

The Court also does not have unfettered control over the implementation of its decisions. That is, the Court is dependent on the lower courts; federal, state, or local governments; and/or administrators to carry out the policies it has articulated. Further, the Court cannot sit in judgment over the day-to-day decisions of these institutions, but must rely largely on their willingness to carry out the decisions. It cannot sit in judgment over a search and seizure or the quality of counsel in every court. The Court has the potential use of sanctions to enforce its decisions, for example, the reversal of the decision of a lower court, but it is not an overwhelming sanction.[7] What is important to bear in mind is that while the Court generally has success in achieving the effective implementation of its decisions, there may be gaps between its decisions and the actions of those who implement its decisions.[8]

The Court's ability as policymaker is affected by other actors in the political system. Congress or a state legislature, for example, may act to counteract a judicial decision by passing a new law. Congress may propose a constitutional amendment, although the small number of amendments to the Constitutions suggests that this approach is not commonly used to respond to the Court's policy-making authority.

In short, the Supreme Court is a policymaker. That role, however, is affected by a variety of factors that may limit its impact on policy as it is implemented.

ACTIVISM, IDEOLOGY, AND JUDICIAL DECISION MAKING

In addition, the Court's role as policymaker at any point in time is affected by the Court's willingness to play that role. That is, judicial policy making will vary depending upon whether the justices view their role as one of judicial activism or judicial restraint. The former view may be defined as the Court's willingness to make significant changes in public policy, particularly in policies established by other institutions, most visibly overturning legislation. Judicial activism is most directly and clearly exhibited by the Court's use of judicial review—its willingness to overturn the decision of other policymakers on the grounds that the latter's decision violates the Constitution.[9] Judicial restraint views activism as illegitimate, because the Court is a relatively undemocratic institution; risky—opening the Court to attack, if it takes on controversial matters; and unwise, because of the lack of court capacity to make effective policy choices.

The policies promulgated by the Court may be characterized as liberal or conservative. An activist judge or court may be liberal or conservative. In the criminal justice area, the Warren Court has been characterized as liberal insofar as it expanded the rights of the criminal defendant, for example, the right to counsel, protection against incrimination, and limitations on search and seizure. In contrast, the Burger Court, and even more so the Rehnquist Court, have been characterized as conservative in their criminal justice decisions, narrowing the rights of criminal defendants and giving government more authority to regulate certain behaviors.

THE SUPREME COURT AND THE JUVENILE JUSTICE SYSTEM

The Supreme Court exercised its power of judicial review to effect changes in the juvenile justice system. It began to reshape the juvenile court in the case of Gerald Gault, which was brought to it on appeal from the State Supreme Court of Arizona. In its decision, the Supreme Court agreed that the constitutional guarantee of due process applied in delinquency proceedings.

INCLUDED SELECTIONS

The first selection in this chapter summarizes the Supreme Court's decision in the case, *In Re Gault* (387 U.S. 1 (1967)). The second article by law professor Barry C. Feld discusses the impact of Gault and subsequent

Supreme Court decisions on the functioning of the juvenile court. Professor Feld asserts that the Court's decisions resulted in the continuing evolution of juveniles' procedural due process requirement and, as such, transformed the juvenile court to one very different from that envisioned by its creators.

FOR DISCUSSION

In this chapter the reader should consider:

1. The source of judicial decision-making power.
2. The limitations of judicial decision-making power.
3. How the Supreme Court has affected criminal justice policy and practice in the adult system.
4. How the Supreme Court has affected criminal justice policy and practice in the juvenile justice system.
5. The strengths and weaknesses of judicial decision making in the criminal justice field.

RECOMMENDED READINGS AND OTHER SOURCES

Specific References

Baum, Lawrence. *The Supreme Court.* 4th ed. Washington, DC: Congressional Quarterly Press, 1992.

Feld, Barry C. "Criminalizing Juvenile Justice: Rules of Procedure for the Juvenile Court." *Minnesota Law Review,* vol. 69, no. 2 (December 1984): 141–276.

Lewis, Anthony. *Gideon's Trumpet.* New York: Vintage Books, 1966.

Woodward, Bob, and Armstrong, Scott. *The Brethren: Inside the Supreme Court.* New York: Simon and Schuster, 1979.

Web Sites

Cornell University <http://www.supct.law.cornell.edu>

Federal Legal Information Through Electronics (Flite) <http://www.fedworld.gov>

Findlaw <http://www.findlaw.com/casecode/supreme.html>

Supreme Court http://www.supremecourtus.gov

IN RE GAULT

Case #: 387 U.S. 1 (1967) Argued December 6, 1966.
Decided May 15, 1967. 99 Ariz. 181, 407 p. 2d 760,
reversed and remanded

SUMMARY

Appellants' 15-year-old son, Gerald Gault, was taken into custody as the result of a complaint that he had made lewd telephone calls. After hearings before a juvenile court judge, Gerald was ordered committed to the state industrial school as a juvenile delinquent until he should reach majority. Appellants brought a habeas corpus action in the state courts to challenge the constitutionality of the Arizona Juvenile Code and the procedure actually used in Gerald's case, on the ground of denial of various procedural due process rights. The State Supreme Court affirmed dismissal of the writ. Agreeing that the constitutional guarantee of due process applies to proceedings in which juveniles are charged as delinquents, the Court held that the Arizona Juvenile Code impliedly includes the requirements of due process in delinquency proceedings, and that such due process requirements were not offended by the procedure leading to Gerald's commitment. Held:

1. Kent v. United States, 383 U.S. 541, 562 (1966), held "that the waiver hearing must measure up to the essentials of due process and fair treatment." This view is reiterated here in connection with a Juvenile Court adjudication of "delinquency," as a requirement which is part of the due process clause of the fourteenth amendment of our Constitution. The holding in this case relates only to the adjudicatory stage of the juvenile process, where commitment to a state institution may follow. When proceedings may result in incarceration in an institution of confinement, "it would be extraordinary if our Constitution did not require the procedural regularity and exercise of care implied in the phrase 'due process.' "

2. Due process requires, in such proceedings, that adequate written notice be afforded the child and his parents or guardian. Such notice must inform them "of the specific issues that they must meet" and must be given "at the earliest practicable time, and in any event sufficiently in advance of the hearing to permit preparation." Notice here was neither timely nor adequately specific, nor was there waiver of the right to constitutionally adequate notice.

3. In such proceedings the child and his parents must be advised of their

Reprinted from the Federal Legal Information Through Electronics (Flite) <http://www.fedworld.gov>.

right to be represented by counsel and, if they are unable to afford counsel, that counsel will be appointed to represent the child. Mrs. Gault's statement at the habeas corpus hearing that she had known she could employ counsel, is not "an 'intentional relinquishment or abandonment' of a fully known right."

4. The constitutional privilege against self-incrimination is applicable in such proceedings: "An admission by the juvenile may not be used against him in the absence of clear and unequivocal evidence that the admission was made with knowledge that he was not obliged to speak and would not be penalized for remaining silent." "[T]he availability of the privilege does not turn upon the type of proceeding in which its protection is invoked, but upon the nature of the statement or admission and the exposure which it invites. . . . Juvenile proceedings to determine 'delinquency,' which may lead to commitment to a state institution, must be regarded as 'criminal' for purposes of the privilege against self-incrimination." Furthermore, experience has shown that "admissions and confessions by juveniles require special caution" as to their reliability and voluntariness, and "[it] would indeed be surprising if the privilege against self incrimination were available to hardened criminals but not to children." "[S]pecial problems may arise with respect to waiver of the privilege by or on behalf of children, and . . . there may well be some differences in technique—but not in principle—depending upon the age of the child and the presence and competence of parents. . . . If counsel was not present for some permissible reason when an admission was obtained, the greatest care must be taken to assure that the admission was voluntary. . . . "Gerald's admissions did not measure up to these standards, and could not properly be used as a basis for the judgment against him.

5. Absent a valid confession, a juvenile in such proceedings must be afforded the rights of confrontation and sworn testimony of witnesses available for cross-examination.

6. Other questions raised by appellants, including the absence of provision for appellate review of a delinquency adjudication, and a transcript of the proceedings, are not ruled upon.

IN RE GAULT APPEAL FROM THE SUPREME COURT OF ARIZONA.

Mr. Justice Fortas delivered the opinion of the Court. This is an appeal under 28 U.S.C. sec. 1257(2) from a judgment of the Supreme Court of Arizona affirming the dismissal of a petition for a writ of habeas corpus. 99 Ariz. 181, 407 p. 2d 760 (1965). The petition sought the release of Gerald Francis Gault, appellants' 15 year-old son, who had been committed as a juvenile delinquent to the state industrial school by the juvenile court of Gila County, Arizona. The Supreme Court of Arizona affirmed dismissal of the writ against various arguments which included an attack upon the constitutionality of Arizona Juvenile Code because of its alleged denial of procedural due process rights to juveniles charged with being "delinquents." The Court agreed that the constitutional guarantee of due process of law is applicable in such proceedings. It held that Arizona's juvenile code is to be read as "impliedly" implementing the "due process concept." It then proceeded to identify and describe "the particular elements which constitute due process in a juvenile hearing." It concluded that the proceedings ending in commitment of Gerald Gault did not offend those requirements. We do not agree, and we reverse. . . .

CRIMINALIZING JUVENILE JUSTICE: RULES OF PROCEDURE FOR THE JUVENILE COURT[10]

Barry C. Feld

I. INTRODUCTION

The 1967 United States Supreme Court decision *In re Gault*[11] precipitated a procedural revolution that has transformed the juvenile court into a legal institution very different from that envisioned by its Progressive creators.[12] In the years since *Gault* states have struggled to bring the administration of their juvenile courts into harmony with the requirements of the Constitution,[13] aided by professional commentary and the continuing evolution of juvenile procedural due process requirements.

This article studies the effects of these efforts on the juvenile justice system. The article briefly reviews the Progressive conception of the juvenile court and examines both the changes resulting from the Supreme Court's due process decisions and the legislative impetus those decisions provided . . . The article concludes that the juvenile court has been effectively criminalized in that its current administrative assumptions and operations are virtually indistinguishable from those of adult criminal courts. At the same time, however, the procedures of the juvenile court often provide protections for juveniles less adequate than those afforded adult criminal defendants. As a result, juveniles receive the worst of both worlds, and the reasons for the very existence of a separate juvenile court are called into question.

II. HISTORICAL BACKGROUND

A. The Progressive Juvenile Court

Between 1870 and World War I, the railroads changed America from an agrarian to an industrial society by fostering economic growth, changing the processes of manufacturing, and ushering in a period of rapid economic modernizations.[14] Simultaneously, traditional social patterns faced challenges as new immigrants, primarily from southern and eastern Europe,

Reprinted and excerpted from *Minnesota Law Review*, vol. 69, no. 2 (December 1984), by Barry C. Feld, "Criminalizing Juvenile Justice: Rules of Procedure for the Juvenile Court," pp. 141–63, Copyright 1984, with permission from the author and the University of Minnesota Law Review.

and rural Americans flooded into the burgeoning cities and crowded into ethnic enclaves and urban slums.[15] Overburdened by numbers, cities proved unable to provide even basic needs.[16] As a result, urban ghettos, poverty, congestion, disorder, crime, and inadequate social services accompanied the development of modern urban industrial life.

Accompanying these developments were changes in family structure and function, including a reduction in the number and spacing of children, a shift of economic functions from the family to other work environments, and a modernization and privatization of the family that substantially modified the roles of women and children.[17] The latter development was especially noticeable in the upper and middle classes, which had begun to view children as corruptible innocents whose upbringing required special attention, solicitude, and instruction.[18] As a result, women, especially in the middle and upper classes, assumed a greater role in supervising the child's moral and social development.[19]

At the same time, the general social and economic problems sparked the Progressive Movement.[20] Progressivism included a host of ideologies and addressed issues ranging from economic regulation to criminal justice and political reform.[21] A unifying theme, however, was the development by professionals and experts of rational and scientific solutions that would be administered by the State.[22] Progressive reliance on the State reflected a fundamental belief that state action could be benevolent, that government could rectify social problems, and that Progressive values could be inculcated in others.[23]

The Progressive trust of state power combined with changes in the cultural conceptions of children and child-rearing to lead Progressives into the realm of "child-saving"—child labor laws, child welfare laws, compulsory education laws, and the juvenile court system.[24] The Progressive programs were intended to structure child development and to control and mold children while protecting them from exploitation. The goals and the methods of these programs, however, often reflected antipathy to the immigrant hordes and a desire to save the second generation from perpetuating the old world ways.[25]

Similarly, the development of new theories about human behavior and social deviance led Progressives to new views on criminal justice and social control policies.[26] The Progressives saw crime not as a product of the deliberate exercise of an individual's free will[27] but as a result of external, antecedent forces.[28] They focused, therefore, on reforming the offender rather than on punishing the offense.[29] The result was the "Rehabilitative Ideal" that permeated all Progressive criminal justice reforms.[30] The Ideal emphasized open-ended, informal, and highly flexible policies so that the criminal justice professional had the discretion necessary to formulate individualized, case-by-case strategies for rehabilitating the deviant.[31]

The juvenile court was based on this Rehabilitative Ideal. It was conceived as a specialized, bureaucratic agency, staffed by experts and designed to serve the needs of a specific category of client: the "child at risk," whether offender, dependent, or neglected. The juvenile court professionals were to make discretionary, individualized treatment decisions to achieve benevolent goals and social uplift by substituting a scientific and preventative approach for the traditional punitive philosophy of the criminal law.[32] The legal justification for intervention was parens patriae—the right and responsibility of the state to substitute its own control over children for that of the natural parents when the latter were unable or unwilling to meet their responsibilities or when the child posed a community crime problem.[33] The parens patriae doctrine drew no distinction between criminal and noncriminal youth conduct, a view that supported the Progressive position that juvenile court proceedings were civil rather than criminal in nature. The civil nature of the proceedings fulfilled the reformers' desire to remove children from the adult criminal system and allowed greater supervision of the children and greater flexibility in treatment.[34] Because the reformers eschewed punishment, they could reach behavior such as smoking, sexual activity, truancy, immorality, stubbornness, vagrancy, or living a wayward, idle, and dissolute life—behavior that had previously been ignored but that the Progressives wished to end because it betokened premature adulthood.[35] Such "status jurisdiction" reflected the dominant concept of childhood and adolescence that had taken root during the nineteenth century and authorized predelinquent intervention to forestall premature adulthood, enforce the dependent conditions of youth, and supervise children's moral upbringing.[36]

The Progressives envisioned a juvenile court administered by an expert judge and assisted by social service personnel, clinicians, and probation officers. They hoped judges would be specialists, trained in the social sciences and child development, whose empathic qualities and insight could aid in making individualized dispositions in the "best interests of the child."[37] Because it was assumed that a rational, scientific analysis of facts would reveal the proper diagnosis and prescribe the cure, the juvenile court's methodology encouraged collecting as much information as possible about the child. The resulting factual inquiry into the whole child accorded minor significance to the specific criminal offense because the offense indicated little about a child's "real needs."[38] Because the reformers' aims were benevolent, their solicitude individualized, and their intervention guided by science, they saw no reason to narrowly circumscribe the power of the state. They maximized discretion to provide flexibility in diagnosis and treatment and focused on the child and the child's character and lifestyle rather than on the crime.

In distinguishing children from adult offenders, the juvenile court also rejected the procedures of criminal prosecution. It introduced a euphemistic vocabulary and a physically separate court building to avoid the stigma of adult prosecutions, and it modified courtroom procedures to eliminate any implication of a criminal proceeding.[39] For example, proceedings were initiated by a petition in the welfare of the child, rather than by a criminal complaint. Because the important issues involved the child's background and welfare rather than the commission of a specific crime, courts dispensed with juries, lawyers, rules of evidence, and formal procedures. To avoid stigmatization, hearings were confidential and private, access to court records was limited, and youths were found to be "delinquent" rather than guilty of an offense. To make proceedings more personal and private, the judge was supposed to sit next to the child while court personnel presented a treatment plan to meet the child's needs as determined by a background investigation identifying the sources of the child's misconduct. Dispositions were indeterminate and nonproportional and could continue for the duration of minority. The events that brought the child before the court affected neither the degree nor the duration of intervention because each child's needs differed and no limits could be defined in advance. The dispositional process was designed to determine why the child was in court in the first instance and what could be done to change the character, attitude, and behavior of the youth to prevent a reappearance.[40]

B. The Constitutional Domestication of the Juvenile Court

Despite occasional challenges and criticism of some conceptual or administrative aspects of juvenile justice, no sustained and systematic examination of the juvenile court occurred until the 1960's.[41] In 1967, however, *In re Gault*[42] began a "due process revolution" that substantially transformed the juvenile court from a social welfare agency into a legal institution. This "constitutional domestication"[43] was the first step in the convergence of the procedures of the juvenile justice system with those of the adult criminal process.[44]

In re Gault involved the delinquency adjudication and institutional commitment of a youth who allegedly made a lewd telephone call of the "irritatingly offensive, adolescent, sex variety" to a neighbor.[45] Fifteen-year-old Gerald Gault was taken into custody, detained overnight without notification of his parents, and made to appear at a hearing the following day. A pro forma petition alleged simply that he was a delinquent minor in need of the care and custody of the court. The complaining witness did not appear, no sworn testimony was taken, and no transcript or formal memorandum of the substance of the proceedings was made. The judge interrogated Gault, who apparently made incriminating responses. At no time was Gault assisted by an attorney or advised of a right to counsel. Following his hearing, the judge returned Gault to a detention cell for several days. At his dispositional hearing the following week, the judge committed Gault as a juvenile delinquent to the State Industrial School "for the period of his minority [that is, until 21], unless sooner discharged by due process of law."[46]

The Court examined the realities of juvenile incarceration rather than accepting the rehabilitative rhetoric of Progressive juvenile jurisprudence. In reviewing the history of the juvenile court, the Court noted that the traditional rationales for denying procedural safeguards to juveniles included the belief that the proceedings were neither adversarial nor criminal and that, because the State acted as parens patriae, the child was entitled to custody rather than liberty.[47] The Court rejected these assertions, however, because denial of procedures frequently resulted in arbitrariness rather than "careful, compassionate, individualized treatment."[48] Although the Court hoped to retain the potential benefits of the juvenile process, it insisted that the claims of the juvenile court process had to be candidly appraised in light of the realities of recidivism, the failures of rehabilitation, the stigma of a "delinquency" label, the breaches of confidentiality, and the arbitrariness of the process.[49] The Court noted that a juvenile justice process free of constitutional safeguards had not abated recidivism or lowered the high crime rates among juvenile offenders. It also emphasized that the realities of juvenile institutional confinement mandated elementary procedural safeguards.[50] These safeguards included advance notice of charges, a fair and impartial hearing, assistance of counsel, opportunity to confront and cross-examine witnesses, and a privilege against self-incrimination.[51]

Although the Court discussed the realities of the juvenile system and mandated procedural safeguards, it limited its holding to the adjudicatory hearing at which a child is determined to be a delinquent.[52] It asserted that its decision would in no way impair the value of the unique procedures for processing and treating juveniles and that the procedural safeguards associated with the adversarial process were essential in juvenile proceedings, both to determine the truth and to preserve individual freedom by limiting the power of the state.[53]

In contrast to the narrow holding, the basis for the Court's constitutional analysis of what rights must be afforded juveniles in adjudicatory hearings was broad. The Court used the "fundamental fairness" requirements of the fourteenth amendment due process to grant the rights to notice, counsel, and confrontation and did not even refer specifically to the explicit requirements of the sixth amendment.[54] The Court did, however, explicitly invoke the fifth amendment to establish that juveniles were protected against self-incrimination in delinquency proceedings.[55] The Court's extension of the self-incrimination protection provides the clearest example of the dual functions of such safeguards in juvenile court adjudications: assuring accurate fact finding and protecting against government oppression.[56] In this respect, *Gault* is a premier example of the Warren Court's belief that expansion of constitutional rights and limitation on the coercive powers of the State could be obtained through the adversary process, which in turn would assure the regularity of law enforcement and reduce the need for continual judicial scrutiny.[57]

In subsequent juvenile court decisions, the Supreme Court further elaborated upon the criminal nature of delinquency proceedings. In *In re Winship*,[58] the Court decided that proof of delinquency must be established "beyond a reasonable doubt," rather than by lower civil standards of proof.[59] Because there is no explicit provision of the Bill of Rights regarding the standard of proof in criminal cases, the *Winship* Court first held that proof beyond a reasonable doubt was a constitutional requirement in adult criminal proceedings.[60] The Court then extended the same standard of proof to juvenile proceedings because of the standard's equally vital role there.[61] The Court concluded that the need to prevent unwarranted convictions and to guard against government power was sufficiently important to outweigh the dissenters' concerns that the juvenile court's unique therapeutic function would be thwarted and that "differences between juvenile courts and traditional criminal courts [would be eroded]."[62]

Five years later, the Court in *Breed v. Jones*[63] held that the protections of the double jeopardy clause of the fifth amendment prohibit the adult criminal prosecution of a youth after a conviction in juvenile court for the same offense. Although the Court framed the issue in terms of the applicability of an explicit provision of the Bill of Rights to state proceedings,[64] it resolved the question by recognizing the functional equivalence and the identical interests of the defendants in a delinquency proceeding and an adult criminal trial.[65]

Only in *McKeiver v. Pennsylvania*[66] did the Court decline to extend the procedural safeguards of adult criminal prosecutions to juvenile court proceedings.[67] The Court in *McKeiver* held that a jury is not required in a juvenile proceeding because the only requirement for "fundamental fairness" in such proceedings is "accurate factfinding," a requirement that can be as well satisfied by a judge as by a jury.[68] In suggesting that due process in the juvenile context required nothing more than accurate fact-finding, however, the Court departed significantly from its own prior analyses, which relied on the *dual* rationales of accurate fact-finding and protection against governmental oppression.[69] Furthermore, in insisting that the accuracy of the fact-finding process is the only concern of fundamental fairness, the Court ignored its own analysis in *Gault* in which it held that the fifth amendment's privilege against self-incrimination was necessary in order to protect against governmental oppression even though accurate fact-finding might be impeded.[70] Justice Brennan's concurring-dissenting opinion in *McKeiver* notes that protection from governmental oppression might also be afforded by an alternative method, such as a public trial that would render the adjudicative process visible and accountable to the community.[71] The Court, however, denied that protection against government oppression was required at all[72] and, invoking the mythology of the sympathetic, paternalistic juvenile court judge, rejected the argument that the inbred, closed nature of the juvenile court could prejudice the accuracy of fact-finding.[73]

In denying juveniles the constitutional right to jury trials, the Court in *McKeiver* departed from its earlier mode of analysis[74] and emphasized the adverse impact that this right would have on the informality, flexibility, and confidentiality of juvenile court proceedings.[75] Rather than asking whether the constitutional right in question would have an adverse impact on any unique benefits of the juvenile court, the Court asked whether the right to a jury trial would positively aid or strengthen the functioning of the juvenile justice system.[76] Although the *McKeiver* Court found faults with the juvenile process, it asserted that imposing jury trials would in no way correct those deficiencies and would make the juvenile process unduly formal and adversarial. The Court did not consider, however, whether there might be any offsetting advantages to increased formality in juvenile proceedings[77] or to what extent its earlier decision in *Gault*[78] had effectively foreclosed its renewed concern with flexibility and informality at the ad-judicatory stage. The Court also gave no indication why a more formal hearing was incompatible with the therapeutic dispositions that a young delinquent might receive. Although the Court decried the possibility of a public trial,[79] it presented no evidence or arguments to support its conclusion that publicity would be undesirable and that confidentiality of juvenile court proceedings was an indispensable element of the juvenile justice process.[80]

Together, *Gault*, *Winship*, and *McKeiver* precipitated a procedural revolution in the juvenile court system that has unintentionally but inevitably transformed its original Progressive conception. Progressive reformers envisioned the commission of an offense as essentially secondary to a determination of the "real needs" of a child—the child's social circumstances and environment. Intervention was premised on the need for rehabilitation and social uplift, not on the commission of an offense. Although *McKeiver* refused to extend the right to a jury trial to juveniles, *Gault* and *Winship* imported the adversarial model, the privilege against self-incrimination, attorneys, the criminal standard of proof, and the primacy of factual and legal guilt as a constitutional prerequisite to intervention. By emphasizing criminal procedural regularity in the determination of delinquency, the Supreme Court shifted the focus of the juvenile court from the Progressive emphasis on the "real needs" of the child to proof of the commission of criminal acts, thereby effectively transforming juvenile proceedings into criminal prosecutions.[81]

Since these decisions, the transformation of the juvenile court has continued through legislative, judicial, and administrative action. In addition to increased procedural formality, there have been major changes in other parts of the system. The Supreme Court's recognition that the Progressive juvenile court failed to realize its benevolent therapeutic promise has led to

changes in the jurisdiction of the juvenile court. Diversion, deinstitutionalization, and "decriminalization" of status offenders have altered the role
of the juvenile court[82] as states have removed status jurisdiction from their
juvenile codes entirely,[83] redefined it to avoid the stigma of crime/delin-
quency adjudications,[84] and limited the dispositions that noncriminal offenders can receive.[85] Similarly, legislatures and courts have extensively
scrutinized the handling of serious young offenders, and the most difficult
youths in the juvenile justice process are now removed to criminal courts
for prosecution as adults.[86] These jurisdictional modifications narrow the
scope of the juvenile court both at the "hard" end, through the removal
of serious juvenile offenders, and at the "soft" end, through the removal
of status offenders. At the same time that juvenile jurisdiction is being nar-
rowed, the dispositions of the remaining delinquents increasingly reflect the
impact of the "justice model," in which "just deserts" rather than "real
needs" prescribe the appropriate sentence.[87] Principles of proportionality
and determinacy based on the present offense and prior record, not the best
interests of the child, dictate the length, location, and intensity of intervention.[88] Finally, as the dispositions by the juvenile court increasingly subordinate the "needs" of the offender to the nature of the offense and
traditional justifications for punishment, the formal procedural safeguards
of the juvenile court increasingly resemble those of the adult criminal process.[89] These four developments—the removal of status offenders, the
waiver of serious offenders into the adult system, the increasing punitive-
ness of dispositions, and the growing emphasis on procedural formality—
have contributed to the criminalization of the juvenile court. . . .

NOTES

1. Barry Feld, "Criminalizing Juvenile Justice: Rules of Procedure for the Juvenile Court," *Minnesota Law Review*, vol. 69, no. 2 (December 1984): 141–276.
    2. Howard Ball, *Courts and Politics: The Federal Judicial System* (Englewood
Cliffs, NJ: Prentice Hall, 1980), p. 11.
    3. Ibid., p. 13.
    4. Lawrence Baum, *The Supreme Court*, 4th ed. (Washington, DC: Congres-
sional Quarterly Press, 1992), p. 122.
    5. Ibid., p. 132.
    6. Ibid., p. 218.
    7. Ibid., pp. 226–27.
    8. Ibid., p. 229.
    9. Ibid., p. 186.
    10. Professor of Law, University of Minnesota. I benefited from the critical com-
ments of a number of colleagues who reviewed an earlier draft of this Article,
including Ms. Kathy Bishop and Professors Daniel Farber, Richard Frase, and Robert Levy. Of course, they bear no responsibility for my failure to heed their advice.
This Article could not have been completed without the research contributions of

a number of students whose assistance is gratefully acknowledged, including Maria Wyant Cuzzo, Gadi Hill, Elizabeth Neufeld-Smith, Polly Peterson, Jeff Saunders, Agnes Schipper, Ann Underbrink, and Mary Ann Wray.

11. 387 U.S. 1 (1967).

12. For various interpretations of the development of the juvenile justice system, see generally J. INVERARITY, P. LAUDERDALE & B. FELD, LAW AND SOCIETY: SOCIOLOGICAL PERSPECTIVES ON CRIMINAL LAW 173 (1983); A. PLATT, THE CHILDSAVERS: THE INVENTION OF DELINQUENCY (2d ed. 1977); D. ROTHMAN, CONSCIENCE AND CONVENIENCE: THE ASYLUM AND ITS ALTERNATIVES IN PROGRESSIVE AMERICA (1980); E. RYERSON, THE BEST-LAID PLANS: AMERICA'S JUVENILE COURT EXPERIMENT (1978); S. SCHLOSSMAN, LOVE AND THE AMERICAN DELINQUENT: THE THEORY AND PRACTICE OF "PROGRESSIVE" JUVENILE JUSTICE 1825–1920 (1977); JUVENILE JUSTICE: THE PROGRESSIVE LEGACY AND CURRENT REFORMS (L. Empey ed. 1979) [hereinafter cited as Juvenile Justice]; Fox, *Juvenile Justice Reform: An Historical Perspective*, 22 STAN. L. REV. 1187 (1970); Mack, *The Juvenile Court*, 23 HARV. L. REV. 104 (1909).

13. *See, e.g.*, Note, *Minnesota Juvenile Court Rules: Brightening One World for Juveniles*, 54 Minn. L. Rev. 303, 303 (1969).

14. *See generally* T. COCHRAN, BUSINESS IN AMERICAN LIFE (1972); S. HAYS, THE RESPONSE TO INDUSTRIALISM 1885–1914 (1957); R. HOFSTADTER, THE AGE OF REFORM: FROM BRYAN TO F.D.R. (1955); G. KOLKO, THE TRIUMPH OF CONSERVATISM: A REINTERPRETATION OF AMERICAN HISTORY, 1900–1916 (1963); D. NOBLE, AMERICA BY DESIGN: SCIENCE, TECHNOLOGY, AND THE RISE OF CORPORATE CAPITALISM (1977); H. THORELLI, THE FEDERAL ANTI-TRUST POLICY (1954); A. TRACHTENBERG, THE INCORPORATION OF AMERICA (1982); J. WEINSTEIN, THE CORPORATE IDEAL IN THE LIBERAL STATE 1900–1918 (1968); R. WIEBE, THE SEARCH FOR ORDER 1877–1920 (1967).

15. The "new immigrants" differed in language, religion, political heritage, and culture from the dominant Anglo-Protestant Americans. They predominantly were peasants, and their cultural and linguistic differences from the dominant culture, coupled with their numbers, hindered their assimilation. *See, e.g.*, R. HOFSTADTER, *supra* note 14, at 8. *See generally* U.S. BUREAU OF THE CENSUS, HISTORICAL STATISTICS OF THE UNITED STATES, COLONIAL TIMES TO 1970 (Bicentennial ed. 1976) (statistics about immigration and the changing demographics of the United States population).

16. *See, e.g.*, W. TRATTNER, FROM POOR LAW TO WELFARE STATE: A HISTORY OF SOCIAL WELFARE IN AMERICA 135 (3d ed. 1984); H. WILENSKY & C. LEBEAUX, INDUSTRIAL SOCIETY AND SOCIAL WELFARE 115–32 (1958). The needs of the urban masses increased by the end of the nineteenth century because of changes in the economic structure and the difficulties of assimilation created by linguistic and cultural difference. *See, e.g.*, H. HIGHAM, STRANGERS IN THE LAND: PATTERNS OF AMERICAN NATIVISM, 1860–1925, at 87 (1974); R. HOFSTADTER, *supra* note 14, at 8.

17. *See, e.g.*, J. KETT, RITES OF PASSAGE: ADOLESCENCE IN AMERICA 1790 TO THE PRESENT 114–16 (1977); HAREVEN, *The Dynamics of Kin in an Industrial Community*, in TURNING POINTS: HISTORICAL, AND SOCIOLOG-

ICAL ESSAYS ON THE FAMILY 151 (J. Demos & S. Boocock eds. 1978); HAR-
EVEN & VINOVSKIS, *Patterns of Childbearing in Late Nineteenth-Century
America: The Determinants of Marital Fertility in Five Massachusetts Towns in
1880*, in FAMILY AND POPULATION IN NINETEENTH-CENTURY AMERICA
85 (T. Hareven & M. Vinovskis eds. 1978). *But see* C. Degler, AT ODDS:
WOMEN AND THE FAMILY IN AMERICA FROM THE REVOLUTION TO
THE PRESENT 9, 178–209 (1980) (industrialization is an inadequate explanation
of the mid-nineteenth century decline in fertility; that decline is caused by women's
"increasing consciousness of themselves as individuals" and, consequently, their
desire to control reproduction). *See generally* C. LASCH, HAVEN IN A HEART-
LESS WORLD: THE FAMILY BESIEGED 6–10 (1977) (effects on family life of
the nineteenth-century emancipation of women and the growth of industrialization);
E. SHORTER, THE MAKING OF THE MODERN FAMILY 205–68 (1975) (ex-
plaining changes in family life as consequences of the growth of laissez-faire
capitalism); Wells, *Women's Lives Transformed: Demographic and Family Patterns
in America, 1600–1970*, in WOMEN IN AMERICA: A HISTORY 16, 18–24 (C.
Berkin & M. Norton eds. 1979) (comparing changes in household structure and
women's place in that structure to the increase in life expectancies, the decrease in
fertility, and the migration to the cities that resulted from industrialization).

18. *See generally* P. ARIES, CENTURIES OF CHILDHOOD 329 (1962) (sum-
marizing the development of the "modern theory" of childhood that suggests that
children are not small adults, but rather that childhood is a separate stage of development); C. DEGLER, *supra* note 17, at 86–110 (change in child-rearing methods of nineteenth century related to new perception of children as innocent and
trainable); J. GILLIS, YOUTH AND HISTORY: TRADITION AND CHANGE: IN
EUROPEAN AGE RELATIONS 1770-PRESENT 98–105 (1974) (concern for children extended to older youths); D. HUNT, PARENTS AND CHILDREN IN HIS-
TORY: THE PSYCHOLOGY OF FAMILY LIFE IN EARLY MODERN FRANCE
33–36 (1970) (slow emergence of the concept of "childhood" in France, beginning
in the Middle Ages and attaining full realization during the ancien regime); J. KETT,
supra note 17, at 109–43 (origins of the idea of "adolescence" from 1840–1880);
B. WISHY, THE CHILD AND THE REPUBLIC 94–114 (1968) (new ideas of childhood and child rearing as reflected in children's books and child-rearing manuals
for parents from 1860–1900); deMause, *The Evolution of Childhood*, in THE HIS-
TORY OF CHILDHOOD 1 (L. deMause ed. 1974) (noting the gradual shift from
a norm of physical and sexual abuse of children to one promoting socialization;
the new norm viewed children as malleable creatures to be trained by adults to
conform to societal mores).

Childhood as a recognizable developmental stage is a recent phenomenon. Prior
to the past two or three centuries, there was neither a fully separate, highly valued
social status based on age nor a corresponding age segregation. Young people were
perceived as miniature adults or inadequate versions of their parents who did not
require any special protection or discrete legal status. Even in the early nineteenth
century the newer views of children were only beginning to alter child-rearing practices. This trend was accentuated as commercial and industrial developments en-
abled young people to achieve economic independence. *See* Marks, *Detours on the
Road to Maturity: A View of the Legal Conception of Growing Up and Letting
Go*, 39 LAW & CONTEMP. PROBS. 78, 80 (1975). By the end of the nineteenth

century, however, the preparation of children for adult roles and their autonomous departures from home became much more restrictive. See authorities cited *supra* notes 12 & 17.

19. *See, e.g.*, A. PLATT, *supra* note 12, at 75–83; *see also* B. WISHY, *supra* note 18, at 116 (discussing increased role of mothers in child development).

20. *See generally* authorities cited *supra* note 14.

21. *See generally* B. BRINGHURST, ANTITRUST AND THE OIL MONOPOLY (1979) (Antitrust); L. CREMIN, THE TRANSFORMATION OF THE SCHOOL: PROGRESSIVISM IN AMERICAN EDUCATION, 1876–1957 (1961) (compulsory education); G. KOLKO, RAILROADS AND REGULATION 1877–1916 (1965) (railroad regulation); D. ROTHMAN, *supra* note 12 (criminal justice reform); H. THORELLI, *supra* note 14 (antitrust); S.TIFFIN, IN WHOSE BEST INTEREST? CHILD WELFARE REFORM IN THE PROGRESSIVE ERA (1982) (child welfare); W. TRATTNER, CRUSADE FOR THE CHILDREN: A HISTORY OF THE NATIONAL CHILD LABOR COMMITTEE AND CHILD LABOR REFORM IN NEW YORK STATE (1965) (child labor laws); W. TRATTNER, *supra* note 16 (urban welfare reform); R. WIEBE, BUSINESSMEN AND REFORM (1962) (business regulation); Hays, *The Politics of Reform in Municipal Government in the Progressive Era*, PAC. NW. Q., Oct. 1964, at 152 ("good government").

22. *See, e.g.*, S. HAYS, *supra* note 14, at 156; R. WIEBE, *supra* note 14, at 166–70. Professors Hays and Wiebe attribute Progressive reforms to the newly emerging middle class of college-educated technocrats, corporate managers, and professionals who viewed the decline of the older order as an opportunity to realize their own potentials through the development of rational, scientific, and managerial solutions to a host of social problems. *See* S. HAYS, *supra* note 14, at 73–74; R. WIEBE, *supra* note 14, at 111–32. This interpretation explains the role of the detached, objective professional and scientific rationality and expertise that recurs throughout most Progressive reform efforts. *See* Kennedy, *Overview: The Progressive Era*, 37 HISTORIAN 453, 460 (1975); Stone, *A Spectre is Haunting America: An Interpretation of Progressivism*, 3 J. LIBERTARIAN STUD. 239, 243–44 (1979). There have been extensive and often conflicting interpretations of the origins and goals of the Progressive reformers. *Compare* R. HOFSTADTER, *supra* note 14 and Kennedy, *supra* (Progressive era was an era of transition) with R. WIEBE, *supra* note 14 and G. KOLKO, *supra* note 14 (emphasizing conservative aspects of Progressivism).

23. *See, e.g.*, F. ALLEN, *Legal Values and the Rehabilitative Ideal*, in THE BORDERLAND OF CRIMINAL JUSTICE 25, 26–27 (1964) [hereinafter cited as BORDERLAND]; F. ALLEN, THE DECLINE OF THE REHABILITATIVE IDEAL: PENAL POLICY AND SOCIAL PURPOSE 11–15 (1981) [hereinafter cited as F. ALLEN, DECLINE]; D. ROTHMAN, *supra* note 12, at 60–61; Allen, *The Decline of the Rehabilitative Ideal in American Criminal Justice*, 27 CLEV. ST. L. REV. 147, 150–51 (1978). Progressives felt no reservations when they attempted to "Americanize" the immigrants and poor through a variety of agencies of assimilation and acculturation to become sober, virtuous, middle-class Americans. D. ROTHMAN, *supra* note 12, at 49.

24. As one author noted, many Progressive programs shared a unifying child-centered theme. "The child was the carrier of tomorrow's hope whose innocence

and freedom made him singularly receptive to education in rational, humane be-
havior. Protect him, nurture him, and in his manhood he would create that bright
new world of the Progressives' vision." R. WIEBE, *supra* note 14, at 169; *see also*
J. KETT, *supra* note 17, at 226–27 (many groups were instrumental in structuring
the activities of children); REPORT OF PANEL ON YOUTH OF THE PRESI-
DENT'S SCIENCE ADVISORY COMMITTEE, YOUTH: TRANSITION TO
ADULTHOOD 34 (1974) [hereinafter cited as YOUTH: TRANSITION TO
ADULTHOOD] (the United States adopted a variety of laws to protect children
against dangerous labor and neglect, to require them to attend school, and to secure
for them a better future); D. ROTHMAN, *supra* note 12, at 206–07 (Progressives
attempted to influence immigrant children to adopt the American way of life); E.
RYERSON, *supra* note 12, at 27–31 (the establishment of the juvenile court was
an outgrowth of a more comprehensive child-study movement, based on a view of
children as innocents); S. TIFFIN, *supra* note 21, at 61–83 (institutional child care
in the nineteenth and early twentieth centuries was based on children's innocence
and malleability of character); Schlossman & Wallach, *The Crime of Precocious
Sexuality: Female Juvenile Delinquency in the Progressive Era*, 48 HARV. EDUC.
REV. 65, 67 (1978) (girls were discriminated against in the early twentieth century
juvenile court because it was believed that they needed more protection than boys).

25. *See* Empey, *Introduction: The Social Construction of Childhood and Juvenile
Justice*, in THE FUTURE OF CHILDHOOD AND JUVENILE JUSTICE, 1, 19–21
(L. Empey ed. 1979); Empey, *The Progressive Legacy and the Concept of Childhood*, in JUVENILE JUSTICE, *supra* note 12, at 3, 25–28. All four of these reforms—child labor laws, child welfare laws, compulsory education requirements,
and the juvenile court system—reflected the central Progressive assumption that the
ideal way to prepare children for life was to strengthen the nuclear family, shield
children from adult roles, and formally educate them for upward mobility. *See, e.g.*,
D. ROTHMAN, *supra* note 12, at 206–09; YOUTH: TRANSITION TO ADULT-
HOOD, *supra* note 24, at 25.

26. *See* D. ROTHMAN, *supra* note 12, at 43.

27. *See, e.g.*, D. MATZA, DELINQUENCY AND DRIFT 5 (1964); D. ROTH-
MAN, *supra* note 12, at 50–51.

28. The new criminology, as distinguished from the old theory of "free will,"
asserted a scientific determinism of deviance and sought to identify the causal var-
iables producing crime and delinquency. In its quest for scientific legitimacy, criminology borrowed both methodology and vocabulary from the medical profession.
Medical metaphors such as pathology, infection, diagnosis, and treatment were
popular analogues for criminal justice professionals, who also prescribed an individualized approach to the diagnosis and cure of each offender. *See, e.g.*, A. PLATT,
supra note 12, at 18; D. ROTHMAN, *supra* note 12, at 56.

29. *See* E. RYERSON, *supra* note 12, at 22. These deterministic interpretations
of human behavior caused a redirection of research efforts in order to identify the
causes of crime by scientifically studying the offender, because the ability to identify
the causes of crime also implied the correlative ability to "cure" crime. Although
early positivistic criminology attributed criminal behavior to hereditary and biological factors, these views were soon challenged by social and environmental explanations of crime. The social science professionals in psychology, sociology, and
social work who were emerging from colleges and universities acquired a profes-

sional stake in environmental explanations of deviance, because environmental factors allowed for greater possibilities of intervention and cure than did imperious biological determinism. *See, e.g.,* J. HAWES, CHILDREN IN URBAN SOCIETY: JUVENILE, DELINQUENCY IN NINETEENTH-CENTURY AMERICA 192 (1971); R. LUBOVE, THE PROFESSIONAL ALTRUIST 56 (1967); A. PLATT, *supra* note 12, at 53, E. RYERSON, *supra* note 12, at 24; W. TRATTNER, *supra* note 16, at 186. The environmental interpretations of deviance attributed deviance to the social and economic conditions associated with immigrant ghettos and urban slums into which the benefits of the American society could not penetrate. Environmentalists emphasized the impacts of industrialization and urbanization in the process of crime causation. Although there was always a touch of moralism condemning those who succumbed to these deleterious influences, there was also an appreciation of the vulnerability of the urban poor to economic forces and social conditions beyond their control. *See, e.g.,* E. RYERSON, *supra* note 12, at 24.

30. These reforms included increased use of probation and indeterminate sentencing, parole supervision following release, and the juvenile court. *See* F. ALLEN, *Legal Values and the Rehabilitative Ideal* in BORDERLAND, *supra* note 23, at 25, 26; *see also* F. ALLEN, DECLINE, *supra* note 23, at 6 (twentieth century innovations in criminal justice reflect the Rehabilitative Ideal); ALLEN, *supra* note 23, at 149 (same).

31. A pervasive feature of all Progressive criminal justice reforms was discretionary decision making by experts. Discretion was necessary because identifying the causes and prescribing the cures for delinquency required an individualized approach that precluded uniformity of treatment or standardization of criteria. *See* D. ROTHMAN, *supra* note 12, at 54. It is probably not coincidental that the increased flexibility, indeterminacy, and discretion in social control practices corresponded to the increasing volume and changing characteristics of offenders during this period. *See id.* at 77; *see also* Feld, *supra* note 12, at 182 (discretion afforded flexibility in social control of immigrants and their children).

A flourishing Rehabilitative Ideal requires both a belief in the maleability of human behavior and a basic moral consensus about the appropriate directions of human change. It also requires agreement about means and ends, the goals of change, and the strategies necessary to achieve them. Progressives believed that the new sciences of human behavior provided them with the tools for systematic human change. They also believed in the virtues of the social order and the propriety of imposing the values of a middle-class lifestyle on immigrants and the poor. *See* F. ALLEN, *Legal Values and the Rehabilitative Ideal,* in BORDERLAND, *supra* note 23, at 25.

32. *See* Hazard, *The Jurisprudence of Juvenile Deviance,* in PURSUING JUSTICE FOR THE CHILD 4 (M. Rosenheim ed. 1976) [hereinafter cited as PURSUING JUSTICE]; Mennel, *Attitudes and Policies Toward Juvenile Delinquency in the United States: A Historigraphical Review,* in 4 CRIME AND SOCIAL JUSTICE 191, 207–15 (M. Tonry & N. Morris eds. 1983); Platt, *The Triumph of Benevolence: The Origins of the Juvenile Justice System in the United States,* in CRIMINAL JUSTICE IN AMERICA 356, 377–84 (R. Quinney ed. 1974); Schultz, *The Cycle of Juvenile Court History,* 19 CRIME & DELINQ. 457, 458–59 (1973). *See generally* authorities, cited *supra* note 12.

Many of the characteristics of the Progressive juvenile court can be traced to the

Houses of Refuge that emerged in the first third of the nineteenth century. The Houses were the first specialized agency for the control of youth. *See, e.g.,* H. FINESTONE, VICTIMS OF CHANGE: JUVENILE DELINQUENTS IN AMERICAN SOCIETY 25–27 (1976); J. HAWES, *supra* note 29, at 144–45; J. KETT, *supra* note, 17, at 122, 222; R. MENNEL, THORNS AND THISTLES: JUVENILE DELINQUENTS IN THE UNITED STATES 1825–1940 at 130–35 (1973); R. PICKETT, HOUSE OF REFUGE: ORIGINS OF JUVENILE REFORM IN NEW YORK STATE 1815–1857, at v (1969); D. ROTHMAN, THE DISCOVERY OF THE ASYLUM: SOCIAL ORDER AND DISORDER IN THE NEW REPUBLIC 207 (1971); Fox, *supra* note 12, at 1187–89, 1207–12. One authority contends that

developments in the 19th century laid the foundation for the subsequent development of the juvenile justice system in the United States. . . . [L]egislation establishing the juvenile court in Chicago did no more than formalize long-standing practices for dealing with juveniles in Illinois. . . . [I]n almost every state the legal and ideological innovations typically associated with the juvenile court (e.g., the extension of legal control over noncriminal children, the denial of due process, and the legalization of the rehabilitative ideal) had occurred before the advent of children's courts, as a result of earlier legislation establishing juvenile reformatories.

Sutton, *Social Structure, Institutions, and the Legal Status of Children in the United States,* 88 AM. J. SOC. 915, 917 (1983)

33. *See, e.g.,* Cogan, *Juvenile Law, Before and After the Entrance of "Parens Patriae,"* 22 S.C.L. REV. 147, 181 (1970); Curtis, *The Checkered Career of Parens Patriae: State as Parent or Tyrant?,* 25 DE PAUL L. REV. 895, 901–02 (1976); Pisciotta, *Saving the Children: The Promise and Practice of Parens Patriae, 1838– 98,* 28 CRIME & DELINQ. 410, 410 (1982); Rendleman, *Parens Patriae: From Chancery to the Juvenile Court,* 23 S.C.L. REV. 205, 207–10 (1971). The leading case of the period, *Ex parte* Crouse, 4 Whart. 9 (Pa. 1838), reflects not only the ideology of environmentalism and preventive intervention, but also the breadth of the parens patriae doctrine and the futility of legal challenges to state intervention. *See id.* at 11; *see also* D. ROTHMAN, *supra* note 12, at 212 (reformers' use of parens patriae to justify state intervention); Fox, *supra* note 12, at 1192–93 (the emergence of the doctrine of parens patriae).

34. The juvenile court sought to aid children as well as to control their criminal behavior. Historically, controlling youth through the criminal law presented the stark alternatives of a criminal conviction and punishment as an adult or an acquittal or dismissal that freed the youth from all supervision. Jury or judicial nullification to avoid punishment excluded many youths from control, particularly minor offenders. Desires for greater supervision and control, rather than leniency, animated many reformers. They sought a system that would allow the law to intervene affirmatively in the lives of young offenders, rather than only to impose punishment. The rehabilitative juvenile court provided Progressives with a middle ground between punishing behavior through the criminal process, thereby criminalizing a youth, and ignoring it altogether, thereby encouraging a resumption of a criminal career. *See, e.g.,* J. HAWES, *supra* note 29, at 162; A. PLATT, *supra* note 12, at 46–55, 101–36; D. ROTHMAN, *supra* note 12, at 213; E. RYERSON, *supra* note 12, at 33; Fox, *supra* note 12, at 1194, 1212–15.

35. *See* authorities cited *supra* notes 12 & 32; *see also* Andrews & Cohn, *Un-*

governability: The Unjustifiable Jurisdiction, 83 YALE L.J. 1383, 1388 (1974) (discussing the significance of juvenile adjudications for status offenses); Garlock, *"Wayward" Children and the Law, 1820–1900: The Genesis of the Status Offense Jurisdiction of the Juvenile Court,* 13 GA. L. REV. 341, 342–43 (1979) (questioning whether juvenile courts should refuse to exercise jurisdiction over status offenses); Rosenberg & Rosenberg, *The Legacy of the Stubborn and Rebellious Son,* 74 MICH. L. REV. 1097, 1098–99 (1976) (noting that every state and the District of Columbia have statutes giving the juvenile court jurisdiction over status offenses); Schlossman & Wallach, *supra* note 24, at 70, 81 (discussing the purpose of the Progressives' concern with certain behavior).

36. *See* A. PLATT, *supra* note 12, at 135. Ironically, the juvenile court simultaneously affirmed the primacy of the nuclear family and expanded the power of the state to intervene in instances of parental inadequacy. See D. ROTHMAN, *supra* note 12, at 212. Child rearing had become too complex to relegate to unsupervised family control. Immigrant and lower class families, caught in the conflict of cultures, could not be expected adequately to Americanize their children, and state supervision was imposed to assure that the next generation adopted an acceptable middle-class way of life. *See id.* at 206. The juvenile court provided the agency through which Anglo-Protestant Americans defined the norms of family and childhood to which the outsiders were to adhere. *See* E. RYERSON, *supra* note 12, at 48.

37. One consequence of judicial discretion, however, "was a system that made the personality of the judge, his likes and dislikes, attitudes and prejudices, consistencies and caprices, the decisive element in shaping the character of his courtroom." D. ROTHMAN, *supra* note 12, at 238.

38. *See id.* at 215. A system of decision making in which literally everything is relevant to the ultimate determination of a child's "best interests" necessarily is heavily dependent on sound judgment and professional expertise. The Progressives envisioned a well-trained probation staff schooled in the principles of psychology and social work, aided by mental hygiene clinics and psychological diagnostic services, and able to provide the scientific undergirding that would assure consistency in dispositions. *Id.* at 242–43.

39. *See, e.g.,* PRESIDENT'S COMMISSION ON LAW ENFORCEMENT AND ADMINISTRATION OF JUSTICE, TASK FORCE REPORT: JUVENILE DELINQUENCY AND YOUTH CRIME 92 (1967) [hereinafter cited as JUVENILE DELINQUENCY AND YOUTH CRIME]; D. ROTHMAN, *supra* note 12, at 218; see also authorities cited *supra* notes 12 & 32.

40. *See* E. RYERSON, *supra* note 12, at 38.

41. *See, e.g.,* Handler, *The Juvenile Court and the Adversary System: Problems of Function and Form* 1965 WIS. L. REV. 7, 8; Note, *Juvenile Delinquents: The Police, State Courts, and Individualized Justice,* 79 HARV. L. REV. 775, 775–76 (1966).

42. 387 U.S. 1 (1967).

43. *Id.* at 22.

44. On the "criminalization" of the juvenile court, see, e.g., Feld, *Juvenile Court Legislative Reform and the Serious Young Offender: Dismantling the "Rehabilitative Ideal,"* 65 MINN. L. REV. 167, 202 (1980). On the due process revolution in the juvenile court, *see, e.g.,* Paulsen, *The Constitutional Domestication of the*

Juvenile Court, 1967 SUP. CT. REV. 233, 237; Paulsen, *Kent v. United States: The Constitutional Context of Juvenile Cases,* 1966 SUP. CT. REV. 167, 168–69 [hereinafter cited as Paulsen, *Constitutional Context*].

45. 387 U.S. at 4.

46. Gault 387 U.S. at 7–8 (brackets in original). If Gault had been an adult his offense would have resulted in no more than a $50 fine or two months' imprisonment; as a juvenile, however, he was subject to incarceration for up to six years, the duration of his minority. Id. at 8–9. Although Arizona has increased the penalties than can be imposed in misdemeanor cases, they still are much less severe than the dispositions juveniles can receive. *Cf.* ARIZ. REV. STAT. ANN. §§ 13–2904 (1978) (Gault's conduct is a class 1 misdemeanor); 13–707 (a 12–802(A) (class 1 misdemeanor carries a maximum fine of $1000).

47. *See Gault,* 387 U.S. at 14–17.

48. *Id.* at 18.

49. *See id.* at 21.

50. The Supreme Court noted that:

The fact of the matter is that, however euphemistic the title, a "receiving home" or an "industrial school" for juveniles is an institution of confinement in which the child is incarcerated for a greater or lesser time. His world becomes "a building with whitewashed walls, regimented routine, and institutional hours . . ." Instead of mother and father and sisters and brothers and friends and classmates, his world is peopled by guards, custodians, state employees, and "delinquents" confined with him for anything from waywardness to rape and homicide. . . . [U]nder our Constitution, the condition of being a [child] does not justify a kangaroo court.

Id. at 27–28.

51. *See id.* at 31–57; *see also id.* at 22, 24, 27 (discussing whether juveniles should be afforded constitutional protection through procedural safeguards); Rosenberg, *The Constitutional Rights of Children Charged with Crime: Proposal for a Return to the Not So Distant Past,* 27 UCLA L. REV. 656, 662–63 (1980) (constitutional protections should attach in proceedings that may result in incarceration of a child). The *Gault* opinion is unclear regarding whether the various rights afforded juveniles attach because of the possibility of institutional commitment, *see, e.g., Gault,* 387 U.S. at 13, or if they attach only when the youth is actually committed to a state correctional facility, *see id.* at 36–37, 41, 44, 49, 56, 57; *cf.* Schultz & Cohen, *Isolationism in Juvenile Court Jurisprudence,* in PURSUING JUSTICE, *supra* note 32, at 20, 28 (*Gault* opinion unclear about basis of extension of right to juveniles). *Compare* Duncan v. Louisiana, 391 U.S. 145 (1968) (sixth amendment right to jury trial in state criminal proceedings determined by the penalty authorized by law rather than the sentence actually imposed) *with* Scott v. Illinois, 440 U.S. 367 (1979) (sixth amendment right to counsel in state misdemeanor trials attaches only if a jail sentence is actually imposed).

52. *See Gault,* 387 U.S. at 13. The Court specifically held that "[w]e do not in this opinion consider the impact of these constitutional provisions upon the totality of the relationship of the juvenile and the state. We do not even consider the entire process relating to juvenile 'delinquents.' " *Id.; see also* McCarthy, *Pre-Adjudicatory Rights in Juvenile Court: An Historical and Constitutional Analysis,* 42 U. PITT. L. REV. 457, 459–60 (1981) (discussing the limitations on juveniles'

procedural rights). The Court's holding did not address a juvenile's rights in either the preadjudicatory (i.e., intake and detention) or postadjudicatory (i.e., disposition) stages of the proceeding, but narrowly confined itself to the actual adjudication of guilt or innocence in a trial-like setting. *See Gault* 387 U.S. at 13, 31 n.48. As will be suggested in the analysis of the Minnesota Supreme Court's Rules of Procedure for Juvenile Court, the United States Supreme Court's reluctance to address the nonadjudicatory stages of the juvenile process has resulted in the consistently "second class" procedural characteristics of the juvenile court. *See* Feld, *supra* note 1 at notes 284–331, 344–387, and accompanying text.

53. *See Gault* 387 U.S. at 21. In its subsequent delinquency decisions, the Court balanced the particular function that a constitutional right served against its impact on the unique processes of the juvenile court and used the degree of impairment of the traditional juvenile court's functions as one of the criteria in determining whether a right would be afforded to juveniles. *See, e.g.,* Breed v. Jones, 421 U.S. 519, 535–39 (1975); McKeiver v. Pennsylvania, 403 U.S. 528, 547 (1971). In *Gault*, however, the Court was adjudicating constitutional rights in a procedural void.

54. The sixth amendment provides:

In all criminal prosecutions, the accused shall enjoy the right to a speedy and public trial, by an impartial jury of the State and district wherein the crime shall have been committed . . . and to be informed of the nature and cause of the accusation; to be confronted with the witnesses against him; to have compulsory process for obtaining witnesses in his favor, and to have the Assistance of Counsel for his defence.

U.S. Const. amend. VI. The discussion of the notice requirement in *Gault* made no reference to the sixth amendment's provision for notice; rather, the Court held that "due process of law requires notice of the sort we have described—that is, notice which would be deemed constitutionally adequate in a civil or criminal proceeding." *Gault* 387 U.S. at 33. Similarly, although the Court described a delinquency proceeding as "comparable in seriousness to a felony prosecution," *id.* at 36, the right to counsel in a juvenile proceeding is grounded in the "due process clause of the fourteenth amendment" rather than the sixth amendment's right to counsel, *id.* at 41. Finally, the Court's analysis of the right to confront and examine witnesses rested on "our law and constitutional requirements" rather than the specific language of the sixth amendment. *Id.* at 57. In deciding the applicability of the fifth amendment privilege against self-incrimination, the majority resorted to an analytical strategy akin to selective incorporation, finding a "functional equivalence" between a delinquency proceeding and an adult criminal trial. *See id.* at 50.

Cases such as Adamson v. California, 332 U.S. 46 (1947); Betts v. Brady, 316 U.S. 455 (1942), *overruled*, Gideon v. Wainwright, 372 U.S. 335 (1963); Palko v. Connecticut, 302 U.S. 319 (1937); and Twining v. New Jersey, 211 U.S. 78 (1908), reflect the historical constitutional debate between proponents of "selective incorporation" and proponents of "fundamental fairness" and "total incorporation" of the Bill of Rights. *See, e.g.,* Henkin, *"Selective Incorporation" in the Fourteenth Amendment,* 73 YALE L.J. 74 (1963); Kadish, *Methodology and Criteria in Due Process Adjudication—A Survey and Criticism,* 66 YALE L.J. 319, 327–33 (1967); Rosenberg, *supra* note 51, at 666–67.

The irony of the "fundamental fairness" strategy employed by the Court in *Gault* to provide procedural safeguards is that this same strategy later permitted the Court to deny juveniles a jury trial by finding that the right was not fundamental. *See* McKeiver v. Pennsylvania, 403 U.S. 528 (1971); *infra* notes 66–80 and accompanying text. The irony stems from the fact that in the years between *Gault* and *McKeiver*, the Supreme Court decided Duncan v. Louisiana, 391 U.S. 145 (1968), which held that the sixth amendment right to a jury trial was applicable to the states via the fourteenth amendment due process clause because it was "fundamental to the American scheme of justice." *Duncan*, 391 U.S. at 149.

55.

It would be entirely unrealistic to carve out of the Fifth Amendment all statements by juveniles on the ground that these cannot lead to "criminal" involvement. In the first place, juvenile proceedings to determine "delinquency," which may lead to commitment to a state institution, must be regarded as "criminal" for purposes of the privilege against self-incrimination. . . . [C]ommitment is a deprivation of liberty. It is incarceration against one's will, whether it is called "criminal" or "civil."

In re Gault, 387 U.S. at 49–50; accord Addington v. Texas, 441 U.S. 418, 428 (1979) (criminal and delinquency proceedings are distinguishable from involuntary civil commitment because the former are punitive).

As a consequence of the Court's decision in *Gault* recognizing the applicability of the privilege against self-incrimination, juvenile adjudications no longer could be characterized as either "noncriminal" or as "nonadversarial," because the fifth amendment privilege, more than any other provision of the Bill of Rights, is the fundamental guarantor of an adversarial process and the primary mechanism for maintaining a balance between the state and the individual.

The Court, in Murphy v. Waterfront Comm'n, 378 U.S. 52 (1964), described the multiple policies underlying the fifth amendment:

The privilege against self-incrimination . . . reflects many of our fundamental values and most noble aspirations: our unwillingness to subject those suspected of crime to the cruel trilemma of self-accusation, perjury, or contempt; *our preference for an accusatorial rather than an inquisitional system of criminal justice,* our fear that self-incriminating statements will be elicited by inhumane treatment and abuses, *our sense of fair play which dictates "a fair state-individual balance by requiring the government to leave the individual alone until good cause is shown for disturbing him and by requiring the government in its contest with the individual to shoulder the entire load,"* . . . our distrust of self-deprecatory statements; and our realization that the privilege, while sometimes "a shelter to the guilty," is often "a protection to the innocent."

378 U.S. at 55 (emphasis added) (citations omitted). *See generally* L. Levy, ORIGINS OF THE FIFTH AMENDMENT (1968) (historical analysis of the fifth amendment as a limitation on state power over the individual); Ritchie, *Compulsion That Violates the Fifth Amendment: The Burger Court's Definition* 61 MINN. L. REV. 383, 385–86 (1977) (discussing the importance of the policies requiring the government to leave the individual alone and of prohibiting the government from the act of compelling self-incrimination).

56. If the Court in *Gault* had been concerned solely with the reliability of juvenile confessions and the accuracy of fact finding, safeguards other than the fifth amendment privilege, such as a requirement that all confessions must be shown to have been made voluntarily, would have sufficed. In both Gallegos v. Colorado,

370 U.S. 49 (1962), and Haley v. Ohio, 332 U.S. 596 (1948), the U.S. Supreme Court considered the admissibility of confessions made by juveniles and, employing the "voluntariness" test, concluded that youthfulness was a special circumstance requiring close judicial scrutiny. *Gallegos*, 370 U.S. at 54–55; *Haley*, 332 U.S. at 599–601. The Court, however, recognized that fifth amendment safeguards are not required simply because they ensure accurate fact finding or reliable confessions, but also because they serve as a means of maintaining a proper balance between the individual and the state:

> The privilege against self-incrimination is, of course, related to the question of the safeguards necessary to assure that admissions or confessions are reasonably trustworthy, that they are not mere fruits of fear or coercion, but are reliable expressions of the truth. The roots of the privilege are, however, far deeper. They tap the basic stream of religious and political principle because the privilege reflects the limits of the individual's attornment to the state and—in a philosophical sense—insists upon the equality of the individual and the state. In other words, the privilege has a broader and deeper thrust than the rule which prevents the use of confessions which are the product of coercion because coercion is thought to carry with it the danger of unreliability. One of its purposes is to prevent the state, whether by force or by psychological domination, from overcoming the mind and will of the investigation and depriving him of the freedom to decide whether to assist the state in securing his conviction.

Gault 387 U.S. at 47 (footnotes omitted); *see also* Rosenberg, *supra* note 51, at 668 (discussing the *Gault* Court's argument that a juvenile proceeding may be "functionally equivalent" to an adult criminal proceeding). One author distinguishes between those aspects of procedural due process that ensure the reliability of the process of determining guilt and those that are designed to ensure respect for the dignity of the individual. *See* Kadish, *supra* note 54, at 346–67, *see also* McCarthy, *supra* note 52, at 464 (distinguishing between procedure "designed to lead to accurate determinations" and those designed to safeguard the "balance in the relationship between an individual and the government"), Feld, *supra* note 1 at notes 101–64 and accompanying text (analyzing the Minnesota Rules of Procedure for Juvenile Court's treatment of the admissibility of juvenile confessions).

57. *See* Allen, *The Judicial Quest for Penal Justice: The Warren Court and The Criminal Cases*, 1975 U. ILL.. L.F. 518, 530–31.

58. 397 U.S. 358 (1970).

59. *See id.* at 368.

60. *See id.* at 361–64.

61. *See id.* at 365–67. It is instructive to compare the *Winship* Court's treatment of the standard of proof in delinquency cases with that required for involuntary civil commitment of the mentally ill, which requires only "clear and convincing" evidence. Addington v. Texas, 441 U.S. 418, 433 (1979). In *Addington*, Chief Justice Burger distinguished both criminal and delinquency prosecutions from involuntary civil commitments and, in so doing, equated criminal trials and delinquency proceedings:

> The Court [in *Winship*] saw no controlling difference in loss of liberty and stigma between a conviction for an adult and a delinquency adjudication for a juvenile. Winship recognized that the basic issue—whether the individual in fact committed a criminal act—was the same in both proceedings. There being no meaningful distinctions between the two proceedings, we required the state to prove the juvenile's act and intent beyond a reasonable doubt.

... Unlike the delinquency proceeding in *Winship*, a civil commitment proceeding can in no sense be equated to a criminal prosecution.

441 U.S. at 427–28. Chief Justice Burger also noted that proof "beyond a reasonable doubt" is a critical component of criminal cases because it helps to preserve the " 'moral force of the criminal law,' ... and we should hesitate to apply it too broadly or casually in noncriminal cases." *Id.* at 428 (citation omitted).

62. *See Winship*, 397 U.S. at 376–77 (Burger, C.J., dissenting). Although parens patriae intervention may be a desirable method of dealing with wayward youths, "that intervention cannot take the form of subjecting the child to the stigma of a finding that he violated a criminal law and to the possibility of institutional confinement on proof insufficient to convict him were he an adult." 397 U.S. at 367.

63. 421 U.S. 519 (1975).

64. *See id.* at 520.

65. The Court reiterated:
Although the juvenile-court system had its genesis in the desire to provide a distinctive procedure and setting to deal with the problems of youth, including those manifested by antisocial conduct, our decisions in recent years have recognized that there is a gap between the originally benign conception of the system and its realities.

... [I]t is simply too late in the day to conclude ... that a juvenile is not put in jeopardy at a proceeding whose object is to determine whether he has committed acts that violate a criminal law and whose potential consequences include both the stigma inherent in such a determination and the deprivation of liberty for many years.

Id. at 528–29. The Court concluded that, with respect to the risks associated with double jeopardy, "we can find no persuasive distinction in that regard between the [juvenile] proceeding ... and a criminal prosecution, each of which is designed to 'vindicate [the] very vital interest in enforcement of criminal laws.' " *Id.* at 531 (quoting United States v. Jorn, 400 U.S. 470, 479 (1971) (plurality opinion)) (brackets in *Breed*).

66. 403 U.S. 528 (1971).

67. *McKeiver* was ultimately decided on the basis of fourteenth amendment due process and "fundamental fairness," even though the Court noted that the sixth amendment jury trial guarantee was applicable to state criminal proceedings by its incorporation into the fourteenth amendment. *See id.* at 540. The Court insisted, however, that "the juvenile court proceeding has not yet been held to be a 'criminal prosecution,' within the meaning and reach of the Sixth Amendment, and also has not yet been regarded as devoid of criminal aspects merely because it usually has been given the civil label." *Id.* at 541. The Court cautioned that "[t]here is a possibility, at least, that the jury trial, if required as a matter of constitutional precept, will remake the juvenile proceeding into a fully adversary process and will put an effective end to what has been the idealistic prospect of an intimate, informal protective proceeding." *Id.* at 545.

68. *See id.* at 543.

69. *See, e.g., In re Winship*, 397 U.S. 358, 363–64 (1970); *In re Gault*, 387 U.S. 1, 47 (1967).

70. *See supra* notes 55–56 and accompanying text.

71. *See McKeiver*, 403 U.S. at 553–55 (Brennan, J., concurring and dissenting). The *McKeiver* decision involved two cases raising the issues of jury trials in juvenile

proceedings, one arising in Pennsylvania and the other in North Carolina. Although Justice Brennan acknowledged that delinquency prosecutions were not criminal proceedings for purposes of implicating the sixth amendment right to a jury trial and required only the "essentials of due process and fair treatment," *id.* at 553 (Brennan, J., concurring and dissenting), he differentiated between the Pennsylvania and North Carolina proceedings. Justice Brennan noted that "the States are not bound to provide jury trials on demand so long as some other aspect of the process adequately protects the interests that Sixth Amendment jury trials are intended to serve." *Id.* at 554 (Brennan, J., concurring and dissenting). He noted that the availability of trial by jury protects the individual against oppression by providing a mechanism to appeal to the conscience of the community. *Id.* (Brennan, J., concurring and dissenting). The Pennsylvania juvenile procedures permitted a public trial, which Justice Brennan regarded as providing a functionally equivalent safeguard for the core values protected by the jury trial rights. *See id.* at 554–55 (Brennan, J., concurring and dissenting). He dissented in the North Carolina case, however, because the North Carolina procedures either permitted or required the exclusion of the public, and the public had in fact been excluded from the proceedings, which arose out of demonstrations by black students and adults against public school discrimination. *Id.* at 556–57 (Brennan, J., concurring and dissenting); *see also* Feld, *supra* note 1 at notes 480–83 and accompanying text.

72. *See McKeiver*, 403 U.S. at 547–48.

73. *See id.* at 550–51.

Concern about the inapplicability of exclusionary and other rules of evidence, about the juvenile court judge's possible awareness of the juvenile's prior record and of the contents of the social file; about repeated appearances of the same familiar witnesses in the persons of juvenile and probation officers and social workers—all to the effect that this will create the likelihood of pre-judgment—chooses to ignore, it seems to us, every aspect of fairness, of concern, of sympathy, and of paternal attention that the juvenile court system contemplates.

Id. at 550. There is, however, ample reason for concern about the accuracy of the fact-finding process in a justice system in which the same probation officers and the same child appear repeatedly before the same judge, who has access to the minor's previous social history and delinquency record in the course of deciding different aspects of the case at different stages. *See* Feld, *supra* note 1 at notes 378–79 and accompanying text (describing the inherently prejudicial nature of such repeated contacts and excessive familiarity).

74. The *McKeiver* case is a "peculiar" decision because it required the Court both to misread its own precedents regarding the dual functions of procedural safeguards and the appropriate method of constitutional adjudication, and to ignore its own legal premises in *Winship* regarding the standard of proof beyond a reasonable doubt. *See, e.g.,* F. ZIMRING, THE CHANGING LEGAL WORLD OF ADOLESCENCE 83 (1982); Rosenberg, *supra* note 51, at 677.

75. The result clearly was dictated by the Court's concern that the right to a trial by jury would be the one procedural safeguard most disruptive of the traditional juvenile court and would require substantial alteration of traditional juvenile court practices because "it would bring with it . . . the traditional delay, the formality, and the clamor of the adversary system and, possibly, the public trial." *McKeiver*, 403 U.S. at 550. Ultimately, the Court realized that such an imposition would render the juvenile court virtually indistinguishable from a criminal court

and would raise the more basic question of whether there is any need for a separate juvenile court at all. *See id.* at 551.

76. *See id.* at 547.

77. As one of its rationales for imposing procedural formality in *In re Gault*, 387 U.S. 1 (1967), the Court opined that the absence of formality "frequently resulted not in enlightened procedure, but in arbitrariness." *Id.* at 18–19.

78. 387 U.S. 1 (1967). *Gault* particularly with its importation of the fifth amendment as the bulwark of the adversary system, had determined that an informal, flexible, nonadversarial procedure was inconsistent with the requirements of due process. *See, e.g.,* Gardner, *Punishment and Juvenile: A Conceptual Framework for Assessing Constitutional Rights of Youthful Offenders*, 35 VAND. L. REV. 791, 830 (1982).

79. *See McKeiver*, 403 U.S. at 550. The *McKeiver* plurality did not respond to the point made by Justice Brennan in his partial dissent that the possibility of a public trial was an alternative mechanism that satisfied the core values of a jury trial. *See supra* note 71.

80. In other cases, the Court has held to the contrary, finding that the confidentiality of juvenile proceedings must in some circumstances give way to other important interests. *See, e.g.,* Smith v. Daily Mail Publishing Co., 443 U.S. 97,104 (1978) (freedom of the press in publishing lawfully obtained information prevails over state's interest in protecting juvenile's privacy); Davis v. Alaska, 415 U.S. 308, 319 (1974) (the defendant's right of confrontation in a criminal case is paramount to the state's interest in preserving the confidentiality of a juvenile record).

81. *See* E. RYERSON, *supra* note 12, at 156.

82. *See, e.g.,* Empey, *Juvenile Justice Reform: Diversion, Due Process, and De-institutionalization* in PRISONERS IN AMERICA 13 (L. Ohlin ed. 1973). Although "[t]he juvenile court's jurisdiction over children's noncriminal misbehavior has long been seen as a cornerstone of its mission," that foundation is rapidly eroding. INSTITUTE OF JUDICIAL ADMINISTRATION AND AMERICAN BAR ASSOCIATION, JUVENILE JUSTICE STANDARDS PROJECT (1977) (hereinafter cited as JUVENILE JUSTICE STANDARDS). The quotation is from JUVENILE JUSTICE STANDARDS, *supra*, STANDARDS RELATING TO NONCRIMINAL MISBEHAVIOR 2. The STANDARDS continue: "These standards take the position that the present jurisdiction of the juvenile court over noncriminal behavior—the status offense jurisdiction—should be cut short and a system of voluntary referral to services provided outside the juvenile justice system adopted in its stead." *Id.*

The Juvenile Justice Standards Project was a cooperative effort of the Institute of Judicial Administration and the American Bar Association. The result of the Project's efforts was a multivolume set of standards that was intended to be to the juvenile justice process what the Standards Relating to Criminal Justice was to the criminal process. Most of these standards were approved by the ABA at its mid-year meeting in 1979. The remainder, with the exception of one volume, were approved at the ABA's mid-year meeting in 1980. The STANDARDS RELATING TO NONCRIMINAL MISBEHAVIOR were published in 1982. *See also* E. SCHUR, RADICAL NON-INTERVENTION: RETHINKING THE DELINQUENCY PROBLEM 46–51 (1973) (discussing the failure of programs for predicting delinquency); Rosenheim, *Notes on Helping Juvenile Nuisances*, in

PURSUING JUSTICE, *supra* note 32, at 52 (courts persist in handling status offenses despite studies recommending alternative treatment).

Virtually every professional group that has considered the issue of status jurisdiction has recommended either its elimination from the juvenile court or drastic restrictions on the grounds for and intensity of intervention. These recommendations also have sustained the "deinstitutionalization" movement. *See, generally* NEITHER ANGELS NOR THIEVES: STUDIES IN THE DE-INSTITUTIONALIZATION OF STATUS OFFENDERS (J. Handler & J. Zatz eds. 1982) [hereinafter cited as NEITHER ANGELS NOR THIEVES].

83. *See, e.g.,* MINN. STAT. 260.015 (5) (e) (1971), *repealed by* Act of April 11, 1974, ch. 469, § 1, Minn. Laws 1149.

84. One version of the redefinitional process was the removal of status offenses from the delinquency jurisdiction of the juvenile court and the creation of a separate legal category of "Persons in Need of Supervision" (PINS). M. LEVIN & R. SARRI, JUVENILE DELINQUENCY: A COMPARATIVE ANALYSIS OF LEGAL CODES IN THE UNITED STATES 12 (1974).

Minnesota has chosen not to label truants, runaways, alcohol and controlled substance offenders, and petty offenders as "delinquent." *See* MINN. STAT. §§ 260.015 (5), (19)–(23) (1982). Although the juvenile court still has jurisdiction over these offenders, *see, e.g.,* MINN. STAT. §§ 260.111 (1982), the dispositions it may impose are more limited than those that can be imposed on delinquent children. *Compare id.* § 260.194 (dispositions available to children who are habitually truants, runaways, or juvenile petty offenders) *and id.* § 260.195 (dispositions available to juvenile alcohol and controlled substance offenders) *with id.* § 260.185 (Supp. 1983) (dispositions available to delinquent children).

85. *See, e.g., In re Ellery* C., 32 N.Y.2d 588, 591, 300 N.E.2d 424, 425, 347 N.Y.S.2d 51, 53 (1973) (prohibiting the commitment of status offenders to the same institutions as youths who committed crimes); Harris v. Calendine, 233 S.E.2d 318, 325 (W. Va. 1977) (prohibiting incarceration of status offenders in a secure institution with children guilty of criminal conduct).

The deinstitutionalization of status offenders received substantial impetus with the passage of the Juvenile Justice and Delinquency Prevention Act of 1974, 42 U.S.C. §§ 5601–5640 (1976 & Supp. III 1979), *as amended by* Juvenile Justice Amendments of 1980, Pub. L. No. 96–509, 94 Stat. 2750 (1980). That Act provided, inter alia, that "juveniles . . . charged with . . . offenses that would not be criminal if committed by an adult. . . . , shall not be placed in juvenile detention or correctional facilities." 42 U.S.C. § 5633 (a) (12) (a) (1976 & Supp. III 1979) (current version at 42 U.S.C. § 5633(a)(12)(a) (1982)). *See generally* NEITHER ANGELS NOR THIEVES, *supra* note 82 (evaluative studies of impact in the states of J.J.D.P. deinstitutionalization mandate).

86. *See, e.g.,* Feld, *Reference of Juvenile Offenders for Adult Prosecution: The Legislative Alternative to Asking Unanswerable Questions,* 62 MINN. L. REV. 515, 519–20 (1978) [hereinafter cited as Feld, *Reference of Juvenile Offenders*]; Feld, *supra* note 44, at 172; Feld, *supra* note 1 at notes 497–522 and accompanying text.

87. Feld, *supra* note 1 at notes 428–53 and accompanying text.

88. *Id.,* notes 442–53 and accompanying text.

89. *Id.,* notes 391–95 and accompanying text.

Chapter 8

Non–Decision Making and Criminal Justice Policy

INTRODUCTION

The preceding chapters of this text introduced the reader to the federal criminal justice policy-making process. Drawing on the political science literature, these chapters included readings that provide insight into the role of the three branches of government in this process. A general limitation of traditional political science, however, is that it has focused on observable policy decisions. Such an approach rests on the assumption that power and influence are always observable.

What if, however, these observed decisions are only the decisions that are allowed to come to the political forefront? What if, there are other potential decisions—other policy choices—that do not reach the public arena? This chapter considers the possibility that not all criminal justice policy options reach the criminal justice policy-making arena. Just as some policy options are "organized into" the arena, others are "organized out." According to the non–decision-making framework, research begins by asking what are the myths, rituals, and political procedures and which persons, if any, benefit. The researcher would then examine how status quo–oriented persons and groups influence community values and groups and, finally, analyze participation in concrete decisions.

NON–DECISION MAKING, THE SECOND FACE OF POWER

Critical of the approaches to the study of power of both political scientists and sociologists, Peter Bachrach and Morton S. Baratz offer an alternative approach.[1] Their central thesis is that there are two faces of power. They assert that sociologists, who view power as centralized or "elitist," miss both faces of power; whereas, political scientists, who recognize power as the participants in the decision-making process exercise it, see only the first face of power.[2] Bachrach and Baratz posit a second face of power—power that is exercised when one party reinforces practices that limit the scope of the political process to public consideration of those issues, which are comparatively innocuous. The party is considered successful, if another party is prevented from raising an issue that would be detrimental to the former.[3]

Drawing on the work of Schattschneider,[4] Bachrach and Baratz suggest that organizations have a bias in favor of certain conflicts and suppression of others because "organization is the mobilization of bias." The mobilization of bias includes the dominant values and the political myths, rituals, and institutions, which tend to favor the vested interests of one or more groups, relative to others. Although political scientists propose to study power by examining the decision-making process surrounding "key decisions," Bachrach and Baratz assert that it is not possible to distinguish between key and unimportant decisions.[5]

Alternatively, to study both faces of power, the authors advocate an approach that begins by investigating the "mobilization of bias" in the institution under scrutiny. Having analyzed the myths, procedures, and who benefits from the existing bias, the next step is to examine non–decision making to determine the extent and manner in which persons oriented to the status quo influence community values and the political institutions under study. Finally, understanding this restrictive face of power allows the researcher to distinguish between key and unimportant decisions.[6]

NON–DECISION MAKING AND CRIMINAL JUSTICE POLICY MAKING

Applying Bachrach and Baratz's approach to the study of criminal justice policy making, the reader may speculate that current criminal justice policies, including those being debated do not exhaust the possibility of criminal justice policies. It is readily evident, for example, in the area of corrections that treatment as an approach to offenders has been more acceptable at times in our history than others. Even then, however, the underlying myth is that prisoners are to be punished. This perspective limits the extent to which treatment is acceptable. Right or wrong, drugs that are now illegal are viewed as bad, in contrast to alcohol, which is legal. For the most part, these assumptions—the mobilization of bias—are accepted and not analyzed.

Bachrach and Baratz assert that the analysis of the "mobilization of bias" in the community involves the analysis of the dominant values and political myths, rituals, and institutions that tend to favor the vested interests of one or more groups relative to others.[7] Generally, one would expect that such an analysis would be difficult, and determining those issues that are kept off the political agenda by the "mobilization of bias" would not be readily evident. In the "Anti-Drug Abuse Act of 1988," however, Congress clearly stated that the legalization of drugs was not a subject for congressional debate.[8] Democrats and Republicans, liberals and conservatives agreed to the proposal. In so doing, Congress used its power to make laws to act in favor of those who opposed drug legalization and against those who supported it, or were at least open to discussing alternatives to existing policy. Although such public statements of system bias are unusual, the example gives support to the assertion that all possible criminal justice policy options are not on the public policy agenda. Not all criminal justice policy options have the same chance of being considered by the public and policymakers.

In short, as significant and important as the study of the criminal justice policy-making process is, the reader should bear in mind that this approach to the study of criminal justice only addresses one face of the power and politics of criminal justice policy making. The study of criminal justice policy making also must consider and examine what policies are not being considered, the obstacles that prevent the consideration of those policies, and how this situation might be changed. That is, to examine the criminal justice policy-making process requires the informed reader to consider the second face of power and whether there may be other criminal justice policies and approaches that the political system has excluded from the criminal justice policy arena.

INCLUDED SELECTIONS

This chapter includes a selection by Peter Bachrach and Morton S. Baratz, which sets forth the possibility that the institutions of power may prevent certain decisions from reaching the public policy arena.[9] The second selection, which is from the "Anti-Drug Abuse Act of 1988" (P.L. 100–690-November 18, 1988), states Congress's position that the legalization of drugs is not a subject for congressional debate.

FOR DISCUSSION

In this chapter the reader should consider:

1. What are the dominant values, myths, procedures, and rules that affect criminal justice policy making.
2. How the status quo and groups supporting the status quo in criminal justice might tend to limit criminal justice decision making to "safe issues."

3. Which other groups might influence the criminal justice policy-making process.

4. Which issues and policies might be added to the criminal justice policy agenda and how might that be achieved.

5. How the "mobilization of bias" affects criminal justice policy making and policy at the state and local levels.

RECOMMENDED READING

Bachrach, Peter, and Baratz, Morton S. *Power and Poverty: Theory and Practice.* New York: Oxford University Press, 1970.

TWO FACES OF POWER[10]

Peter Bachrach and Morton S. Baratz

The concept of power remains elusive despite the recent and prolific out-pourings of case studies on community power. Its elusiveness is dramatically demonstrated by the regularity of disagreement as to the locus of community power between the sociologists and the political scientists. Sociologically oriented researchers have consistently found that power is highly centralized, while scholars trained in political science have just as regularly concluded that in "their" communities power is widely diffused.[11] Presumably, this explains why the latter group styles itself "pluralist," its counterpart "elitist."

There seems no room for doubt that the sharply divergent findings of the two groups are the product, not of sheer coincidence, but of fundamental differences in both their underlying assumptions and research methodology. The political scientists have contended that these differences in findings can be explained by the faulty approach and presuppositions of the sociologists. We contend in this paper that the pluralists themselves have not grasped the whole truth of the matter; that while their criticisms of the elitists are sound, they, like the elitists, utilize an approach and assumptions which predetermine their conclusions. Our argument is cast within the frame of our central thesis: that there are two faces of power, neither of which the sociologists see and only one of which the political scientists see.

I

Against the elitist approach to power several criticisms may be, and have been levelled.[12] One has to do with its basic premise that in every human institution there is an ordered system of power, a "power structure" which is an integral part and the mirror image of the organization's stratification. This postulate the pluralists emphatically—and, to our mind, correctly—reject, on the ground that nothing categorical can be assumed about power in any community. If anything, there seems to be an unspoken notion among pluralist researchers that at bottom nobody dominates in a town, so that their first question is not likely to be, "Who runs this community?," but rather, "Does anyone at all run this community?" The first query is

Reprinted from the *American Political Science Review*, vol. 56, no. 4, by Peter Bachrach and Morton S. Baratz, "Two Faces of Power," pp. 947–52, Copyright 1962, with permission from the American Political Science Association.

somewhat like, "Have you stopped beating your wife?," in that virtually any response short of total unwillingness to answer will supply the researchers with a "power elite" along the lines presupposed by the stratification theory.[13]

Equally objectionable to the pluralists—and to us—is the sociologists' hypothesis that the power structure tends to be stable over time.

Pluralists hold that power may be tied to issues, and issues can be fleeting or persistent, provoking coalitions among interested groups and citizens, ranging in their duration from momentary to semi-permanent. To presume that the set of coalitions which exists in the community at any given time is a timelessly stable aspect of social structure is to introduce systematic inaccuracies into one's description of social reality.[14]

A third criticism of the elitist model is that it wrongly equates reputed with actual power:

If a man's major life work is banking, the pluralist presumes he will spend his time at the bank, and not in manipulating community decisions. This presumption holds until the banker's activities and participations indicate otherwise. . . . If we presume that the banker is "really" engaged in running the community, there is practically no way of disconfirming this notion, even if it is totally erroneous. On the other hand, it is easy to spot the banker who really does run community affairs when we presume he does not, because his activities will make this fact apparent.[15]

This is not an exhaustive bill of particulars; there are flaws other than these in the sociological model and methodology[16]—including some which the pluralists themselves have not noticed. But to go into this would not materially serve our current purposes. Suffice it simply to observe that whatever the merits of their own approach to power, the pluralists have effectively exposed the main weaknesses of the elitist model.

As the foregoing quotations make clear, the pluralists concentrate their attention, not upon the sources of power, but its exercise. Power to them means "participation in decision-making"[17] and can be analyzed only after "careful examination of a series of concrete decisions."[18] As a result, the pluralist researcher is uninterested in the reputedly powerful. His concerns instead are to (a) select for study a number of "key" as opposed to "routine" political decisions, (b) identify the people who took an active part in the decision-making process, (c) obtain a full account of their actual behavior while the policy conflict was being resolved, and (d) determine and analyze the specific outcome of the conflict.

The advantages of this approach, relative to the elitist alternative, need no further exposition. The same may not be said, however, about its defects—two of which seem to us to be of fundamental importance. One is that the model takes no account of the fact that power may be, and often is, exercised by confining the scope of decision-making to relatively "safe" issues. The other is that the model provides no *objective* criteria for distinguishing between "important" and "unimportant" issues arising in the political arena.

II

There is no gainsaying that an analysis grounded entirely upon what is specific and visible to the outside observer is more "scientific" than one based upon pure speculation. To put it another way,

If we can get our social life stated in terms of activity, and of nothing else, we have not indeed succeeded in measuring it, but we have at least reached a foundation upon which a coherent system of measurements can be built up. . . . We shall cease to be blocked by the intervention of unmeasurable elements, which claim to be themselves the real causes of all that is happening, and which by their spook-like arbitrariness make impossible any progress toward dependable knowledge.[19]

The question is, however, how can one be certain in any given situation that the "unmeasurable elements" are inconsequential, are not of decisive importance? Cast in slightly different terms, can a sound concept of power be predicated on the assumption that power is totally embodied and fully reflected in "concrete decisions" or in activity bearing directly upon their making?

We think not. Of course power is exercised when A participates in the making of decisions that affect B. But power is also exercised when A devotes his energies to creating or reinforcing social and political values and institutional practices that limit the scope of the political process to public consideration of only those issues which are comparatively innocuous to A. To the extent that A succeeds in doing this, B is prevented, for all practical purposes, from bringing to the fore any issues that might in their resolution be seriously detrimental to A's set of preferences.[20]

Situations of this kind are common. Consider, for example, the case— surely not unfamiliar to this audience—of the discontented faculty member in an academic institution headed by a tradition-bound executive. Aggrieved about a long-standing policy around which a strong vested interest has developed, the professor resolves in the privacy of his office to launch an attack upon the policy at the next faculty meeting. But, when the moment of truth is at hand, he sits frozen in silence. Why? Among the many possible reasons, one or more of these could have been of crucial importance: (a) the professor was fearful that his intended action would be interpreted as an expression of his disloyalty to the institution; or (b) he decided that, given the beliefs and attitudes of his colleagues on the faculty, he would almost certainly constitute on this issue a minority of one; or (c) he concluded that, given the nature of the lawmaking process in the institution, his proposed remedies would be pigeonholed permanently. But whatever the case, the central point to be made is the same: to the extent that a person or group—consciously or unconsciously—creates or reinforces barriers to the public airing of policy conflicts, that person or group has power. Or, as Professor Schattschneider has so admirably put it:

All forms of political organization have a bias in favor of the exploitation of some kinds of conflict and the suppression of others because *organization is the mobilization of bias*. Some issues are organized into politics while others are organized out.[21]

Is such bias not relevant to the study of power? Should not the student be continuously alert to its possible existence in the human institution that he studies, and be ever prepared to examine the forces which brought it into being and sustain it? Can he safely ignore the possibility, for instance, that an individual or group in a community participates more vigorously in supporting the nondecision-making process than in participating in actual decisions within the process? Stated differently, can the researcher overlook the chance that some person or association could limit decision-making to relatively non-controversial matters, by influencing community values and political procedures and rituals, notwithstanding that there are in the community serious but latent power conflicts?[22] To do so is, in our judgment, to overlook the less apparent, but nonetheless extremely important, face of power.

III

In his critique of the "ruling-elite model," Professor Dahl argues that "the hypothesis of the existence of a ruling elite can be strictly tested only if . . . [t] here is a fair sample of cases involving key political decisions in which the preferences of the hypothetical ruling elite run counter to those of any other likely group that might be suggested."[23] With this assertion we have two complaints. One we have already discussed, viz., in erroneously assuming that power is solely reflected in concrete decisions, Dahl thereby excludes the possibility that in the community in question there is a group capable of preventing contests from arising on issues of importance to it. Beyond that, however, by ignoring the less apparent face of power Dahl and those who accept his pluralist approach are unable adequately to differentiate between a "key" and a "routine" political decision.

Nelson Polsby, for example, proposes that "by pre-selecting as issues for study those which are generally agreed to be significant, pluralist researchers can test stratification theory."[24] He is silent, however, on how the researcher is to determine what issues are "generally agreed to be significant," and on how the researcher is to appraise the reliability of the agreement. In fact, Polsby is guilty here of the same fault he himself has found with elitist methodology: by presupposing that in any community there are significant issues in the political arena, he takes for granted the very question which is in doubt. He accepts as issues what are reputed to be issues. As a result, his findings are fore-ordained. For even if there is no "truly" significant issue in the community under study, there is every likelihood that Polsby (or any like-minded researcher) will find one or some and, after careful study, reach the appropriate pluralistic conclusion.[25]

Dahl's definition of "key political issues" in his essay on the ruling-elite model is open to the same criticism. He states that it is "a necessary although possibly not a sufficient condition that the [key] issue should involve actual disagreement in preferences among two or more groups."[26] In our view, this is an inadequate characterization of a "key political issue," simply because groups can have disagreements in preferences on unimportant as well as on important issues. Elite preferences which border on the indifferent are certainly not significant in determining whether a monolithic or polylithic distribution of power prevails in a given community. Using Dahl's definition of "key political issues," the researcher would have little difficulty in finding such in practically any community; and it would not be surprising then if he ultimately concluded that power in the community was widely diffused.

The distinction between important and unimportant issues, we believe, cannot be made intelligently in the absence of an analysis of the "mobilization of bias" in the community; of the dominant values and the political myths, rituals, and institutions which tend to favor the tested interests of one or more groups, relative to others. Armed with this knowledge, one could conclude that any challenge to the predominant values or to the established "rules of the game" would constitute an "important" issue; all else, unimportant. To be sure, judgments of this kind cannot be entirely objective. But to avoid making them in a study of power is both to neglect a highly significant aspect of power and thereby to undermine the only sound basis for discriminating between "key" and "routine" decisions. In effect, we contend, the pluralists have made each of these mistakes; that is to say, they have done just that for which Kaufman and Jones so severely taxed Floyd Hunter: they have begun "their structure at the mezzanine without showing us a lobby or foundation,"[27] i.e., they have begun by studying the issues rather than the values and biases that are built into the political system and that, for the student of power, give real meaning to those issues which do enter the political arena.

IV

There is no better fulcrum for our critique of the pluralist model than Dahl's recent study of power in New Haven.[28]

At the outset it may be observed that Dahl does not attempt in this work to define his concept, "key political decision." In asking whether the "No-tables" of New Haven are "influential overtly or covertly in the making of government decisions," he simply states that he will examine "three differ-ent 'issue-areas' in which important public decisions are made: nominations by the two political parties, urban redevelopment, and public education." These choices are justified on the grounds that "nominations determine which persons will hold public office. The New Haven redevelopment pro-gram measured by its cost—present and potential—is the largest in the country. Public education, aside from its intrinsic importance, is the cost-liest item in the city's budget." Therefore, Dahl concludes, "It is reasonable to expect . . . that the relative influence over public officials wielded by the . . . Notables would be revealed by an examination of their participation in these three areas of activity."[29]

The difficulty with this latter statement is that it is evident from Dahl's own account that the Notables are in fact uninterested in two of the three "key" decisions he has chosen. In regard to the public school issue, for example, Dahl points out that many of the Notables live in the suburbs and that those who do live in New Haven choose in the main to send their children to private schools. "As a consequence," he writes, "their interest in the public schools is ordinarily rather slight."[30] Nominations by the two political parties as an important "issue-area," is somewhat analogous to the public schools, in that the apparent lack of interest among the Notables in this issue is partially accounted for by their suburban residence—because of which they are disqualified from holding public office in New Haven. Indeed, Dahl himself concedes that with respect to both these issues the Notables are largely indifferent: "Business leaders might ignore public schools or the political parties without any sharp awareness that their in-difference would hurt their pocketbooks. . . ." He goes on, however, to say that

the prospect of profound changes [as a result of the urban redevelopment program] in ownership, physical layout and usage of property in the downtown area and the effects of these changes on the commercial and industrial prosperity of New Haven were all related in an obvious way to the daily concerns of businessmen.[31]

Thus, if one believes—as Professor Dahl did when he wrote his critique of the ruling-elite model—that an issue, to be considered as important, "should involve actual disagreement preferences among two or more groups,"[32] then clearly he has now for all practical purposes written off public education and party nominations as key "issue-areas." But this point aside, it appears somewhat dubious at best that "the relative influence over public officials wielded by the Social Notables" can be revealed by an ex-amination of their nonparticipation in areas in which they were not inter-ested.

Furthermore, we would not rule out the possibility that even on those issues to which they appear indifferent, the Notables may have a significant degree of *indirect* influence. We suggest, for example, that although they send their children to private schools, the Notables do recognize that public school expenditures have a direct bearing upon their own liabilities. This being so, and given their strong representation on the New Haven Board of Finance,[33] the expectation must be that it is in their direct interest to play an active role in fiscal policy-making, in the establishment of the educational budget in particular. But as to this, Dahl is silent: he inquires not at all into either the decisions made by the Board of Finance with respect to education nor into their impact upon the public schools.[34] Let it be understood clearly that in making these points we are not attempting to refute Dahl's contention that the Notables lack power in New Haven. What we are saying, however, is that this conclusion is not adequately supported by his analysis of the "issue-areas" of public education and party nominations.

The same may not be said of redevelopment. This issue is by any reasonable standard important for purposes of determining whether New Haven is ruled by "the hidden hand of an economic elite."[35] For the Economic Notables have taken an active interest in the program and, beyond that, the socioeconomic implications of it are not necessarily in harmony with the basic interests and values of businesses and businessmen.

In an effort to assure that the redevelopment program would be acceptable to what he dubbed "the biggest muscles" in New Haven, Mayor Lee created the Citizens Action Commission (CAC) and appointed to it primarily representatives of the economic elite. It was given the function of overseeing the work of the mayor and other officials involved in redevelopment, and, as well, the responsibility for organizing and encouraging citizens' participation in the program through an extensive committee system.

In order to weigh the relative influence of the mayor, other key officials, and the members of the CAC, Dahl reconstructs "all the *important* decisions on redevelopment and renewal between 1950–58 . . . [to] determine which individuals most often initiated the proposals that were finally adopted or most often successfully vetoed the proposals of the others."[36] The results of this test indicate that the mayor and his development administrator were by far the most influential, and that the "muscles" on the Commission, excepting in a few trivial instances, "never directly initiated, opposed, vetoed, or altered any proposal brought before them. . . ."[37]

This finding is, in our view, unreliable, not so much because Dahl was compelled to make a subjective selection of what constituted *important* decisions within what he felt to be an *important* "issue-area," as because the finding was based upon an excessively narrow test of influence. To measure relative influence solely in terms of the ability to initiate and veto proposals is to ignore the possible exercise of influence or power in limiting the scope of initiation. How, that is to say, can a judgment be made as to the relative influence of Mayor Lee and the CAC without knowing (through prior study of the political and social views of all concerned) the proposals that Lee did not make because he anticipated that they would provoke strenuous opposition and, perhaps, sanctions on the part of the CAC.[38]

In sum, since he does not recognize both faces of power, Dahl is in no position to evaluate the relative influence or power of the initiator and decision-maker, on the one hand, and of those persons, on the other, who may have been indirectly instrumental in preventing potentially dangerous issues from being raised.[39] As a result, he unduly emphasizes the importance of initiating, deciding, and vetoing, and in the process casts the pluralist conclusions of his study into serious doubt.

V

We have contended in this paper that a fresh approach to the study of power is called for, an approach based upon a recognition of the two faces of power. Under this approach the researcher would begin—not, as does the sociologist who asks, "Who rules?," nor as the pluralist who asks, "Does anyone have power?"—but by investigating the particular "mobilization of bias" in the institution under scrutiny. Then, having analyzed the dominant values, the myths and the established political procedures and rules of the game, he would make a careful inquiry into which persons or groups, if any, gain from the existing bias and which, if any, are handicapped by it. Next, he would investigate the dynamics of non–decision-making; that is, he would examine the extent to which and the manner in which the status quo oriented persons and groups influence those community values and those political institutions (as, e.g., the unanimity "rule" of New York City's Board of Estimate[40]) which tend to limit the scope of actual decision-making to "safe" issues. Finally, using his knowledge of the restrictive face of power as a foundation for analysis and as a standard for distinguishing between "key" and "routine" political decisions, the researcher would, after the manner of the pluralists, analyze participation in decision-making of concrete issues.

We reject in advance as unimpressive the possible criticism that this approach to the study of power is likely to prove fruitless because it goes beyond an investigation of what is objectively measurable. In reacting against the subjective aspects of the sociological model of power, the pluralists have, we believe, made the mistake of discarding "unmeasurable elements" as unreal. It is ironical that, by so doing, they have exposed themselves to the same fundamental criticism they have so forcefully leveled against the elitists: their approach to and assumptions about power predetermine their findings and conclusions.

PUBLIC LAW 100–690–NOV. 18, 1988
"THE ANTI-DRUG ABUSE ACT OF 1988"

TITLE V—USER ACCOUNTABILITY

Subtitle A—Opposition to Legalization and Public Awareness

Sec. 5011. *Sense of the Congress Opposing Legalization of Drugs.* The Congress finds that legalization of illegal drugs, on the Federal or State level, is an unconscionable surrender in a war in which, for the future of our country and the lives of our children, there can be no substitute for total victory.

Sec. 5012. *Public Awareness Campaign.* The Director of National Drug Control Policy shall within 90 days after confirmation by the Senate develop a program to inform the American public of the provisions of this Act pertaining to penalties for the use or possession of illegal drugs.

NOTES

1. Peter Bachrach and Morton S. Baratz, "Two Faces of Power," *American Political Science Review*, vol. 56 no. 4 (1962): 947–52.

2. Ibid., p. 947.

3. Ibid., p. 948.

4. E. E. Schattsneider, *The Semi-Sovereign People* (New York: Holt, Rinehart and Winston, 1960), p. 71.

5. Bachrach and Baratz, "Two Faces of Power," p. 950.

6. Ibid., p. 952.

7. Ibid., p. 950.

8. "Anti-Drug Abuse Act of 1988" (P.L. 100–690–Nov. 18, 1988).

9. Bachrach and Baratz, "Two Faces of Power," pp. 947–52.

10. This paper is an outgrowth of a seminar in Problems of Power in Contemporary Society, conducted jointly by the authors for graduate students and undergraduate majors in political science and economics.

11. Compare, for example, the sociological studies of Floyd Hunter, *Community Power Structure* (Chapel Hill, 1953); Roland Pellegrini and Charles H. Coates, "Absentee-Owned Corporations and Community Power Structure," *American Journal of Sociology*, vol. 61 (March 1956): 413–19; and Robert O. Schulze, "Economic Dominants and Community Power Structure," *American Sociological Review*, vol. 23 (February 1958): 3–9; with political science studies of Wallace S. Sayre and Herbert Kaufman, *Governing New York City* (New York, 1960); Robert A. Dahl, *Who Governs?* (New Haven, 1961); and Norton E. Long and George Belknap, "A Research Program on Leadership and Decision-Making in Metropolitan Areas" (New York: Governmental Affairs Institute, 1956). See also Nelson W.

Polsby, "How to Study Community Power: The Pluralist Alternative," *Journal of Politics*, vol. 22 (August 1960), 474–84.

12. See especially Polsby, op. cit. p. 475f.

13. Ibid., p. 476.

14. Ibid., pp. 478–79.

15. Ibid., pp. 480–81.

16. See especially Robert A. Dahl, "A Critique of the Ruling-Elite Model," *American Political Science Review*, vol. 52 (June 1958): 463–69; and Lawrence J. R. Herson, "In the Footsteps of Community Power," *American Political Science Review*, vol. 55 (December 1961): 817–31.

17. This definition originated with Harold D. Lasswell and Abraham Kaplan, *Power and Society* (New Haven, 1950), p. 75.

18. Dahl, "A Critique of the Ruling-Elite Model," loc. cit., p. 466.

19. Arthur Bentley, *The Process of Government* (Chicago, 1908), p. 202, quoted in Polsby, op. cit., p. 481n.

20. As is perhaps self-evident, there are similarities in both faces of power. In each, A participates in decisions and thereby adversely affects B. But there is an important difference between the two: in the one case, A openly participates; in the other, he participates only in the sense that he works to sustain those values and rules of procedure that help him keep certain issues out of the public domain. True enough, participation of the second kind may at times be overt; that is the case, for instance, in cloture fights in the Congress. But the point is that it need not be. In fact, when the maneuver is most successfully executed, it neither involves nor can be identified with decisions arrived at on specific issues.

21. Schattschneider, *The Semi-Sovereign People*, p. 71.

22. Dahl partially concedes this point when he observes ("A Critique of the Ruling-Elite Model," pp. 468–69) that "one could argue that even in a society like ours a ruling elite might be so influential over ideas, attitudes, and opinions that a kind of false consensus will exist—not the phony consensus of a terroristic totalitarian dictatorship but the manipulated and superficially self-imposed adherence to the norms and goals of the elite by broad sections of a community. . . . This objection points to the need to be circumspect in interpreting the evidence." But that he largely misses our point is clear from the succeeding sentence: "Yet here, too, it seems to me that the hypothesis cannot be satisfactorily confirmed without something equivalent to the test I have proposed," and that is "by an examination of a series of concrete cases where key decisions are made. . . ."

23. Op. cit., p. 466.

24. Op. cit., p. 478.

25. As he points out, the expectations of the pluralist researchers "have seldom been disappointed . . . " (Ibid., p. 477).

26. Op. cit., p. 467.

27. Herbert Kaufman and Victor Jones, "The Mystery of Power," *Public Administration Review*, vol. 14 (Summer 1954): 207.

28. Dahl, *Who Governs?* (New Haven, 1961).

29. Ibid., p. 64.

30. Ibid., p. 70.

31. Ibid., p. 71.

32. Op. cit., p. 467.

33. *Who Governs?*, p. 82. Dahl points out that "the main policy thrust of the Economic Notables is to oppose tax increases; this leads them to oppose expenditures for anything more than minimal traditional city services. In this effort their two most effective weapons ordinarily are the mayor and the Board of Finance. The policies of the Notables are most easily achieved under a strong mayor if his policies coincide with theirs or under a weak mayor if they have the support of the Board of Finance. . . . New Haven mayors have continued to find it expedient to create confidence in their financial policies among businessmen by appointing them to the Board" (pp. 81–82).

34. Dahl does discuss in general terms (pp. 79–84) changes in the level of tax rates and assessments in past years, but not actual decisions of the Board of Finance or their effects on the public school system.

35. Ibid., p. 124.

36. Ibid. "A rough test of a person's overt or covert influence," Dahl states in the first section of the book, "is the frequency with which he successfully initiates an important policy over the opposition of others, or vetoes policies initiated by others, or initiates a policy where no opposition appears" (Ibid., p. 66).

37. Ibid., p. 131.

38. Dahl is, of course, aware of the "law of anticipated reactions." In the case of the mayor's relationship with the CAC, Dahl notes that Lee was "particularly skillful in estimating what the CAC could be expected to support or reject." (p. 137). However, Dahl was not interested in analyzing or appraising to what extent the CAC limited Lee's freedom of action. Because of his restricted concept of power, Dahl did not consider that the CAC might in this respect have exercised power. That the CAC did not initiate or veto actual proposals by the mayor was to Dahl evidence enough that the CAC was virtually powerless; it might as plausibly be evidence that the CAC was (in itself or in what it represented) so powerful that Lee ventured nothing it would find worth quarrelling with.

39. The fact that the initiator of decisions also refrains—because he anticipates adverse reactions—from initiating other proposals does not obviously lesson the power of the agent who limited his initiative powers. Dahl missed this point: "It is," he writes, "all the more improbable, then, that a secret cabal of Notables dominates the public life of New Haven through means so clandestine that not one of the fifty prominent citizens interviewed in the course of this study—citizens who had participated extensively in various decisions—hinted at the existence of such a cabal . . ." (p. 185).

In conceiving of elite domination exclusively in the form of a conscious cabal exercising the power of decision-making and vetoing, he overlooks a more subtle form of domination; one in which those who actually dominate are not conscious of it themselves, simply because their position of dominance has never seriously been challenged.

40. Sayre and Kaufman, op. cit., p. 640. For a perceptive study of the "mobilization of bias" in a rural American community, see Arthur Vidich and Joseph Bensman, *Small Town in Mass Society* (Princeton, 1958).

Chapter 9

Conclusion

The purpose of this text was to apply the discipline of political science to the study of criminal justice in order to examine how criminal justice policy is made and implemented. To do so involved examining the political structures and processes through which (1) behavior is defined as criminal; (2) policies, processes, and procedures regulating criminal behavior are determined; and (3) criminal justice policies are implemented. The focus of the discussion was on federal criminal justice policy making. Accordingly, after describing the evolution of the federal role in criminal justice policy making and the ideologies underlying criminal justice policy in chapter 2, chapters 3 through 7 examine the role of each of the three branches of the federal government—executive (president and bureaucracy), legislature, and courts in federal criminal justice policy making. The reader must also bear in mind, however, that criminal justice policy making is also affected by the politics of interaction between and among the branches of government and between and among the levels of government.

CRIMINAL JUSTICE POLICY MAKING: WITHIN THE BRANCHES OF THE FEDERAL GOVERNMENT

To analyze the criminal justice policy-making process in each branch, articles were included that applied various political science frameworks to the study of criminal justice. The frameworks applied included symbolic politics, interest groups, political culture, and implementation.

The symbolic framework was applied to presidential, congressional, and bureacratic criminal justice policy making. Presidential and congressional criminal justice initiatives can often be explained in terms of the symbolic functions they serve. The initiatives may reflect the desire of the president or members of Congress to (1) reassure their audience, the public, that they are addressing a crime problem or threatening lawbreakers; (2) send a message to the law breaker and law-abiding citizen that certain behavior is not acceptable; (3) educate about a problem; or (4) provide model policies for the states. The criminal justice bureaucracy, by providing information to policymakers and the public, was also shown to perform the symbolic functions of education and model for the states.

Congressional policy making was further examined from the perspective of interest groups. Interest groups participating in the congressional criminal justice policy-making process were found to exhibit diverse types of goals; have different types of resources available to them; and use a variety of techniques, at different points in the legislative process, in order to influence the legislative outcome. While many groups, particularly professional criminal justice organizations, seek to affect the content of criminal justice legislation, other groups, such as social reform groups, may seek to block legislation from congressional consideration. Interest groups often seek to influence the process, by presenting their views in testimony before congressional subcommittees and committees during hearings.

The function of the criminal justice bureaucracy is to execute criminal justice policy. Through the implementation of criminal justice policy, bureaucracy affects the public perception of what that policy is. It has been asserted in this text that policy making does not stop once legislation has been enacted, but that policy is subject to the interpretation of the "street-level bureaucrat." Moreover, the parameters within which the bureaucracy operates is affected by the community's political culture, which supports particular political structures; political and police styles; and, ultimately, what is acceptable regarding law enforcement practice. Furthermore, the flexibility of law enforcement's bureaucratic environment supports the development of a police culture, which may lead to problems of police corruption.

Using juvenile justice policy as an example, the Supreme Court was shown to have affected criminal justice policy. Through the complexities of judicial decision-making and the implementation of those decisions, the Court's decisions, according to Feld, resulted in the continuing evolution of juveniles' procedural due process requirement and, as such, transformed the juvenile court to one very different from that envisioned by its creators.

Finally, the reader was introduced to the non–decision-making framework, which observes that the dominant values and the political myths, rituals, and institutions tend to favor the vested interests of one or more groups, relative to others. As a consequence of the "mobilization of bias" some potential policies may not be included on the public policy agenda.

To understand criminal justice policy and criminal justice policy making, the reader must consider not only how policy is made, but the factors and influences that exclude other policies from the public policy agenda.

CRIMINAL JUSTICE POLICY MAKING: BETWEEN AND AMONG THE BRANCHES OF THE FEDERAL GOVERNMENT

The study of federal criminal justice policy making does not end with the examination of policy making within each branch, but must also consider the contribution of the interaction among and between the branches. As noted in chapter 1, the three branches of government are separate institutions that share functions. On the one hand, this sharing of functions by the branches establishes a general need for cooperation among the branches, if policy is to be enacted and implemented. On the other hand, sharing functions provides a check by each branch on the policy making of the others, at least in theory—the so-called checks and balances. Sharing functions may also lead to a stalemate, if the branches cannot agree. Drawing the text to a conclusion, it is important to underscore these relationships.

Within the executive branch, the president affects the bureaucracy through executive appointments, executive orders, and policy initiatives. Although many policies and programs continue from one administration to the next, dominated by one political party and then the other, the head of an agency may shift the priorities of the department, bureau, or office.

As described in chapter 5, bureaucracies may be sources of information. In providing that information, it may help to define a problem for policymakers, indicate how programs and policies are working, or identify new problems. In so doing, the bureaucracy may affect the policymaking decisions of the other branches of government.

Since the president must sign most legislation, presidents may affect Congress's policy-making efforts. As discussed in chapter 3, presidents may present legislation to Congress, thereby seeking to influence Congress's crime agenda. Presidents may also seek to thwart congressional policy making. During the 1980s, the threat of a presidential veto of proposed crime legislation, if it included a drug czar, resulted in the provision not being included in omnibus crime legislation. Neither President Reagan nor his attorney general, Ed Meese, wanted the position, which would allow Congress to call its incumbent to Capitol Hill for hearings to testify, thereby bringing media attention to the drug problem. Several years later, however, the same president signed anti-drug legislation that included a drug czar. The drug czar was among the recommendations of a White House Congress on Drugs, which had been mandated in the 1986 anti-drug legislation.

Moreover, in 1988, President Reagan was concluding his term of office, and the carrying out of the drug czar provision would be left to his successor, George Bush.

Congress, through its legislative and appointment powers, may affect a president's crime agenda. For example, in 1986, Congress passed anti-drug legislation without active support from the White House. As indicated above, that legislation mandated a White House Conference on Drugs. Two years later, the proposed and enacted anti-drug package included White House–supported provisions and recommendations from the drug conference participants. These proposals were introduced in Congress, through the Republican congressional leadership. The 1988 anti-drug package included punitive provisions directed at drug users, supported by the White House, which caused discomfort for many Democrats who, generally, supported the legislation.

On an annual basis, and perhaps more important, Congress affects an agency's appropriation. The budget process is complex, beginning several years in advance of the budget submitted for a particular fiscal year. Congress has to enact the legislation, which as with other legislation has to be signed by the president. Sometimes negotiations take so long that agencies must operate under a continuing resolution, which allows them to operate until their regular appropriation is enacted. Congress also authorizes or can fail to reauthorize policies and programs that the bureaucracy then has to implement or not.

Through its appointment authority, Congress can affect the bureaucracy. Although Congress rarely turns down a presidential executive branch nominee, it does happen. In recent years, the threat of in-depth personal interrogations during the confirmation process may have deterred some individuals from even considering such positions.

The Supreme Court may challenge decisions of the Congress or the president. Dependent on cases being brought to it, the Court cannot seek out decisions that it would like to hear. While the solicitor general may bring cases on behalf of the administration, as Attorney General Ashcroft suggested in his confirmation hearings, it is unwise for an administration to ask the Court to review policies that it has declared to be the "settled" law of the land. Both the president and Congress through the appointment process influence who sits on the Court, and, therefore, at least to some degree the views expressed by the Court through its decisions.

The Court may directly or indirectly, affect the laws enacted by Congress. During the 1970s, through its interpretation of state death penalty statutes, the Court sent a message that such statutes had to include certain procedures. Congress revised federal statutes, providing for the death penalty, to ensure that the Court would not overturn a federal death penalty case, if it were challenged.

The interactions among the branches of the federal government, which affect criminal justice policy, are many and complex. A discussion of these interactions requires a text in and of itself. These interactions, however, must be considered for a full understanding of the federal criminal justice policy-making process.

CRIMINAL JUSTICE POLICY MAKING: BETWEEN AND AMONG THE LEVELS OF GOVERNMENT

As noted in chapter 1 of this text, the U.S. system of government is a federal system. There are three levels of government—federal, state, and local. Moreover, the state and local government bear most of the responsibility for criminal justice, despite the expansion of the federal role in criminal justice. Requisite to an understanding of criminal justice policy and policy making is an examination of the interaction of the three levels of government.

The discussion of symbolic politics, in relation to the president, Congress, and bureaucracy asserts that one of the symbolic functions of federal criminal justice policy is to provide a model for the states. In this way, the federal government may influence state and local criminal justice policies. By providing funds for initiatives at the state and local level, through grants programs, especially formula grant programs, the federal government has sought to facilitate—using a carrot approach—the implementation of what it views as good policy, at the state and local level. In some cases, federal legislation has also employed the stick, threatening to take away other federal funds if states and localities did not implement certain policies. By enacting new federal penalties, for example, in the drug area, the federal government also sends a message to state and local officials regarding federal criminal justice priorities.

As with the interactions among the federal branches of government and how they affect criminal justice policy, those between and among the levels of government are complex. They too require a text.

NEW ISSUES IN CRIMINAL JUSTICE

In recent years, new criminal justice policy challenges have arisen. Domestic violence and domestic terrorism have been subjects of concern for policymakers. Transnational crimes, such as terrorism, international drug trafficking, money laundering, trafficking in women and girls, and the dissemination of weapons of mass destruction have raised new fears and challenges for policymakers. In cases of transnational crime, for example, the line between intelligence investigations, those directed against foreign citizens or governments, and investigations gathering evidence for criminal prosecution has become blurred. Intelligence investigators want to know who the international contacts of those threatening terrorism in the United

States are, while criminal prosecutors want to pursue the prosecution of the individuals for crimes committed in the United States, for example, bombings or conspiracy to bomb a U.S. facility.

Congress, the president, and the bureaucracy have taken steps to meet these new criminal justice challenges, but it will be necessary for them to continue to develop and implement policies to address these problems. These efforts bear watching by those interested in criminal justice policy making. The analytical tools provided in this text provide the means to study and analyze these developments.

TOOLS FOR FURTHER STUDY

This text has focused on the role of each of the federal branches of government in the criminal justice policy-making process. It provides analytical tools for examining what has happened, as well as policy making yet to occur. The study of criminal justice policy making is a continuing exercise as new crimes emerge and new policies are proposed, enacted, and implemented to meet those challenges. This book provides the tools for continuing study.

Selected Bibliography

Bachrach, Peter, and Baratz, Morton S. *Power and Poverty: Theory and Practice.* New York: Oxford University Press, 1970.

Bachrach, Peter, and Baratz, Morton S. "Two Faces of Power." *American Political Science Review*, vol. 56, no. 4 (December 1962): 947–52.

Ball, Howard. *Courts and Politics: The Federal Judicial System.* Englewood Cliffs, NJ: Prentice Hall, 1980.

Cavanagh, Suzanne. *Crime Control: The Federal Response.* Congressional Research Service Issue Brief for Congress, May 26, 1999.

The Challenge of Crime in a Free Society: A Report of the President's Commission on Law Enforcement and Administration of Justice. New York: Avon Books, 1968.

The Challenge of Crime in a Free Society Looking Back . . . Looking Forward. Washington, DC: U.S. Department of Justice, Office of Justice Programs, May 1998.

City of New York, The Commission to Investigate Allegations of Police Corruption and the Anti-Corruption Procedures of the Police Department. *The Report.* New York: July 7, 1994.

Drug Courts: Overview of Growth, Characteristics, and Results. (GAO/GGD-97-106.) Washington, DC: U.S. General Accounting Office, 1997.

The Federalization of Criminal Law. Washington, DC: The American Bar Association, 1998.

Feld, Barry C. "Criminalizing Juvenile Justice: Rules of Procedure for the Juvenile Court." *Minnesota Law Review*, vol. 69, no. 2 (December 1984): 141–276.

Lipsky, Michael. "Street-Level Bureaucracy and the Analysis of Urban Reform." *Urban Affairs Quarterly* (June 1971): 391–409.

Lipsky, Michael. *Street-Level Bureaucracy: Dilemmas of the Individual in Public Services.* New York: Russell Sage Foundation, 1980.

Marion, Nancy E. *A History of Federal Crime Control Initiatives, 1960–93.* Westport, CT: Praeger, 1994.

Marion, Nancy E. *A Primer in the Politics of Criminal Justice.* Albany, NY: Harrow and Heston, 1995.

Marion, Nancy E. "Symbolic Policies in Clinton's Crime Control Agenda." *Buffalo Criminal Law Review*, vol. 1, no.1 (1997): 67–108.

Miller, Walter B. "Ideology and Criminal Justice Policy: Some Current Issues." *The Journal of Criminal Law and Criminology*, vol. 64, no. 2 (1973): 141–62.

Office of Justice Programs. *Fiscal Year 1999 Program Plan.* Washington, DC: U.S. Department of Justice, Office of Justice Programs.

The Report of the Commission on Police Integrity. Chicago, Illinois, November 1997.

Stolz, Barbara Ann. "Congress and Capital Punishment: An Exercise in Symbolic Politics." *Law and Policy Quarterly* 5 (April 1983): 157–79.

Stolz, Barbara Ann. "Congress and Criminal Justice Policy Making: The Impact of Interest Groups and Symbolic Politics." *Journal of Criminal Justice*, vol. 13, no. 4 (1985): 307–19.

Stolz, Barbara Ann. "Congress and the War on Drugs: An Exercise in Symbolic Politics." *Journal of Crime and Justice*, vol. 15, no. 1 (1992): 119–36.

Stolz, Barbara Ann. "Congress, Symbolic Politics and the Evolution of 1994 'Violence Against Women Act.' " *Criminal Justice Policy Review*, vol. 10, no. 3 (1999): 401–28.

Stolz, Barbara Ann. "Interest Groups and Criminal Law: The Case of Federal Criminal Code Revision." *Crime and Delinquency*, vol. 30, no.1 (1984): 91–106.

Wilson, James Q. *Varieties of Police Behavior.* Cambridge, MA: Harvard University Press, 1968.

Index

ABOUT THE AUTHOR

BARBARA ANN STOLZ is a political scientist and criminologist who has worked in academia and government. She has published numerous articles on the role of symbolic politics, interest groups, subgovernments in determining U.S. criminal justice policies regarding capital punishment, juvenile delinquency, drug control, corrections, and domestic violence. As a Fulbright scholar in Russia, she taught American politics at Yaroslav State University. Currently, she is a senior analyst engaged in research on criminal justices issues at a federal agency.